MOURNING ANIMALS

THE ANIMAL TURN

SERIES EDITOR
Linda Kalof

SERIES ADVISORY BOARD
Marc Bekoff, Juliet Clutton-Brock, Nigel Rothfels

Making Animal Meaning
   Edited by Linda Kalof and Georgina M. Montgomery
Animals as Domesticates: A World View through History
   Juliet Clutton-Brock
Animals as Neighbors: The Past and Present of Commensal Species
   Terry O'Connor
French Thinking about Animals
   Edited by Louisa Mackenzie and Stephanie Posthumus
Animals as Food: (Re)connecting Production, Processing, Consumption, and Impacts
   Amy J. Fitzgerald
Mourning Animals: Rituals and Practices Surrounding Animal Death
   Edited by Margo DeMello

MICHIGAN STATE UNIVERSITY LIBRARY
AUG 22 2025
WITHDRAWN

PLACE IN RETURN BOX
to remove this checkout from your record.
TO AVOID FINES return on or before date due.
MAY BE RECALLED with earlier due date if requested.

DATE DUE	DATE DUE
IL: JAN 29 2017	MelCat NOV 26 2017

10/13 p:/CIRC/FoldedDateDueForms_2013.indd - pg.8

MOURNING ANIMALS

*Rituals and Practices
Surrounding Animal Death*

Edited by Margo DeMello

Michigan State University Press
East Lansing

Copyright © 2016 by Michigan State University

∞ The paper used in this publication meets the minimum requirements of ANSI/NISO Z39.48-1992 (R 1997) (Permanence of Paper).

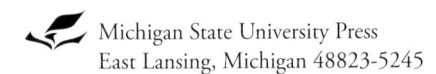

Michigan State University Press
East Lansing, Michigan 48823-5245

Printed and bound in the United States of America.
22 21 20 19 18 17 16   1 2 3 4 5 6 7 8 9 10

LIBRARY OF CONGRESS CATALOGING-IN-PUBLICATION DATA

Names: DeMello, Margo, editor.
Title: Mourning animals : rituals and practices surrounding animal death / edited by Margo DeMello.
Description: East Lansing : Michigan State University Press, [2016] | Series: The animal turn | Includes bibliographical references and index.
Identifiers: LCCN 2015033659| ISBN 9781611862126 (cloth : alk. paper) | ISBN 9781609174989 (pdf) | ISBN 9781628952711 (epub) | ISBN 9781628962710 (kindle)
Subjects: LCSH: Dead animals. | Pets—Death. | Pets—Funeral rites and ceremonies. | Animal cemeteries. | Human-animal relationships.
Classification: LCC QL87.5 .M68 2016 | DDC 591.6—dc23 LC record available at http://lccn.loc.gov/2015033659

Book design by Scribe Inc. (www.scribenet.com)
Cover design by Erin Kirk New
Cover image is ©Emma Kisiel (emmakisiel.com) and is used with permission.

green press INITIATIVE Michigan State University Press is a member of the Green Press Initiative and is committed to developing and encouraging ecologically responsible publishing practices. For more information about the Green Press Initiative and the use of recycled paper in book publishing, please visit www.greenpressinitiative.org.

Visit Michigan State University Press at www.msupress.org

Contents

Preface	vii
Acknowledgments	xv
Introduction	xvii
Discarded Property, *Mary Shannon Johnstone*	xxvii

PART 1: WHEN DID WE START CARING ABOUT ANIMAL DEATH?

More than a Bag of Bones: A History of Animal Burials, *Ivy D. Collier*	3
Mourning the Sacrifice: Behavior and Meaning behind Animal Burials, *James Morris*	11
Horses, Mourning: Interspecies Embodiment, Belonging, and Bereavement in the Past and Present, *Gala Argent*	21
The Issue of Animals' Souls within the Anglican Debate in the Eighteenth to Nineteenth Centuries, *Alma Massaro*	31
Hartsdale Pet Cemetery, *Liza Wallis Margulies*	39

PART 2: COMPANION ANIMALS: THOSE WE LOVE

All the World and a Little Bit More: Pet Cemetery Practices and Contemporary Relations between Humans and Their Companion Animals, *Michał Piotr Pręgowski*	47
To All that Fly or Crawl: A Recent History of Mourning for Animals in Korea, *Elmer Veldkamp*	55
Freeze-Drying Fido: The Uncanny Aesthetics of Modern Taxidermy, *Christina M. Colvin*	65
Clutching at Straws: Dogs, Death, and Frozen Semen, *Chrissie Wanner*	73
I Remember Everything: Children, Companion Animals, and a Relational Pedagogy of Remembrance, *Joshua Russell*	81
On Cats and Contradictions: Mourning Animal Death in an English Community, *Becky Tipper*	91

So Sorry for the Loss of Your Little Friend: Pets' Grievability in Condolence
    Cards for Humans Mourning Animals, *David Redmalm*   101

Claire: Last Days, *Julia Schlosser*   109

PART 3: MEMORIALS AND THE "SPECIAL" TREATMENT OF THE DEAD

Britain at War: Remembering and Forgetting the Animal Dead of the Second
    World War, *Hilda Kean*   115

Now on Exhibit: Our Affection for, Remembrance of, and Tributes to Nonhuman
    Animals in Museums, *Carolyn Merino Mullin*   123

Another Death, *Emma Kisiel*   131

PART 4: ANIMALS WE DO NOT MOURN

In the Heart of Every Horse: Combating a History of Equine Exploitation and
    Slaughter through the Commemoration of an "Average" Thoroughbred
    Racehorse, *Tamar V. S. McKee*   137

Creating Carnivores and Cannibals: Animal Feed and the Regulation of Grief,
    Keridiana Chez   143

Mourning the Mundane: Memorializing Road-Killed Animals in North America,
    Linda Monahan   151

The Unmourned, *Linda Brant*   159

PART 5: PROBLEMS WITH COPING AND HUMAN RESPONSIBILITY

Beyond Coping: Active Mourning in the Animal Sheltering Community, *Jessica Austin*   165

Mourning for Animals: A Companion Animal Veterinarian's Perspective, *Anne Fawcett*   171

You're My Sanctuary: Grief, Vulnerability, and Unexpected Secondary Losses for
    Animal Advocates Mourning a Companion Animal, *Nicole R. Pallotta*   179

Keeping Ghosts Close: Care and Grief at Sanctuaries, *pattrice jones and Lori Gruen*   187

Grieving at a Distance, *Teya Brooks Pribac*   193

Who Is It Acceptable to Grieve? *Jo-Anne McArthur*   201

Bibliography   205

About the Contributors   221

Index   227

Preface

WHILE WE ARE SURROUNDED BY ANIMAL DEATH—ONE CAN ARGUE, IN FACT, THAT THE deaths of animals, companion, farmed, or other, is one of the defining features of humans' relationships with them—there are very few texts that deal with this sensitive issue. *Mourning Animals: Rituals and Practices Surrounding Animal Death* is the first book to look at the question of what happens after animals die, how we mourn them, and whether or not we think they have an afterlife—which itself often determines the kind of posthumous care and attention that they get.

Part 1, "When Did We Start Caring about Animal Death?," opens with Ivy D. Collier's chapter on the history of animal burial practices. By closely examining these very personal and emotional activities, we see the multilayered impacts of culture, religion, and social structures, all of which tell the story of the human–animal bond. This chapter focuses on a few major historical examples in order to set the stage for the chapters that will follow.

Then archaeologist James Morris discusses the interpretation of animal burials from British archaeological sites ranging from 4000 BCE to 1850 CE. Morris shows that, although often viewed as "waste" or "sacrifices," animal burials are often polysemic, created through multiple human actions and meanings. Through a reconstruction of the human actions behind animal burials, he shows it is possible to detect the caring for and mourning of animals by communities and individuals and questions if these actions are linked to the classification of nonhuman animals.

Archaeologist Gala Argent's chapter looks at the practice of sacrificing horses for Pazyryk burials some 2,500 years ago. Argent employs both ethological studies of horses and an autoethnographic research strategy that uses her own position as a horse rider to try to understand the human–horse intersubjectivities occurring at the time.

In the final chapter in this section, we have an essay by Alma Massaro that provides an overview of the works of some Anglican pastors who, during the eighteenth to nineteenth centuries, began to inquire about the status of animals' afterlife from a biblical perspective. Massaro shows that while some of these pastors were concerned with the theological problems that resulted from animals' lack of a soul and other pastors were more concerned with the real condition of animals' lives, the very fact they did start to speak on these topics makes it possible to see in them a sort of "common voice" in favor of Christian compassion toward animals.

Part 2, "Companion Animals: Those We Love," addresses the animals whom most people think about when we think about mourning animals—pets. Not surprisingly, this is the largest section of the book. We begin with Michał Piotr Pręgowski's chapter on pet cemeteries, and in particular on gravestone inscriptions, based on his fieldwork at Psi Los, the oldest and largest pet cemetery in Poland. His chapter gives us insight into a very private, intimate world people share with their companion animals. Such animals are commemorated in many ways:

as representatives of their breed or species, as beloved friends, but also as members of families. The gravestones highlight key virtues of the deceased, feature poems in their honor, or focus on expressing the owners' grief and longing to the world. Last farewells can also be an expression of faith in animal friends' immortality and their hopeful reunion.

Elmer Veldkamp looks at another culture, and one that is not typically thought of as animal friendly to Western eyes—Korea. Veldkamp notes that Westerners who think of Korea often think of the consumption of dog meat when they think of animals at all. In this chapter, the different meanings that are attached to animal death and mourning in Korea are explored. By looking closely at the rhetoric, ideologies, and historical dimensions behind a selection of related practices—including the rise of memorial services for military and laboratory animals introduced during the Japanese occupation, the emergence of the Korean animal protection movement, and the explosion of Western-style pet-keeping, along with the rise in pet funerals—Veldkamp gives us a dynamic and multidimensional view of animal death and mourning in Korea.

One relatively recent practice that has emerged for those who cannot bear to be separated from their companion animals after death is pet taxidermy. Christina M. Colvin interrogates the complex relationship between grief work and aesthetics in taxidermic representations of companion animals. Her chapter shows how dead animals insist on being both recognized and remembered in many instances of modern taxidermy. A closer look at the pet preservation industry, experimental (or "rogue") taxidermy, as well as two recent reality television shows featuring taxidermy and taxidermists—*Immortalized* and *American Stuffers*—shows that much modern taxidermy actually facilitates the work of memory by emphasizing an animal's death and the particularity of the animal who died. This chapter further demonstrates how modern taxidermy as an aesthetic practice both codifies and destabilizes the divide between "human" and "animal" by establishing animals as possible subjects of grief.

Technology is used in a different way to help dog owners and breeders overcome their grief at the death of their canine companions, as we see in Chrissie Wanner's chapter. Wanner's ethnographic research led her to dog shows, breeders' kennels, and a veterinary clinic specializing in canine reproduction that offered cryopreservation—a process by which semen is frozen to be later used in artificial insemination. Wanner considers how the preservation of semen collected from dogs allowed owners to "hold on"—both figuratively and practically—to a part of their deceased animals. For owners facing the loss of their dogs, semen preservation is a process through which parts of the body come to stand in for the dogs themselves. Despite the veterinarian's warnings of low success rates, and the fact that many owners never do use the semen for artificial insemination anyway, the important thing, it seems, is the fact that semen has been preserved. Ultimately, Wanner argues, the process of cryopreservation is transformed from a method of regeneration into a gesture of grieving. But for those owners, and especially breeders, who do use the technology to produce litters from frozen semen (either to be "reunited" with their dogs through their offspring, or in the case of the breeders, to ensure that the bloodline is perpetuated), Wanner considers how the concepts of pedigree and lineage shape the way owners and breeders of pedigree dogs experience the loss of their animals.

Joshua Russell's chapter looks at a different demographic and how they mourn in their own ways. Russell, whose work focuses on children's experiences of companion animal death, finds that the role of memory emerged as a significant factor within children's lives and experiences with companion animals. Above all, children's recollections of deceased pets emphasized the importance of significant others—caregivers, parents, siblings, and even himself as a researcher—in accessing the past. Given the highly relational context of companion animals, as members of the domestic sphere and as subjects within the family structure, children's memories of their pets are distinctly tied to those places and individuals who share in that context. Yet, despite the highly social character of children's memory work, they often expressed a deep sense of their memories as "their own," emphasizing the accuracy of their own recall and establishing a sense of individual identity and responsibility for remembering others. In his conclusion, Russell explores the implications of remembering deceased companion animals as a meaningful pedagogical and moral action engaged in by children and others.

In Becky Tipper's chapter, she looks at an unusual case of death and loss, by presenting the case study of an English community's response to the death of a neighborhood cat. While Tipper was doing fieldwork in the community, the cat, Vince, was hit by a car. She noted the ways in which members of the community began to mourn him and mark his passing. This incident challenged the idea that the deaths of companion animals are marked only by their "owners." The response to Vince's death also offers a compelling example of how animals may be publicly mourned not only as members of the generic category "animals" (as, for instance, in public memorials to animals who have died in wars), but more specifically as "persons," and in ways that might parallel the mourning of human deaths. In addition, this case also highlighted how human grief for animal death can be controversial in the context of British (and, perhaps, Western) society. Although Vince's death touched many people, others felt it was inappropriate to mourn an animal's death in such a public manner.

Then we move on to David Redmalm's look at one of the primary ways in which we help other people cope with the loss of their companion animals today—the condolence card. Redmalm notes that to send a condolence card is not only to recognize someone's pain, but to recognize this pain in a specific way, contributing to a shared social understanding of what the loss in question might mean to the bereaved person and the people around him or her. While many themes in condolence cards for companion animals resemble "human" condolence cards, these cards also challenge nonhuman animals' status as grievable: companion animals are recurrently represented as replaceable to some extent, the loss is sometimes framed as predictable or in other ways manageable, and the many objectifying depictions of nonhuman bodies in the cards suggest a lack of embodied empathy with nonhuman animals. Redmalm thus argues that this risks belittling or rejecting the grief for a lost companion animal. On the other hand, this genre of condolence cards also makes possible ways to represent loss and death in quite explicit ways, challenging the Western taboo around death. Some cards also challenge the hierarchical human/animal distinction, emphasizing nonhuman animals' status as kin, in spite of the difference in kind.

In Part 3, "Memorials and the 'Special' Treatment of the Dead," we look at animals who died in war and animals on display in museums—animals who stand out as somehow above and beyond other animals based on their special purpose or use for humans, and who were then treated very differently after their deaths.

We begin with a chapter that deals with animals who died at war and how they have, and have not, been commemorated. Hilda Kean notes that the home front in Britain during the Second World War continues to engage the popular historical imagination and that it is a time that the British still wish to remember. The interest in commemoration extends beyond the human to particular animals who are deemed to have fitted within the war myths constructed around humans. Thus particular, named, animals such as Jet of Lada, a German shepherd who rescued people from bombed out buildings, or Faith, the London church cat who protected her kittens in a night of terrible bombardment during the Blitz, are remembered. However, the deaths of other animals, such as the four hundred thousand cats and dogs killed by their owners at the start of the war or the French dogs who were embraced by the retreating British Expeditionary Forces in Dunkirk only to be summarily shot by the military police before embarking to England, are overlooked. While (some) animals are remembered, this is usually only the case when their narratives are seen to be easily subsumed by discourses showing humans in a favorable light. Kean's chapter looks at why it is that the British have so easily forgotten all of the other animals who died and were killed during the Second World War.

From the war memorials we move to another kind of memorialization—the exhibiting of taxidermic animals in museums. Carolyn Merino Mullin, the director of the National Museum of Animals and Society, tells us that museums play an important role in preserving, interpreting, and sharing the collective memory of society. Her chapter looks at animal bodies on display in museums. In particular, she focuses on *individuals* with a biographical sketch of historical importance, such as Japan's Hachikō or Germany's Knut the polar bear. This chapter explores visitor impressions, related programming, and the educational value of having them on display. In addition, she looks at the museological treatment and views of these animals. While their bodies stand upon pedestals or in glass cases, the exhibition of these animals brings about larger questions: Can these displays be considered tributes or memorials? Is there a distinct line between memorial and exhibition? Are museums objectifying these animals and thus losing respect for their bodies?

In our next section, Part 4, "Animals We Do Not Mourn," we look at those animals who are ungrievable: the animals we kill for meat, animals who are killed by cars and left by the side of the road, and those who fall somewhere in between, such as racehorses. Some racehorses, when they reach the height of fame, achieve a peaceful retirement, while others are slaughtered after their careers are over, never to be thought about again. And still other animals—most animals, in fact—will never be thought of at all.

Tamar V. S. McKee opens this section by looking at the deaths of racehorses in the United States. McKee notes that if horse slaughter has sparked considerable outrage in the contemporary United States due to cultural taboos on the consumption of horse meat, the slaughter of Thoroughbred ex-racehorses has pushed this outrage into new territory. As evidenced in the slaughter of the 1986 Kentucky Derby winner, Ferdinand, in Japan in 2002, this stallion's death demonstrated how a once-celebrated, almost-humanized champion racehorse could turn into not just a killable commodity, but one whose death was rendered so anonymous and hidden that it did not come to light until a year after it had happened. The outrage over Ferdinand's death consequently mobilized myriad efforts to save Thoroughbred racehorses from going to slaughter, such as the establishment of, or further investment in, equine rescue and retirement facilities. In light of these events, McKee's chapter looks at another way Ferdinand's death has been both mourned and mobilizing: in the interment ceremony of a Thoroughbred racehorse called Invisible Ink at the Kentucky Horse Park in 2011. McKee recounts attending his memorial service and explores the meaning of such a ceremony in terms of the statement it intended to make about how Thoroughbred racehorses should be celebrated throughout their lives—in sickness and in health as was the case of Invisible Ink—and not just when they are productive champions.

Keridiana Chez looks at animals used for meat, but through a historical lens. In the streets of nineteenth-century London and the United States, the "dog's-meat man" would hawk horseflesh for the dogs who were being refashioned into beloved companions. For dogs, this was a step up the food ladder: accorded the privilege of eating the meat of other animals, dogs were moved closer to humanity. Yet horse meat remained inedible to humans, who preserved their status through different representations of the quality of the flesh of different animals. This chapter explores the ways that humans have determined which nonhuman animals can eat others and how this process intersects with race, gender, and class. Chez highlights key shifts in the way the discourse of edibility and "posthumous utility" shaped the deaths, and therefore the lives, of nonhuman animals. The more ingeniously and extensively humans used animal bodies, the less grievable their lives became, which she then links to twentieth-century representations of animals as factories and, later, the conception of nonhuman animals as cash crops to be harvested.

And finally, Linda Monahan ends this section with a category of animal that very few people even think about: roadkill. These animals, which include our beloved dogs and cats, are both visible—lying on every nation's roads and highways—and invisible, as we often become so used to seeing them, depending on where we live, that we don't even notice them. Historically, road-killed animals have been outside the realm of acceptable human mourning. In the twentieth century, for example, roadkill was commonly the subject of cartoon and culinary humor that culturally disengaged the deaths of actual animals. In the early twenty-first century, however, road-killed animals have begun to be integrated into larger narratives of subjectivity and interspecies community through activism, art, and policy. One example of emergent collective mourning practices is the petitioning of state legislatures to erect highway memorials for mass road kills. In the United States, People for the Ethical Treatment of Animals (PETA) petitioned state legislatures in 2006, 2011, and 2014 to erect highway memorials for farmed animals killed in transport. While none of the petitions has thus far been approved, the attempts have generated revealing discussions in news media about contemporary American attitudes toward road-killed animals. Considered alongside policy initiatives such as wildlife corridors that work to prevent animal mortality on North American roadways, recent art and activist work suggest that roadkill has successfully begun its cultural transformation from laughably grotesque to grievable animal death.

In our final section, Part 5, "Problems with Coping and Human Responsibility," we deal with our human responsibility for animal death and how we variously cope, and do not cope, with our roles in those deaths.

We begin with Jessica Austin's chapter that deals with how animal shelter workers cope with the roles that they play in death. Animal shelter employees face each day with the possibility of inhabiting two conflicting roles: the caretaker, charged with ensuring the safety and well-being of the wards in their custody; and the executioner, overseer of these same animals' premature deaths. With shelter euthanasia estimates climbing to nearly three million adoptable animals per year, shelter workers shoulder a considerable burden of grief, resulting in stress and manifesting in depression and even physical complaints, such as sleep disturbance. While several authors offer coping mechanisms for those whose work involves death, both in general and specifically tailored toward shelter employees, little is written about how shelter workers specifically mourn the animals they euthanize and how grieving for these beings affects their mental health. Austin's chapter explores the myriad emotions that inform shelter workers' outlook on their role in animal death and how personal mourning rituals and practices occur and empower them to continue in their dichotomous role as both protector and life-taker.

Veterinarians, too, play that dual role, as is discussed in veterinarian Anne Fawcett's chapter. They are primarily caretakers, but they also must act as partner in end-of-life decision making and effectors of euthanasia. As such, they are often witness to anticipatory and early grief. The first part of Fawcett's essay deals with the type of mourning that veterinarians may witness—known as disenfranchised grief, thanks to the fact that our relationships with our companion animals are not sufficiently recognized by others. The second part of her chapter discusses the mourning that veterinarians do not see: some owners are mourning, in part, the loss of their relationship with the veterinary team. Finally, the chapter concludes with a discussion of mourning from the veterinarian's perspective—the impact of witnessing grief, the veterinarian's mourning, their denial of their own need to mourn, and the frequency of grief to the very short lifespan of their animal patients.

Our final three chapters in this section deal with how animal advocates deal with animal death. Nicole R. Pallotta looks at what she calls secondary losses that may emerge when mourning a companion animal. For some animal advocates, a strong bond with a companion animal may serve an additional, latent function (and hence represent a unique secondary loss): a psychological buffer. For those who are heavily involved in animal advocacy work, companion animals can serve as a psychological shield between themselves and the traumatic knowledge that constantly filters in about the multitude of other animals, whom they can't save, on a daily basis. Losing the buffer this special relationship provides can exacerbate the experience of acute grief and contribute to heightened feelings of social alienation and emotional vulnerability. This chapter explores how losing a cherished pet can induce not only depression over the loss of that animal and one's particular relationship with him or her, but also about all the other animals suffering and dying in slaughterhouses, etc., every minute of every day. While animal advocates may have been aware of these other animal deaths, losing a beloved pet may compromise their coping mechanisms in a way that complicates their grief experience. With this one precious relationship gone—the one animal whose happiness was in the bereaved person's hands, and that hence gave a modicum of control—it can become more difficult to shut out the horrors visited on the nameless others.

In pattrice jones and Lori Gruen's chapter, the authors discuss how sanctuary workers deal with the abundance of death that surrounds them, and in particular, the deaths of animals who are not typically mourned, such as farmed animals—raised for meat and intended to be killed and consumed. Gruen and jones cover the few people who not only care for—and about—these animals while they are alive, but mourn for them after they are dead, providing a permanent resting spot, where feasible, for their bodies, and a memorial site for people to grieve for them. Finally, jones and Gruen discuss how donors who sponsor sanctuary animals are notified (or not) of their deaths and what all of these practices say about living and dying with other animals.

This section ends with Teya Brooks Pribac's chapter, which directly addresses those "nameless others" mentioned in Pallotta's chapter. Brooks Pribac focuses on the legitimacy and modes of mourning for nonhuman animals who are personally unknown to the human mourner and who suffer and die either as subjects of organized exploitation practices or as victims of systemic or random slaughter in their natural habitats. Because people who do grieve over nonhuman animals (and over unknown nonhuman animals particularly) not only lack social support and their grief is not socially recognized (and is often derided), their suffering is magnified. This final chapter, however, argues that this kind of grief, which she calls "grief at a distance," is both possible and legitimate. And finally, she argues that the outward expression of grief is compulsory as it bears witness to both the reality of the human mourner's internal turmoil as well as the reality of the animals who have died.

Each section of the book is accompanied by a photo essay produced for this book by a photographer whose work engages in one way or another with the subject matter. The book opens with an essay by North Carolina photographer Mary Shannon Johnstone whose essay, "Discarded Property," looks at the wasted lives and deaths produced in the American pet industry. Part 1 ends with an essay titled "Hartsdale Pet Cemetery" by Liza Wallis Margulies whose photos were taken at Hartsdale, America's oldest pet cemetery. Her photos are a touching look at the love that many people had for their animals in a time when most animals simply went out with the trash. Part 2 concludes with a series of photos titled "Claire's Last Days" by artist Julia Schlosser in which she memorializes the life of her companion Claire. Claire, a rabbit, suffered from a painful and dangerous bone infection, and eventually Schlosser made the decision to have her euthanized. Schlosser created a series of scanned images of Claire's body and some of the objects associated with her life, which serve as a tribute to Claire and their relationship.

Part 3 ends with an essay by photographer Emma Kisiel, who also provided the cover photo for the book. Kisiel's series, "Another Death," depicts museum taxidermic animals who are depicted being killed by another animals—thus "another death." Multimedia artist Linda Brant's essay concludes Part 4. Her photos depict found animal bones that she has lovingly cleaned and posed as a form of respect for the dead. And finally, photographer Jo-Anne McArthur's series wraps up the final section. Her photos, taken at animal sanctuaries around the country, depict three different animals—a pig, a sheep, and a chimpanzee—shortly after death, while being attended to by their human caretakers. Her photos depict scenes of intense love and grief over (nonpet) animals that are rarely seen by the public.

It is still far from universal—even in the United States where Americans, in 2015, spent over $60 billion on our companion animals[1]—that we even grant *pets* loving treatment after death, much less a belief in an afterlife—that we find them grievable. Some people find it both excessive and distasteful that many of us waste both money and emotions on our companion animals when they die. So why should we be surprised that the rest of the animal kingdom falls outside of the bounds of the grievable and can find no room in heaven? It is my hope that as our circle of compassion slowly grows wider, that the afterlife may expand with it, making room for even a few more animals.

NOTE

1. American Pet Products Association, "Pet Industry and Market Size and Ownership Statistics, 2015," http://www.americanpetproducts.org/press_industrytrends.asp.

Acknowledgments

This book was inspired by the work of a number of fellows from the Animals and Society Institute-Wesleyan Animal Studies Human–Animal Studies Fellowship, an annual summer program that allows six to eight scholars to work on important projects in human–animal studies. Over two of the years of this fellowship, a number of the participants (some of whom are represented in this volume) worked on projects dealing with animal death and their responses to it. It occurred to me—as both an animal studies scholar and an animal rescuer who has had to cope with hundreds of animal deaths—that this was an extremely important topic to explore. I am extremely grateful that Linda Kalof, editor of this book series (and the host of the Animals and Society Institute's Human-Animal Studies Fellowship in 1998), also recognized the importance of this topic.

I am also grateful to a number of individuals for their assistance on this project. First, the authors who contributed to this book have not just given it an extremely broad scope, but collectively they have provided a window into the complex and contradictory ways in which humans deal with—and do not deal with—our responsibility for the deaths of so many non-human animals. The six photographers who have shared their often very personal photos have provided an intimate look into the human–animal relationship when death breaks the bonds that we share. I am especially grateful to Emma Kisiel for providing not only a photo essay but the beautiful photo that adorns the cover. Thanks as well to Julie Loehr and Annette Tanner of Michigan State University Press for shepherding this book through the production process.

I want to thank my husband, Tom Young, who has shared with me the joys and pain of living with hundreds of rescued animals over the past twenty-plus years. He has witnessed their deaths and helped me cope with those often unendurable losses. Finally, I want to thank my parents, Bill DeMello and Robin Montgomery, who have always given me love and support throughout all of my projects.

Introduction

You never hear a snake slithering across the Rainbow Bridge.
—CRISS STARR

PEOPLE TODAY, ESPECIALLY IN THE INDUSTRIALIZED AND POSTINDUSTRIALIZED world, live more intimately with nonhuman animals than ever before in history. We share our lives with companion animals in a way that just fifty years ago would have been unheard of. One way to measure this drastic change in our relationships with other animals is to look at the growth of the animal death care industry. According to Brandes, there are over six hundred pet cemeteries in the United States alone, while according to Ambros there are over 900 in Japan.[1] There is even a small but growing movement to allow "whole family cemeteries" in the United States and elsewhere—cemeteries that would allow pets and humans to be buried together, in the same grave (something that had, at one time, been practiced as far back as the late Paleolithic).[2]

In recent years, we have seen the emergence of natural or "green" burial options for pets. Championed by anthropologist Eric Greene's Green Pet-Burial Society, green burials do not feature the metal, wood, or plastic caskets found in traditional burials, with the associated blue, lacquer, and other potential toxins. Not offered in most cemeteries, there are now a handful of green pet cemeteries that are both more economical as well as ecologically friendly; even more innovative, however, is the fact that green human cemeteries (unlike the vast majority of regular cemeteries) allow pets to be buried in (human) family cemetery plots.

Today, there are countless options for dealing with the death of a companion animal, from burial to cremation to taxidermy to wearing or displaying the remains (ashes, fur, or other parts) of the animal in jewelry, a tattoo, or artwork. There are now social workers and counselors who specialize in helping people to mourn their companion animals, as well as classes for veterinarians to help clients grieve, and even tips to help the surviving animals who are grieving their animal friends. Pet psychics will communicate with dead animals for bereaved owners, memorial websites offer support for strangers who don't have people to talk to in their own lives, and universities and veterinary practices offer pet loss support groups and phone lines to assist people who are suffering. (In a new twist, one Indiana funeral home now even offers a support dog to help mourning families to grieve their *human* kin.)

One issue that has emerged in recent years is the question of whether nonhuman animals have an immortal soul and whether they will experience an afterlife, and if so, what kind of an afterlife they will experience. Theologians have debated these questions for centuries, but the issue has taken on more urgency in recent years as the answers to the questions are implicated both in terms of how we treat animals in the profane world in which we live now and in terms of whether we will be reunited with our beloved companion animals in the afterlife. While the first issue may have been of legal or theological interest to a handful of scholars over the past few centuries, it has only really been recently, as our relationship with other animals has become ever more intimate, that people have been concerned about the second issue—being reunited in an afterworld with our companion animals. So the issue of animals' immortal souls and capacity for an afterlife has very real relevance for a great many people today. But as important as these issues are to many of us, the reality is that these questions about souls, afterlives, and mourning practices generally only extend, with very few exceptions, to certain kinds of animals—pets. Most animals, in most cultures, don't get mourned, and the question of an afterlife is not contemplated for them at all.

In this collection, the authors assembled investigate a set of related questions, including what happens after animals die, which animals live on after death, how humans grieve animals (and which animals are, in fact "grievable," to borrow Judith Butler's term), what happens to animals who are not mourned, and finally, how animal lovers suffer from the vast unmourned deaths of animals.

While there are a great many books and articles available regarding how people can cope on an individual level with the death of their companion animals, and there is more recent work on how animals mourn the deaths of other animals,[3] this collection deals with the cultural practices and attitudes that have emerged surrounding human mourning of other animals. When did these practices begin? Are they limited to companion animals? What scope and form do they take? In some ways, this collection is a counterpoint to an edited collection recently published by Jay Johnston and Fiona Probyn-Rapsey called *Animal Death*;[4] while a few chapters in *Animal Death* do cover mourning practices (see Hilda Kean's chapter on historic pet cemeteries, Peta Tait's chapter on plastinated animal corpses, and Chloë Taylor's chapter that asks whether or not we can respect the animal dead, even, for example, when eating them), much of the book is devoted to the question of death: How do the animals themselves anticipate and cope with it? Why do humans feel the right to kill, or cause the deaths of, other animals? How do we as a species cope with the grotesque amount of animal death that we ourselves have created? Ultimately, *Animal Death* both acknowledges and grants significance to the deaths of animals, something that this collection works to do as well.

The idea for this book emerged about fifteen years ago, when my friend Susan Davis and I were researching our book, *Stories Rabbits Tell*.[5] At the time, Susan was lurking on a meat rabbit listserv where people talk about raising and killing rabbits for meat. In between all of the discussions of slaughter methods and the various ways in which they go wrong,[6] one of the women told the other list members that her dog had just died, and the other participants commiserated with her and reassured her that her dog had safely traveled to the "Rainbow Bridge" where he now romped happily.[7] In fact, talking about dead pets is a pretty common occurrence on forums like this one—even those devoted at least in part to discussions of killing other animals.

It struck Susan and me that while in our world, the pet rabbit world, rabbits *do* get to go to the Rainbow Bridge after they die (at least we think they do), just like cats and dogs, in the meat rabbit world, all of the rabbits that these people slaughtered are excluded from the Bridge. In the rabbit growers' world view, rabbits are not pets, so they don't even deserve an afterlife. That thought, and the deep unfairness of it, has stayed with me ever since.

As we will see throughout this book, even though many Americans—65 percent of us, or 79.7 million households, lived with companion animals in 2015 according to the American

Pet Products Association—deeply mourn our pets when they die, not only has this not always been the case (in fact, it is probably a relatively recent development), this sense of grief does not extend to most of the animals with whom we share the planet. This inconsistency is most easily seen by looking at which animals are thought to have an afterlife in which religions, and at the beliefs in the Rainbow Bridge.

LIFE AFTER DEATH

Do nonhuman animals live on after death? Do they have an afterlife? I mean a couple of things when I ask this question. I ask, first, the obvious, but also unanswerable, question: do animals get to go to "heaven," however this may be conceived? Even though the answer to this question is no more available to us than the question of whether humans (or a particular human) will go to heaven, the question is important nevertheless, because how it is answered by a given culture gives us a glimpse into how valued animals are by that culture. It is one thing to welcome animals into our homes and our families, but do we welcome them into our spiritual realms as well? Have we granted them access to salvation, everlasting life, or a soul?

In tribal and traditional religions around the world, animals can have spiritual lives that overlap with humans' lives. The line between human and animal is not always clear in many premodern cultures, especially in the spirit realm. Therefore, the afterlife, too, is often mixed with respect to human and nonhuman. But beliefs like this are rare among the world religions.

Buddhism and Hinduism, the two major Eastern religions, also do not have strictly separated spiritual realms for humans and nonhumans. Animals and humans both have souls and can be reborn, through the cycle of rebirth, into one another. In fact, they are the only two of the major religions that explicitly allow for animals to have an afterlife like humans. But while humans and animals exist in the same continuum of life for Buddhists and Hindus, humans are considered to be the apex of what life should be; humans are thus superior to animals, and the only way that one can be reborn as an animal is through accruing negative karma in one's life. Thus becoming an animal is not something to be desired.

In the Judeo-Christian-Muslim tradition, however, animals don't get an afterlife at all. The Talmud explains that animals do not have the divine soul or spark that humans have. So while they have a material soul, they cannot forge a relationship with the Divine and cannot experience an afterlife. The other religions of the book, Christianity and Islam, follow this same path. St. Augustine wrote that only man has a rational soul, created by the breath of God. Animals have, on the other hand, only sensation and cannot attain eternal life. And finally, animals in Islam also lack the immortal or divine soul; in addition, unlike humans, they will not be judged by Allah, and thus will not be found in paradise.

The second way in which I ask whether animals live on after death has to do with any memorial practices that we may observe after their death. Most animals, throughout history and in the present, die never to be mourned, remembered, or even thought of again. They are simply lost to history. Some animals, on the other hand, live on after death—through a funeral, in a piece of literature or art, or as a museum specimen or through a gravestone. With or without an immortal soul, companion animals, and some other notable animals,[8] have been thought to at least deserve some sort of care or recognition after death.

MOURNING PRACTICES

The archaeological and zooarchaeological record gives us plenty of evidence of dog and cat, as well as other (mostly livestock but occasional wild animals), burials from the Neolithic onwards; some of these burials (although clearly not the majority) seem to indicate that the animals were intentionally buried because of a connection to the humans who buried them. Of those burials, dogs are clearly found in the majority of all the intentional burials.

In the ancient classical world, dogs were sometimes buried with gravestones that survived the ensuing centuries. One touching epitaph read: "I am in tears, while carrying you to your last resting place as much as I rejoiced when bringing you home in my own hands fifteen years ago."[9]

While burials are the oldest method of caring for a beloved animal, it wasn't until the nineteenth century that pet cemeteries emerged. Prior to that time, most animals—especially in urban areas, and even those who were cared for—were not actually buried but were disposed of in the trash. The emergence of pet cemeteries at the turn of the nineteenth century was tied to the new belief among some Europeans and Americans that animals had souls (official church doctrine notwithstanding), the rise in the suffragist and antivivisectionist movements and with them the animal protection movement, and the fact that animals could not be buried on consecrated soil and thus needed their own separate cemeteries.[10] Hilda Kean notes that animal cemeteries are "a place of visible death" in which the animals who are laid to rest there have not been killed for any purpose (as most animals have been), but have simply died naturally.[11] For this reason, pet cemeteries are not simply a mirror of human cemeteries but are an important statement about the changing nature of human–animal relationships.

Another ancient method for dealing with the animal dead, although not nearly as common as burial, was mummification. In ancient Egypt, a variety of animals was mummified. Many families mummified their pet cats and buried them in the family vault in the hope that they would be reunited together in the afterlife. Cats and other sacred animals were also mummified because they were thought to be incarnations of gods, so they were buried in an appropriately respectful fashion. Some animals were sacrificed to other gods, and mummified and buried, while still other animals were mummified and buried as food to be eaten by humans in the afterlife.

Cremation is an ancient method for disposing of the dead—used by Hindus for centuries—but is now commonly used for pets by people with practical reasons (such as the size of the animal, or the fact that many people live in apartments) precluding burial. Others may simply not want to handle the body. Samantha Hurn argues that grave digging is a cathartic act and an important part of the mourning process for human individuals who experience disenfranchised grief as a result of the wider societal objectification of animals—even pets.[12] Cremation, then, is a more sanitized form of animal disposal that removes bereaved humans from the process. On the other hand, some people who cremate their pets choose to become close to their animals in other ways. One way is through wearing one's pet's cremains in jewelry, thereby keeping a part of the animal on one's person at all times. This practice hearkens back to a very old practice called memento mori (Latin for "remember that you will die"). Mourning jewelry, made from the hair of (human) loved ones, sometimes combined with a postmortem portrait, was popular from the sixteenth to the nineteenth centuries and served much the same purpose.

In Japan, where pet cremation is common, many people place their animals' cremains into a shrine in a Buddhist temple where they surround it with a photo of their pet, Buddhist symbols, and mementos of their pet's life and visit it on holidays. Both Elmer Veldkamp and Barbara Ambros have written extensively about the history of animal funeral rites in Japan and how pet funerary practices evolved out of an ancient, pre-Buddhist fear about appeasing the angry spirits of animals who were killed through hunting.[13] For modern Japanese pet owners, however, these rites are primarily about, as they are in the West, dealing with the owners' grief.

Today we also have at our disposal other ways to mourn our companion animals, such as pet obituaries that, according to Jane Desmond, "assert the legitimacy of a pet's family member status and legitimate mourning for that familial loss,"[14] and online memorials that, like pet obituaries, are another venue that provides for socially marginalized grief such as that which is felt for nonhuman animals. In addition, pet memorial websites provide online communities of supporters who help the mourner through their grief in a way that is often not possible in the nonvirtual world.

All of the above methods for dealing with animal remains have been almost exclusively used to deal with the remains of companion animals. One practice that began as a means of immortalizing "game animals," or animals who were killed by hunting, is taxidermy, and this method (as will be discussed in Christina Colvin's chapter) is now being used to memorialize pet animals as well. While this practice has some historical precedents (as, for example, with the mounting and display of Hachikō, the Akita known for his loyalty to his owner, in the National Science Museum of Japan), for the most part, animals were not preserved in this way because someone grieved for them. As Jane Desmond points out, in a comparison of taxidermic animal bodies with plastinated human cadavers (in exhibitions like *Body Worlds*), the human corpses displayed in *Body Worlds* are acceptable (and wildly popular) because they lack skin, making them a form of "anti-taxidermy."[15] This is contrasted with the taxidermic animals displayed both in museums and in private homes that are mostly artificial; the only thing that remains of the living animal is the skin.

THE RAINBOW BRIDGE

Even though for Christians, pets cannot go to heaven,[16] that has not stopped some Christians from creating an afterlife for animals that acts as a sort of a backdoor into heaven. This notion, called the Rainbow Bridge, allows *some animals*—companion animals—to accompany their owners or guardians into heaven and thus provides countless animal lovers a feeling of solace when thinking about the passing of their beloved pets. And yet the notion of a heaven that is restricted to only a certain kind of animal—pets—and only those who were "owned" at the time of their death, simply reinforces the kinds of deeply inconsistent ways in which we treat animals here on earth.

The Rainbow Bridge began as a poem that was written in the 1980s or 1990s by an unknown author and became popular on Internet pet newsgroups. It is probably based on a couple of myths: the Norse myth of a burning rainbow bridge called the Bifröst, which connects earth to the land of the gods, and a Native American belief that the Milky Way connects heaven to earth, with a bridge that is guarded by dogs that lies at the fork of the Milky Way.

The poem reads as follows:

There is a bridge connecting Heaven and Earth.
It is called the Rainbow Bridge because of all its beautiful colors.
Just this side of the Rainbow Bridge there is a land of meadows,
Hills, and valleys with lush green grass.
When a beloved pet dies, the pet goes to this place.
There is always food and water and warm spring weather.
The old and frail animals are young again.
Those who were sick, hurt, or in pain are made whole again.
There is only one thing missing;
They are not with their special person who loved them so much.
So each day they run and play until the day
When one suddenly stops playing and looks up!
The nose twitches! The ears are up!
The eyes are staring, and this one runs from the group!
You have been seen, and when you and your special friend meet,
You take him in your arms and hug him.
He licks and kisses your face again and again—
And you look once more into the eyes of your best friend and trusting pet.
Then you cross the Rainbow Bridge together never again to be apart.

As is clear through reading the poem, the Rainbow Bridge refers to both the temporary place—a land of hills and meadows—to which the animal goes immediately after death, and also to the bridge connecting this world to heaven (which is implied, rather than explicitly stated). It is, therefore, a liminal space; it is fun, certainly, with "food and water and warm spring weather." It is also a magical place where ailments are cured and, as with the beliefs associated with cargo cults and other revitalization movements, the old are young again and the disabled are made whole again. But it is not where the animals are meant to remain, as is demonstrated in the line "there is only one thing missing." That one thing of course is the missing human. The anthropocentrism of the Bridge becomes clear now, because the animal's happiness, even when dead, is not complete until his or her owner appears (after death, of course). That is when their nose twitches and their ears perk up and they can achieve true happiness, crossing the bridge together to their permanent destiny.

Perhaps most importantly, however, the poem reinforces the fact that the afterlife, even one that is made up by animal lovers, is reserved for pets. "When a beloved *pet* dies, the *pet* goes to this place." This poem is ubiquitous on both pet memorial websites as well as animal rescue websites' memorial pages. Occasionally a farm animal sanctuary or non–pet animal website might host the poem on their website, but when it does, the word "pet" will be substituted with the word "animal" to make it more inclusive. But the vast majority of versions of this poem, in all languages into which I've seen it translated, use the word "pet."

There is now a second version of the poem known as the "Rescuer's Rainbow Bridge" that is intended for rescued animals. According to the original poem, only "owned pet" animals get escorted across the bridge, since it is the animal's owner who brings them across, which means that nonowned animals (i.e., street animals, shelter pets, etc.) cannot cross. In the Rescuer's poem, abandoned and shelter animals must wait for a rescuer to die, who then escorts all of the homeless animals across—a moving, but at the same time, extremely sad image indeed.

Today the Rainbow Bridge is found in every Western country as well as in many Asian countries—even Buddhist countries like Japan.

WHOSE LIVES ARE GRIEVABLE?

In all of these cases, the practices discussed are, with very rare exceptions, used for companion animals. Philosopher Judith Butler, in her 2009 book, *Frames of War: When Is Life Grievable?*, discusses the ways in which Americans (the media, politicians, and the public) frame the wars in the Middle East such that we often do not recognize Afghans or Iraqis as fully human, and thus most of us do not grieve their deaths.[17] According to Butler, they don't live "grievable" lives like we do.

Most animals, who die in numbers that defy the imagination, don't live grievable lives, and thus are not mourned when they die. Leslie Irvine, in her discussion of the aftermath of Hurricane Katrina, contrasted the public's concern about a little boy who the media reported was separated from his dog, Snowball, to the lack of concern about the hundreds of thousands of chickens who drowned during the flood.[18] This is just one example of the selective grief that we choose to feel for some animals that we don't feel for other—most—animals. When humans do mourn or memorialize nonpet animals, it is something extraordinary to behold. In 2011, hundreds of South Korean Buddhist monks and believers offered public prayers for the almost two million animals who were killed—mostly burned alive—in an outbreak of foot-and-mouth disease in that country. According to a news report published at the time, the participants wrote condolence notes to the dead. One read, "It must have been painful and you cried a lot. I hope that you go to a good place and enjoy happiness."[19]

And even companion animal guardians, who now have at their disposal a whole host of ways to commemorate their pets, still often face public ridicule when mourning the passing of their beloved companions. It is still far from publicly acceptable to openly grieve the deaths of dogs or cats, the most normative companion animals, and as Chloë Taylor points out, when we cannot mourn the animals whom we have loved, it makes even their lived lives less "real."[20] To make matters worse, with very rare exceptions (living with an Amazon parrot, say, or a giant tortoise), our companion animals will die long before we do. As Jessica Pierce points out in her book *The Last Walk*, we know, as soon as we bring a companion animal home, that we will have to watch them die.[21] Their deaths, then, are preordained and intimately connected with our love for them.

NOTES

1. Stanley Brandes, "The Meaning of American Pet Cemetery Gravestones," *Ethnology* 48, no. 2 (2009): 99–118. See Barbara Ambros, "Vengeful Spirits or Loving Spiritual Companions? Changing Views of Animal Spirits in Contemporary Japan," *Asian Ethnology* 69 (2010): 35–67; Barbara

Ambros, *Bones of Contention: Animals and Religion in Modern Japan* (Honolulu: University of Hawai'i Press, 2012).
2. Steven J. Mithen, *After the Ice: A Global Human History, 20000–5000 BC* (Cambridge, MA: Harvard University Press, 2004).
3. See especially Barbara J. King, *How Animals Grieve* (Chicago: University of Chicago Press, 2013); David Alderton, *Animal Grief: How Animals Mourn* (Dorchester: Veloce Publishing, 2011).
4. Jay Johnston and Fiona Probyn-Rapsey, eds., *Animal Death* (Sydney: Sydney University Press, 2013).
5. Susan Davis and Margo DeMello, *Stories Rabbits Tell: A Natural and Cultural History of a Misunderstood Creature* (New York: Lantern, 2005).
6. Rabbits are not covered under the Humane Methods of Slaughter Act, so there is no officially sanctioned method of killing nor do they have to be stunned before their necks are slit open. In addition, many methods leave rabbits screaming during slaughter, and even many people who do this regularly are squeamish about it, so home "growers" who slaughter their own rabbits are always seeking new methods for killing their rabbits.
7. The Rainbow Bridge is an internet-borne belief about where companion animals go after they die.
8. In particular, animals of historical importance like race horses, animals who served in war, and "famous" animals like well-loved zoo or circus animals often receive a life after death, which often ends up being in a museum after being taxidermied. But it should be noted that nonfamous animals, too, like animals who were killed to be hunting trophies, also experience such a life after death. See Garry Marvin, "Enlivened through Memory: Hunters and Hunting Trophies," in *The Afterlives of Animals: A Museum Menagerie*, ed. Samuel J. M. M. Alberti, 202–17 (Charlottesville: University of Virginia Press, 2011).
9. Anthony L. Podberscek, Elizabeth S. Paul, and James A. Serpell, eds., *Companion Animals and Us: Exploring the Relationships between People and Pets* (Cambridge: Cambridge University Press, 2000), 33.
10. Philip Howell, "A Place for the Animal Dead: Pets, Pet Cemeteries and Animal Ethics in Late Victorian Britain," *Ethics, Place & Environment* 5, no. 1 (2002): 5–22.
11. Hilda Kean, "Human and Animal Space in Historic 'Pet' Cemeteries in London, New York and Paris," in Johnston and Probyn-Rapsey, *Animal Death*, 39.
12. Samantha Hurn, email to the author, July 7, 2014.
13. Elmer Veldkamp, "The Emergence of 'Pets as Family' and the Socio-Historical Development of Pet Funerals in Japan," *Anthrozoös* 22, no. 4 (2009): 333–46; Ambros, *Bones of Contention*.
14. Jane Desmond, "Animal Deaths and the Written Record of History: The Politics of Pet Obituaries," in *Making Animal Meaning*, ed. Linda Kalof and Georgina M. Montgomery (East Lansing: Michigan State University Press, 2011), 104.
15. Jane Desmond, "Postmortem Exhibitions: Taxidermied Animals and Plastinated Corpses in the Theaters of the Dead," *Configurations* 16, no. 3 (2008): 347–78.
16. In late November 2014, Catholic animal lovers around the world had a momentary feeling of hope after an Italian newspaper misquoted Pope Francis as having said that "Paradise is open to all creatures." However, Francis said no such thing. Vecchi Gian Guido, "Il Papa e gli animali 'Il Paradiso è aperto a tutte le creature,'" *Corriere della Sera*, November 27, 2014, 25.
17. Judith Butler, *Frames of War: When Is Life Grievable?* (London: Verso, 2009).
18. Leslie Irvine, *Filling the Ark: Animal Welfare in Disasters* (Philadelphia: Temple University Press, 2009).

19. Haeran Hyun, "South Korean Buddhists Pray for Animals Killed during Foot-and-Mouth Disease Epidemic," *Los Angeles Times*, January 21, 2011. http://latimesblogs.latimes.com/unleashed/2011/01/south-korean-buddhists-pray-for-dead-animals-.html.
20. Chloë Taylor, "Respect for the (Animal) Death," in Johnston and Probyn-Rapsey, *Animal Death*, 85–102, 97.
21. Jessica Pierce, *The Last Walk: Reflections on Our Pets at the End of Their Lives* (Chicago: University of Chicago Press, 2012).

Discarded Property

MARY SHANNON JOHNSTONE

In North Carolina, the state in which I live, every year over one hundred thousand dogs and cats are euthanized because there is no place to put them (North Carolina Department of Health and Human Services). That is almost 300 animals every day, which I find shocking and heartbreaking.

Before I began this project, I knew that animal euthanasia was a fact. When I heard the statistics, I naively wanted to believe that those two hundred thousand euthanized dogs and cats were the bad ones—the sick, aggressive, feral, mean dogs and cats that needed to be put down. But that first visit was crushing. I was devastated to find dogs and cats that looked and acted just like my six beloved pets at home. While there were some very sick animals and several aggressive beasts, the vast majority were docile pets that just couldn't find a home. Several appeared to be "pure" breeds. On that morning, which was a typical one, I witnessed the deaths of eighty-two animals. The only difference between most of these cats and dogs and the ones in my house was that nobody loved them. I cried all the way home.

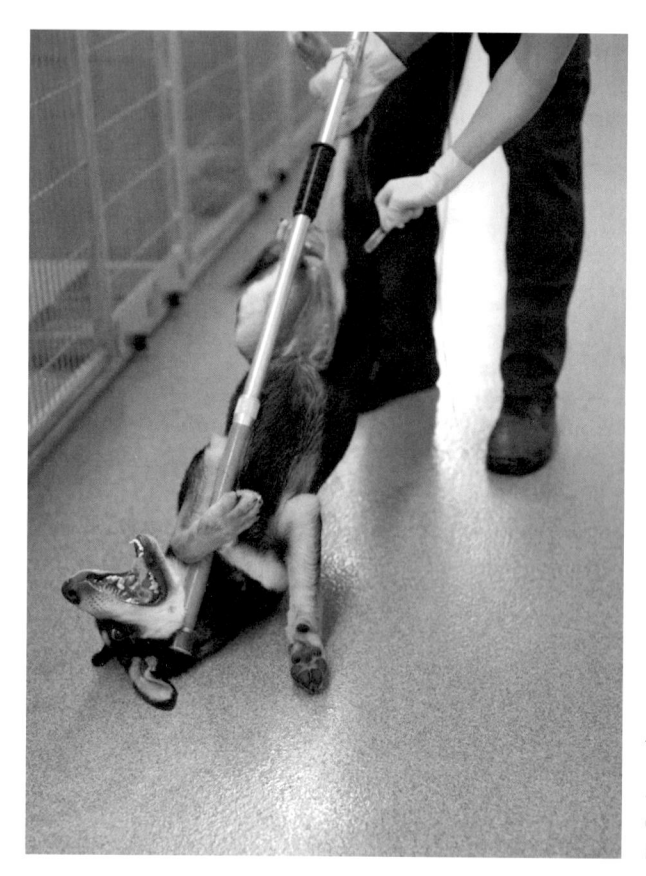

Mary Shannon Johnstone, *Anesthetize*. Cats and dogs are anesthetized before they are euthanized. Although the sedation does not hurt, many fight because they are scared.

Mary Shannon Johnstone, *Blood*. Euthanized dog.

Mary Shannon Johnstone, *Cats in Freezer*. Cat carcasses are stored in a walk-in freezer until they can be picked up and disposed of.

Mary Shannon Johnstone, *Cats Euthanized*. After cats and dogs have been anesthetized, they are then euthanized by injection with an even stronger anesthetic.

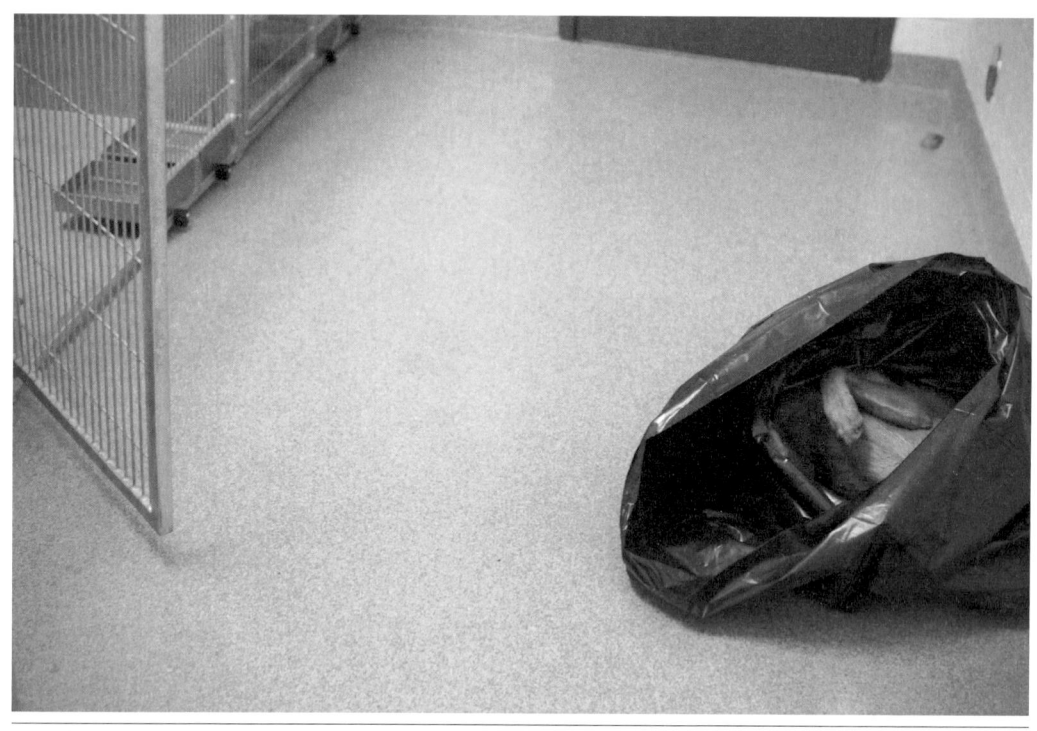

Mary Shannon Johnstone, *Poor Dead Dog*. A euthanized dog is placed in a large plastic garbage bag.

Mary Shannon Johnstone, *Three Scared Puppies*. Three scared puppies await euthanasia.

Mary Shannon Johnstone, *Dead Dogs*. After dogs have been euthanized, their bodies are placed into large black plastic bags and their kennels are sanitized.

Mary Shannon Johnstone, *Cats in Cages*. Euthanized cats are lined up in their cages to be counted.

PART 1

When Did We Start Caring about Animal Death?

More than a Bag of Bones
A History of Animal Burials

IVY D. COLLIER

Love of animals is a universal impulse, a common ground on which all of us may meet. By loving and understanding animals, perhaps we humans shall come to understand each other.

—DR. LOUIS J. CAMUTI

ANIMAL BURIALS HAVE BEEN FOUND THROUGHOUT THE ARCHAEOLOGICAL RECORD dating back to the Neolithic period. The question is, how do we know if those burials are the result of a human–animal bond or if the animals buried are what zooarchaeologists call articulated or associated animal bone groups?

There are a great many reasons why animals could be found buried that may have nothing to do with a relationship with a person. For example, animals could be buried after a sacrifice (the animal was killed but was left whole); the animal could have died of natural causes (it may have simply fallen into a pit); it may have been killed but not consumed (young animals could have been buried alive as a means of population control soon after birth); the animal could have been killed and consumed (it would show marks of butchery); it could have been killed or buried alive with a human as grave goods or food offerings (it may have been partially dismembered or butchered or could be whole); the animal could be a foundation offering (when buried under the foundation of a home); it could be a companion offering (buried alongside a human); it could be intended to accompany a human on his or her journey to the afterworld; or finally, the animal could truly be buried because of a special relationship that the human had with that animal when alive. Clearly, though, there are more reasons that an animal might have been buried if it was not a companion than if it was. The reality is that most animals found buried throughout human history were not buried as companions and were not buried in graves; they were buried in pits and were buried for a functional purpose for humans or were simply discarded by humans.

There are some good indications of animals being buried as companions, however. If the animals were older, were whole, and were buried either near or with humans, those are good indications that they may have been loved or well regarded by humans. Another good sign is if the animal was buried with his or her own grave goods, such as food to accompany the animal to the afterlife. This chapter, however, will deal with the archaeological and historical evidence of true animal burials and how modern animal funerary practices evolved.

ANTIQUITY

Archaeologists, historians, and anthropologists have provided us with a great deal of evidence suggesting that humans and other animals have long shared a special bond. In particular, focusing on the burial rituals and other funerary practices dedicated to nonhuman animals has demonstrated that this bond has grown stronger throughout history. One of the earliest depictions that speaks to this bond is the pre-Natufian[1] (23,000–11,500 BCE) and Natufian (13,000–9,800 BCE) archaeological sites throughout the Eastern Mediterranean.[2] Both of these cultures are considered unique in that, even though they were probably hunter-gatherers, they were semisedentary/sedentary and were among the first known to live in villages. These communities existed in an area that is now dry and barren but was once a lush woodland area where people cultivated numerous types of plants, fruits, nuts, and cereals as well as hunted woodland animals. Within these areas, researchers found burial sites that show evidence that the Natufian kept domesticated animals, which indicates a distinctive human–animal relationship. Although some of these animals may have been used for food, fur, and possibly to guard or hunt with, there is an indication that some animals may have been kept solely as companions.[3]

Uyun al-Hammam,[4] a pre-Natufian burial site, consists of several elaborate human burials, some of which contain human remains and personal ornaments such as shell beading, animal teeth, and jewelry like bracelets, necklaces, and earrings. One of these burial sites included a human buried with a fox; evidence shows that this fox was not treated as an object or an adornment but rather as a companion. It was not uncommon for archeologists to find fox burial sites in this region, although most of the foxes displayed fragmented bones or bones that exhibited butcher marks indicating that these animals were used for food or fur.[5] However, this fox may have been buried alongside the human so they could be reunited in the afterlife. Archaeologists believe that the burial of the fox and human may have a similar symbolic importance as that of a human and dog does today.[6] We may never know the true relationship between this human and fox; we can only speculate that there may have been emotional and social ties connecting the two. What we do know is that we see this type of emotional connection throughout history.

The ancient Egyptians believed animals possessed a soul like humans in addition to their physical beings. Researchers have found that some pharaohs and other elite members of ancient Egyptian society were buried with their prized animals like horses or companion animals such as dogs and cats. Examples of this were in 1400 BCE when Pharaoh Amenhotep II was buried with his hunting dog, and ten years later his successor Pharaoh Thutmose IV was buried with his favorite cat. Clearly pharaohs thought enough of their companion animals to be buried with them, either because they wanted to continue to have them as companions or for utilitarian purposes in their afterlives.[7]

Numerous animals like crocodiles, rams, and dogs were seen as representatives of gods in ancient Egypt, but cats were considered semidivine. There were several gods that were associated with cats, with the most famous being Bast (also spelled Bastet) who was the goddess of protection, fertility, sun, moon, and pleasure. Cats were held in high esteem because they killed vermin that would otherwise destroy crops and supplies. Although cats were often used for utilitarian purposes, only pharaohs could *own* cats, and since they were looked upon as the pharaoh's property, harming any cat was considered treason and carried stiff penalties, including death.[8]

When cats died, a cat's family entered into a period of mourning that included family members shaving their eyebrows to demonstrate to the public their grief. It was common for the deceased cat to be massaged with the best essential oils during the embalming and mummification process and to be wrapped in fine linen. Cats were often either buried in feline-only tombs or interred in Bubastis, which was the Bast center of worship. Cats were usually buried with milk, rats, or mice so they would have the provisions they needed for the journey into the afterlife.[9]

Large numbers of animal cemeteries started to appear after the fall of the New Kingdom around 1075 BCE in Egypt.[10] Once the New Kingdom was succeeded by the Third Intermediate Period,[11] Egypt had no pharaoh to mediate relationships between humans and the gods. This led to a rise in animal mummies, which ordinary citizens used to petition the gods for favors, such as good health, long lives, prosperity, and easing family strife. It has been estimated that thirty-one cemeteries held at least twenty million animal mummies at one time.[12]

THE CONTEMPORARY WORLD

There is no doubt that throughout the years animals have changed history by fulfilling utilitarian needs for herders, farmers, and hunters. They have served in religious ceremonies as well as defined social structures and provided economic status in cultures across the world. And, as can be seen from this brief look at the funerary practices of the ancient world, they have played an intimate part in the familial lives of humans as well.

Japan has been ritually mourning animals for thousands of years, although it has only been recently that those practices have been extended to pets. According to scholars of Japanese culture,[13] these rituals and memorials emerged because the Japanese needed to appease the spirits of those animals—bears, whales, and others—whom they killed while hunting. They were later extended to all animals who were used by the Japanese.[14] In recent decades, with the rise of Western concepts of pet keeping and the afterlife, appeasing angry spirits is no longer the motivation behind modern pet-mourning rituals.

Japan is a primarily Buddhist country in which most people believe that both humans and animals will be reincarnated. Each person tries to live a life of dignity and respect, and when the person dies they hope to be reincarnated as a higher being. This process will repeat until the person reaches nirvana, which is a state of pure happiness. While it is debatable if animals can reach nirvana, what can be agreed upon is that many Japanese believe that it is their responsibility to ensure that their deceased pet, who shares with them the cycle of birth and rebirth, is memorialized properly.[15]

Today, Japanese companion animals are held in the same regard as family members—and in fact experience very similar death rituals as human family members.[16] An example of such a ritual from the early twentieth century follows:

> We got a rectangular grave marker.... On the front, I wrote, "cat grave." On the back, I wrote a haiku.... To the left and right of the grave, we set out two glass vases filled with bush clover flowers. In front we put a teacup of water.... Every month, on the same day of the month the cat had died, my wife offered a slice of salmon and a bowl of rice topped with dried bonito flakes in front of the grave.[17]

Once a pet dies, there are number of ways to honor their life. Some pet owners decide to have their pet cremated or they can elect to purchase a pet grave or shelf in a shrine associated with a temple.[18] Economic limitations may force pet owners to choose a shelf over a grave, but there are other reasons as well, such as the desire to give deceased pets others with whom to play in the spirit world.

Usually pet funerals are a scaled-down version of human funerals and include the deceased animal being placed in a simple, cardboard coffin, and a Buddhist or Shinto priest reciting a series of prayers for the pet.

Once the pet is buried, the family will either purchase a headstone, or if they have rented a shelf, they will have a memorial tablet created. Memorial tablets are similar to tombstones in that they are etched with basic information about the pet but can also contain a favorite quote or endearing statement. Mourning rituals continue after the pet has been laid to rest by offering incense at a temple altar; some family members will offer incense for a period of time after the death while others only offer incense on special holidays and the anniversary of the pet's death. Likewise, many family members will visit the pet's grave or shelf during special times of the year, including the anniversary of the pet's death—sometimes for fifty years after the death, just as for humans. They may show respect by replacing old flowers and in some cases offering the pet's favorite foods or toys. It is important for family members to remember and remain respectful of their dearly loved pet, and some even feel that they will be reunited with their companion animals in another life.

In America, too, we find a long history of mourning practices for nonhuman animals. Indeed, the human–animal relationship is neatly blended into American history and continues to grow and change as society continues to evolve. During the precolonial period, Native Americans formed complex relationships with a variety of animals like bison, deer, and other woodland creatures. Many hunting tribes showed great respect for animals, and even though they needed to hunt them for food and other uses, they felt that they must be killed in a proper, ritualized manner.[19] Some Native Americans believed that animal deaths are temporary and that the animal would be reincarnated and return to our world as the same species. If the hunter did not kill the animal properly, the animal could return as a ghost and haunt the hunter and possibly infect him with a disease.

As European settlers arrived, new animals were introduced to the developing American culture. For example, caged birds like mockingbirds and goldfinches arrived along with cats and new "companion" animals. By the late eighteenth and nineteenth centuries, purpose-bred companion animals including "lap animals" were prevalent in all walks of life and were commonly called "pet."[20] Our affinity for companion animals continued to flourish, which is evident by the arrival of animals like dogs, cats, and squirrels showing up on greeting cards, children's books, and calendars during this period.[21]

During the twentieth century, people sought to better understand their livestock, flocked to roadside circuses and zoos in order to view wildlife, and many companion animals, especially dogs, retired for the night inside their family home. The American Society for the Prevention of Cruelty to Animals (ASPCA), founded in 1866, and its many spin-offs were working to eliminate animal cruelty and educate people on the proper treatment of animals.

It was also around this time period that America's first pet cemetery, Hartsdale Canine Cemetery, was founded in New York.[22] Hartsdale is not only the oldest pet cemetery in the United States but also the largest pet cemetery in the country with over forty thousand animals buried there.[23] "Officially and ritualistically, burying a family pet is probably a logical extension of the evolving nature of human–animal relationships, especially since that relationship has increased in emotional intensity in the twentieth century."[24]

Throughout the years animals slowly moved from farm help to family members who are adored and loved. Pets are so loved that they are now showing up in a loved one's obituary, noted with other family members, and some even have their own obituaries. For example, Legacy.com will allow you to write a tribute to your pet and attach pictures and music. These online obituaries are a way to celebrate the life of a pet while allowing family and friends from near and far to read the obituary to share in the grieving process. It is also a way of understanding the death of a pet by enacting the rituals and memorials that were once reserved only for humans.

The International Association of Pet Cemeteries and Crematories estimates that there are between two hundred and three hundred cemeteries in the United States to provide aftercare services for beloved pets that have passed away.[25] These services range from picking up the deceased pet from the home or veterinary office to full funeral services including music, prayers, flowers, and repast. Hartsdale offers a small chapel for funerals that is accompanied by a priest, scripture readings, poems (usually relating to the Rainbow Bridge),[26] and prayers.

Why do Americans choose to bury their pets in cemeteries or have them cremated? Anthropologist Stanley Brandes writes:

> Pet owners who bury their companion animals in cemeteries are not part of a small group with unique or extreme relationships to those animals. Rather, they seem to hold a pronounced version of widely held beliefs and attitudes, which overall serve to diminish, if not entirely obliterate, the categorical distinction between beast and human.[27]

One such pet owner gave a heartfelt explanation:

> I tried burying our first baby in the back of the house. But every time I looked out the kitchen window, either passing by or while I was washing the dishes, I had to see her out there. Even after a year, when the grass had grown back, I was still crying over that little girl. It was too upsetting for me. When we heard about this place, I had my husband dig her up and bring her out here.[28]

This pet owner may have felt that giving her pet an "appropriate" burial in a cemetery may bring closure to the death and help with grieving. Perhaps having her pet at the cemetery helped memorialize the death and gave the pet owner a place to continue showing her love and respect for the pet for years to come.

One anonymous pet owner who had her pet cremated at a local humane society said that many pet owners choose to cremate their pets because it is affordable and they can take their pet's ashes with them wherever they choose to go. She went on to say that she had a pet cremated a few years ago and found it hard to have the urn in the house the first few months after the pet died. However, she is comforted by the thought that she can still celebrate special holidays like birthdays and Christmas with her pet because her urn is there.[29] The pet owner said that looking at her pet's picture on the urn and reading the urn inscription, a poem that she wrote for her pet, reminds her of how much she loves her pet and of the wonderful bond they shared.

This final anecdote illustrates one key way that the human–animal relationship has evolved. Many animals are no longer valued strictly for their utility—although that is clearly still the case for most noncompanion animals—but rather they are now considered by many as friends, confidants, and family members. From articulated animal bone groups to deeply adored animals who are buried or cremated with love, and are remembered for years afterward, our relationships with these animals have certainly, in some very important ways, been transformed. These rituals and memorials show us just how deep our connection is with other animals and show just how we remember, mourn, and also celebrate our loved ones. One question that these examples beg, however, is whether we will begin extending this connection to other animals as well.

NOTES

1. The *Natufian* culture (pronounced /nəˈtjuːfiən/) was a Mesolithic culture that existed in the Levant, a region in the Eastern Mediterranean.
2. The Eastern Mediterranean includes the countries that are located to the east of the Mediterranean Sea. This region, known as the Levant, is commonly thought of as Syria, Cyprus, Turkey, Greece, and Egypt but also contains Palestine, Lebanon, Jordan, and Israel.
3. Reuven Yeshurun et al., "The Social Role of Food in the Natufian Cemetery of Raqefet Cave, Mount Carmel, Israel," *Journal of Anthropological Archaeology* 32 (2013): 511–26. O. Bar-Yosef, "The Natufian Culture in the Levant: Threshold to the Origins of Agriculture," *Evolutionary Anthropology* 6 (1999): 159–77. Brian F. Byrd, "Death, Mortuary Ritual, and Natufian Social Structure," *Journal of Anthropological Archaeology* 14 (1999): 251–87.
4. Uyun al-Hammam, in northern Jordan, is the oldest (16,500 years old) cemetery in the Middle East.
5. See Lisa A. Maher et al., "A Unique Human-Fox Burial from a Pre-Natufian Cemetery in the Levant (Jordan)," *PLoS ONE* 6, no. 1 (2011): e15815, doi:10.1371/journal.pone.0015815.
6. Maher et al., "A Unique Human-Fox Burial."
7. Eric A. Powell, "Messengers to the Gods," *Archaeology*, March/April 2014, 48–52.
8. Powell, "Messengers to the Gods," 48–52. Giacomo Gnudi et al., "Radiological Investigation of an over 2000-Year-Old Egyptian Mummy of a Cat," *Journal of Feline Medicine and Surgery* 14 (2012): 291–93. Donald J. Hughes, "Sustainable Agriculture in Ancient Egypt," Agriculture History 66, no. 2 (1992): 12–22.
9. Powell, "Messengers to the Gods," 48–52. Gnudi et al., "Radiological Investigation," 291–93. Hughes, "Sustainable Agriculture in Ancient Egypt," 12–22.
10. The New Kingdom of Egypt was a time of tremendous wealth and power. This time period falls between the sixteenth century BCE and the eleventh century BCE and covers the Eighteenth, Nineteenth, and Twentieth Dynasties of Egypt.
11. The Intermediate Period in Egypt ranged from 1070 BCE to 664 BCE and was considered to be a time of political instability and decline.
12. Eric A. Powell, "Messengers to the Gods," *Archaeology*, March/April 2014: 48–52.
13. See Elmer Veldkamp, "The Emergence of 'Pets as Family' and the Socio-Historical Development of Pet Funerals in Japan," *Anthrozoös* 22, no. 4 (2009): 333–46; Barbara Ambros, "Vengeful Spirits or Loving Spiritual Companions? Changing Views of Animal Spirits in Contemporary Japan," *Asian Ethnology* 69 (2010): 35–67; Barbara Ambros, *Bones of Contention: Animals and Religion in Modern Japan* (Honolulu: University of Hawai'i Press, 2012).

14. We see this later in memorials to animals killed in Japanese wars or animals used in laboratories in Japan.
15. Elizabeth Kenney, "Pet Funerals and Animal Graves in Japan," *Mortality* 9, no. 1 (2004): 42–60.
16. Kenney, "Pet Funerals and Animal Graves in Japan."
17. Natsume Sōseki, *Ten Nights' Dreams and Our Cat's Grave*, trans. Sankichi Hata and Dofu Shirai (Tokyo: Tokyo News Service, 1934).
18. Pet graves can be purchased either for an individual pet or as a communal grave. In many cases, the pet is actually cremated, but the grave itself is a part of the memorial process. The grave site that adorns a tombstone allows the pet owners to decorate the graves throughout the year in memory of their beloved pet. Pet cemeteries are primarily for pets only, although there are some that are attached to human cemeteries or adjoined to Buddhist temples. Some pet cemeteries create spaces for pet owners to buy or rent and store their pet's urn. Pet owners are allowed to decorate and memorialize their space as appropriate. These spaces are also known as shelves, apartment graves, or lock-style graves.
19. Lucretia Kelly, "Beyond Food: The Role of Animals in Ritual and Ideology," *Illinois Antiquity* (2010): 8–10.
20. The term "pet" means "tamed animal" and has its origins in Scottish and northern English dialect and was exclusive in those areas until the mid-eighteenth century.
21. Katherine C. Grier, *Pets in America: A History* (Chapel Hill: University of North Carolina Press, 2006).
22. Hartsdale Pet Cemetery was founded in 1896 in Hartsdale, New York, by Dr. Samuel Johnson. Johnson, a veterinarian, opened the cemetery after one of his clients called him in a panic after her dog died. She was concerned about giving her dog a "proper" burial, but there was no legal place to do so within New York. Hartsdale started as a canine-only cemetery but has since expanded to include cats, rabbits, birds, and other companion animals. Hartsdale also provides crematory services for all types of pets, provides funeral services, and offers headstone design and placement (http://www.hartsdalepetcrematory.com/).
23. David D. Witt, "Pet Burial in the United States," in *Handbook of Death and Dying*, ed. Clifton D. Bryant and Dennis L. Peck (Thousand Oaks, CA: Sage Publications, 2003), 757–67.
24. Witt, "Pet Burial in the United States," 757.
25. Witt, "Pet Burial in the United States," 2.
26. "Rainbow Bridge" is a poem that tells the story that when a pet dies, they go to a land that is just before the Rainbow Bridge. This is a happy place, where the pet is restored to health and plays all day with other animals. Although the pet is living a happy life, they still miss their owner. When the owner passes away, they will reunite with their pet and enter into heaven (https://rainbowsbridge.com/poem.htm).
27. Stanley Brandes, "The Meaning of American Pet Cemetery Gravestones," *Ethnology* 48, no. 2 (2009): 101.
28. Witt, "Pet Burial in the United States," 10.
29. Personal communication with the author, 2009.

Mourning the Sacrifice
Behavior and Meaning behind Animal Burials

JAMES MORRIS

THE REMAINS OF ANIMALS, FRAGMENTS OF BONE AND HORN, ARE OFTEN THE MOST common finds recovered from archaeological excavations. The potential of using this material to examine questions of past economics and environment has long been recognized and is viewed by many archaeologists as the primary purpose of animal remains. In part this is due to the paradigm in which zooarchaeology developed and a consequence of practitioners' concentration on taphonomy and quantification.[1] But the complex intertwined relationships between humans and animals have long been recognized, a good example being Lévi-Strauss's oft quoted "natural species are chosen, not because they are 'good to eat' but because they are 'good to think.'"[2] The relatively recent development of social zooarchaeology has led to a more considered approach to the meanings and relationships animals have with past human cultures.[3] Animal burials are a deposit type for which social, rather than economic, interpretations are of particular relevance.

When animal remains are recovered from archaeological sites they are normally found in a state of disarticulation and fragmentation, but occasionally remains of an individual animal are found in articulation. These types of deposits have long been noted in the archaeological record, although their descriptions, such as "special animal deposit,"[4] can be heavily loaded with interpretation. In Europe some of the earliest work on animal burials was Behrens's investigation into the "Animal skeleton finds of the Neolithic and Early Metallic Age," which discussed 459 animal burials from across Europe.[5] Dogs were the most common species to be buried, and the majority of these cases were associated with inhumations. Behrens suggests that animal parts not found in association with human remains may be foundation deposits for the divine blessing of a new construction or perhaps part of an animal cult. For remains recovered with human remains Behrens uses three categories of explanation: *sociological*, the animal is a gift; *spiritual*, the animal is a guide; and *emotional*, the animal may be a favored pet or a gift by the mourners.[6] Inspired by Gabalówna,[7] Behrens accepted that ideas of sacrifice, emotion, and holy status might be applied to humans and animals alike. The concepts of animals as sacrifices and as holy objects are still trends within the interpretation of animal burials today, but Behrens remains one of the few archaeologists to consider, albeit briefly, the human emotion behind these deposits.

ANIMAL BURIALS: PROBLEMS AND POSSIBILITIES

As a discipline that deals mainly in material culture and the ephemeral traces of humanity's past, there is still a lack of consideration of emotion within archaeology. It is often viewed as unrecoverable from the archaeological record, or not suitable for objective analysis.[8] When emotion and mourning are considered in archaeology it is mainly in the context of funerary remains and often not explicitly. For example discussions regarding the inclusion of flowers in prehistoric graves and other material deposits are often discussed in the context of the funerary "ritual" rather than in terms of the personal and emotional, although emotion is implied.[9] As Peterson points out, while the processes are well understood, the emotional damage of grief and loss are often omitted.[10]

The problems archaeologists have with considering emotions, such as mourning, are highlighted by recent experiences. My family has lost and mourned both human and animal family members; both resulted in grief, both public and private, and burial in cemeteries with other mammals of the same species. Henry, an ironically nervous, yet massive black-and-white male cat was interred beside an olive tree, next to our previously deceased cats, Greebo and Pepsi, and another family pet, Tango. That we conducted a ritualized ceremony similar to that undertaken for human family members underlines what these animals meant to us. This ceremony was so important that Henry was transported three hundred miles so he could be buried in this specific locale in the presence of other feline family members.

If future archaeologists were to excavate the site containing these cat burials, and assuming excellent bone survival, what would they be able to ascertain? If there were limited postdepositional disturbance, the remains would be found in articulation and easy to identify to species. Metal buckles would be found with each cat, as the fabric of the collars would have disintegrated; these would probably date the burials as well as suggest the animals were pets.[11] The skeletal morphology and possible further DNA would identify that three males and one female were present, all old adults.[12] Pathological changes associated with osteoarthritis may be present on all four skeletons, and one male (Greebo) would have a false hip joint and metal pins in the pelvis and femur indicating medical intervention during his life. Stable isotope analysis of the teeth using strontium and/or oxygen[13] would indicate two of the males (Greebo and Tango) and the female cat (Pepsi) all grew up in the same local region, although analysis of their bones would give a mixed signature, suggesting they spent some of their life in a different part of the United Kingdom. The teeth, as well as bones, of the other male cat (Henry) would have a different signature, for an area one hundred miles away from the burials, indicating he did not grow up in the area he was buried. Henry was, therefore, born in one part of the United Kingdom, spent a large part of his life in a number of different regions, and was buried in a part of the country he had never lived in.

Archaeologists can therefore use a number of different strands of evidence to examine animal burials. Bones can inform on the life history of the animals; material culture may be associated with the burial, further informing on human involvement; and finally the context/composition of the burial can inform on how the animal was buried. Adding to this is the accumulated knowledge of the time period the burials date to; for example, we know that cats are commonly kept as pets rather than consumed. The above example shows the wealth of information available to archaeologists, but what is difficult to ascertain from the information is the grief and emotion behind the burials. Therefore, archaeologists examining animal burials have not traditionally considered emotion; rather they have concentrated on the purpose of the burials with attention focused between functional or ritualistic interpretations. Behrens may have considered the role of animals in terms of rituals such as foundation offerings, but until the 1990s the majority of archaeologists viewed them as Maltby did, "not of any particular significance that cannot be explained by the events normally associated with pastoral farming."[14] During this time complete animal burials were often viewed as the remains of diseased animals, natural deaths, or the results of population/pest control; partial burials were interpreted as the results of carcass processing.[15] This trend changed in the 1990s due to counterarguments suggesting that both complete and partial animal burials from prehistoric contexts are likely to be the result of ritual activities.[16] This change in the interpretation of prehistoric material eventually influenced archaeologists working in other time periods, with Roman (50–450 CE) and Anglo-Saxon (450–1050 CE) animal burials also viewed as the result of ritual activities.[17] However, the blanket use of prehistoric interpretations on remains from later periods has been questioned.[18]

The dichotomous interpretation of animal burials being viewed as the result of either ritual or functional activities led me to investigate the deposit type in Britain from the Neolithic, 4000 BCE, to the end of the medieval period, 1550 CE.[19] Taking a longue durée approach highlights the fallacy of attempting to define animal burials with one interpretation across time periods or indeed within a single period. Not only is there a great deal of variation between time periods in the species deposited as animal burials (see figure 1), but the composition and context of these burials often differs. For example, studying remains from southern Britain, only one complete Bronze Age (2600 BCE—700 BCE) dog burial was identified.[20] The dog was placed into a pit, dug into a round barrow mound at North Down Barn, Dorset.[21] Due to the age of the excavation, information is limited, but this appears to be the only later inclusion of an animal burial into a round barrow. All other evidence suggests that if present, they are normally included during the primary construction phase.[22] Barrows are commonly reused for further human burials, often cremations,[23] therefore this dog burial could represent a linked behavior.

In comparison, dog burials are much more common on Iron Age and, in particular, Roman sites; however, these remains are primarily found within pits on settlement sites, the context and actions behind the burials being very different. For example, excavations of the twenty-six-meter deep Oakridge Well, which appears to have been filled during the middle and later Roman period, recovered eighty-six dog burials, many neonatal.[24] The dog remains have been interpreted as the result of population control, but it highlights an issue that not only affects the Roman period, in that animal burials are often in contexts that contain "rubbish." Thomas has highlighted the inclusion of dog and cat skeletons in household waste during the medieval (1050–1550 CE) and postmedieval (1550–1900 CE) periods and suggests that in the past the burial of a loved pet may have been the exception.[25] However, this could be a reflection of the influence of Christian doctrine on how animals are treated in death,[26] and it is interesting that the number of dog burials does reduce from the Anglo-Saxon to the medieval period (see figure 1). These two descriptions of dog burials are examples of the variety in context and composition of animal burials. Although they are recovered from each archaeologically defined time period a host of different actions and human motivations are behind their creation.

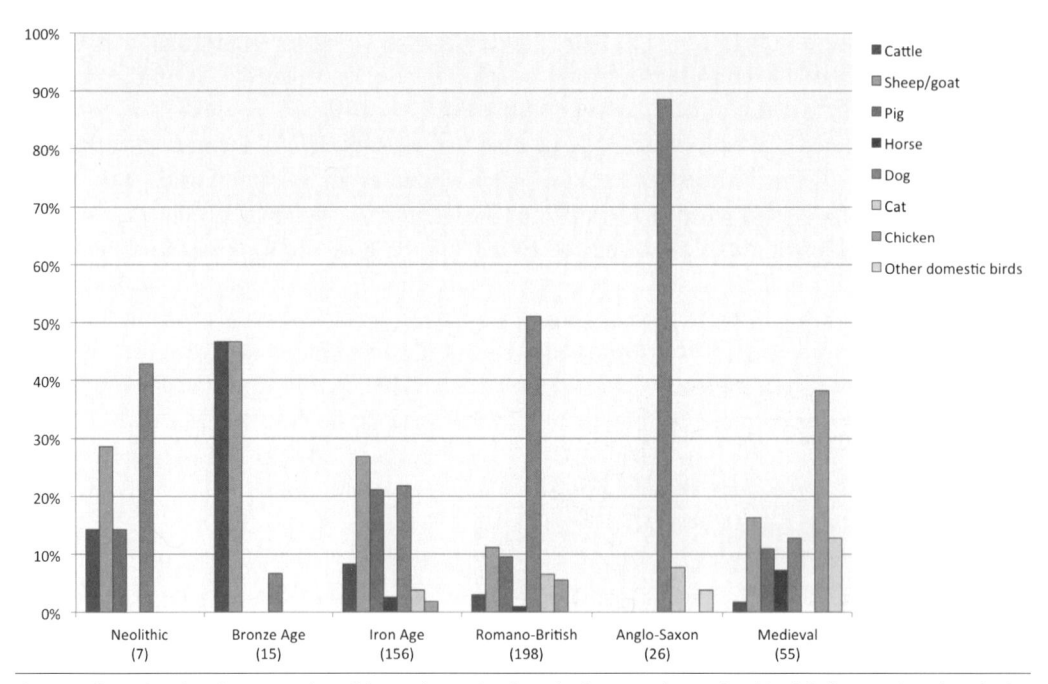

Figure 1. Chart showing the proportion of domestic species deposited as complete animal burials from each archaeological time period in southern Britain (data from Morris, *Investigating Animal Burials*). Number in parentheses indicates the total sample size.

BEHAVIOR AND MEANING: INTIMATE ACTIONS

How then do we work with the mass of archaeological data on animal burials to consider emotion and mourning? An often-used quote when discussing human remains is that "the dead do not bury themselves,"[27] and neither do animals. I have argued that one of the reasons we have struggled with the interpretation of animal burials is the desire to develop an all-encompassing interpretation and a concentration on the final act, the act of burial. This has led to meta-level interpretations: "it's ritual," which should be the start of the conversation not the end.[28] Rather, a biographical approach considering each burial's life history, concentrating on the series of aboveground events behind its creation, would result in better informed interpretations.[29]

An example of this is a reconsideration of the two animal burials recovered from pit 6596 on the Iron Age site of Winnall Down[30] (see figure 2). In his seminal work on Iron Age pit deposits Hill suggests the animal remains from the pit, in the burials, represent a single event of a communal feast and sacrifice that would have involved the consumption of over twelve cattle, a horse, a sheep, a pig, and a hare.[31] In my initial reconsideration I discuss the problems with this interpretation, including a misunderstanding of some of the animal bone data. For example, the pig does have butchery marks present on the right lower leg, suggested to be the result of skinning, but the animal was recovered in articulation indicating soft tissue was still present when deposited,[32] and therefore it was not consumed. Recovered in association with the pig was a complete dog burial, with a strikingly different life history. The pig was a little over two years old, but the female dog had lived well into adulthood. Earlier in its life its left femur had been fractured; the injury had healed but left the limb distorted, and the animal

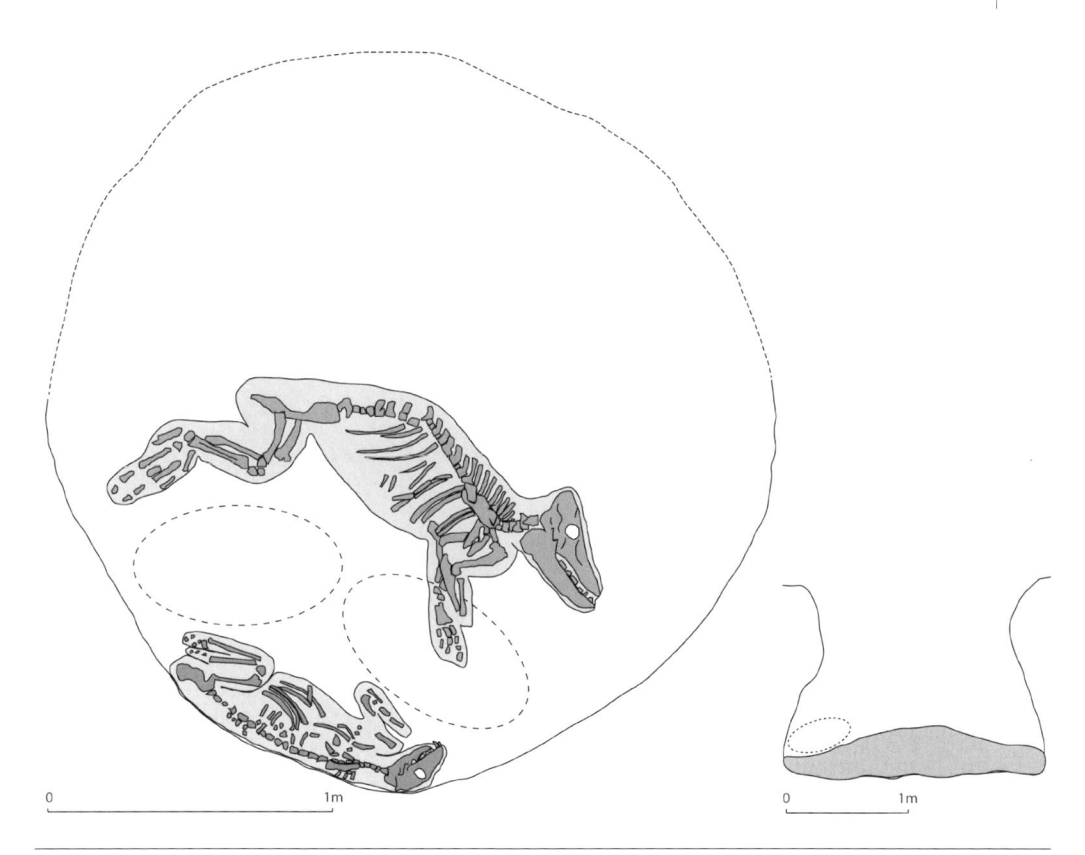

Figure 2. Illustration of the dog and pig burials from Winnall Down pit 6596. Left shows plans of the skeletons with areas of soft tissue suggested; dashed circles indicate the approximate area one human squatting would take up. Bottom right shows the vertical section of pit 6596, with area of the dog burial indicated by dashed line. Top right shows a plan of human burial 505. (Illustrations altered from Hill, *Ritual and Rubbish*, fig. 7.5 and Fasham, *The Prehistoric Settlement at Winnall Down, Winchester*, fig. 21.)

would have limped for the remainder of its adult life. In reconsidering this deposit I have previously suggested the pig could represent a suitable offering to be included with the dog,[33] but I failed to consider emotion and mourning in the interpretation.

Emotion is a difficult subject to tackle for archaeologists, but one possible approach is to consider the human actions during the creation of the burial, and in particular points of intimacy. The placement of the dog and the pig are very different. The pig is placed almost in the middle of the pit, on its left side, with its limbs partially flexed; such a central position might lead one to see it as the "main" deposit. But the dog burial would have required much more effort and contact with the body. The dog is positioned with its back against the side of the pit and would have needed to be physically positioned against the pit wall. It was placed on a layer approximately 1.5 meters deep within the pit, and the body would have needed to be handed down to someone within the pit. Its legs are tightly flexed against its body, which would have required intimate handling and manipulation of the dogs' body. The nature of Iron Age "beehive" pits means the dog is positioned under an overhang, and at this point there would have only been room for two, perhaps three, people to fit around the dog, probably stooped over the body, obscuring the view of anyone standing on the pit edge, resulting in a very personal act that excluded most members of the society. It is interesting to note that the position of the dog mirrors that of some human burials also found on the site (see figure 2 for example). Perhaps the emotions for both events were also mirrored, and if we assume mourning and grief for the human burials, perhaps we should assume similar emotions for the dog burial.

It is tempting to interpret the Winnall Down example as the burial of a beloved pet, but we know very little about pet keeping in the Iron Age. Firmer archaeological evidence for companion animals is present in the Romano-British period, alongside classical literature sources. We know that dogs were kept as pets within the Roman Empire and were mourned. For example a Roman tomb in Mytilene, Greece, is dedicated to the pet dog Parthenope. The dog is shown in relief reclining on a funerary bed with the inscription explaining she will be cherished in life and death.[34] As discussed above, Roman dog burials are normally recovered from pit deposits, but there are some more unusual examples. Excavations at York Road, Leicester, revealed a number of third- and fourth-century CE graves. One in particular was unusual; Grave F85 did not include an inhumation, but rather the skeleton of a dog present on the base of the grave cut.[35] The dog had been deliberately placed toward the center of the grave, on its stomach, with legs splayed out at either side (see figure 3). The dog is male and would have been similar in height to a modern Dachshund, around twenty-six to twenty-eight centimeters at the shoulder.[36] Miniature dogs of this kind are first seen in Britain in the Roman period and appear to be exclusively pets.[37] Epiphyseal fusion of the dog's bones suggest it is fully adult, although the teeth are not very worn and Baxter suggests this may be due to a softer preferential diet.[38] The actions behind the creation of this deposit mirror those of human burial, and like Parthenope it is possible this burial represents a cherished pet.

Another dog burial was present on the York Road excavations; this was recovered from a pit, was largely disarticulated, and was found amid a number of other animal remains. As discussed above this type of deposit is much more common in the archaeological record. However, occasionally evidence of intimate care can be seen in rubbish deposits. Excavations of the northern gatehouse of Silchester Roman town revealed an area of a midden with abundant pottery, tile, and animal bone. Within this midden was a cat burial of an adult animal, with no butchery marks present. What makes this deposit striking is that the cat had been placed within a rough cist made out of reused roof tiles[39] (see figure 4). The cist measures approximately eighty centimeters by fifty centimeters, just big enough for a cat. This certainly would have been an intimate act: the construction of the cist, the placing of the body within it, manipulating the limbs so the cat fits, and then sealing the cist. The context may differ from human burials, but the care and attention do not. The placement within the midden may suggest that the individual burying the cat did not have anywhere more suitable, and the cist would have protected the burial from disturbance, especially from dogs who would have gnawed exposed bones. Whereas the York Road dog is likely to have belonged to a wealthy individual, the cat cist burial may represent the actions of someone from the poorer end of society, caring for an animal, worrying about its burial, and possibly mourning.

CONCLUSION: EMOTIONAL CREATIONS

Animal burials are created by a whole host of human actions, with different associated meanings and values. Rather than searching for wide-ranging culture/period patterns, the bread and butter of archaeology, we should view them as a *polythetic* concept encompassing a multiplicity

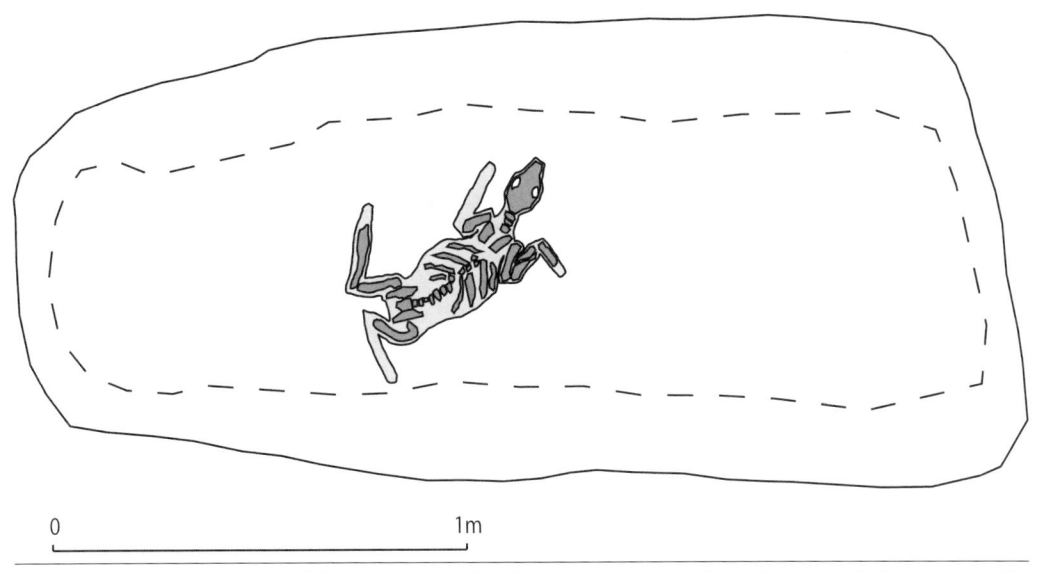

Figure 3. Illustration of the dog burial from Grave F85, York Road, Leicester. Approximate body area illustrated around the skeleton. (Altered from Baxter, "A Dwarf Hound Skeleton," fig. 1.)

Figure 4. Photo of the Silchester cat burial in cist. (From Fulford et al., "Silchester," Plate XIII, with kind permission of Michael Fulford.)

of phenomena, with overlapping familial resemblances but no fixed criteria.[40] In exploring the meaning behind animal burials we have to consider the aboveground human actions behind their creation, and by understanding these actions together with the life history of the animal itself we can move beyond simple ritual/functional dichotomous arguments. However, in doing so we must also include emotion, often at the core of human experiences and elucidation of meaning, yet rarely considered within archaeology. Emotion is not only an important consideration for animal burials that may be driven by mourning and grief. It should also be considered for those deposits that perhaps resulted from ritualized activities such as sacrifice since emotion is an important constituent of ritual and social memory.[41]

For animal burials one approach would be to explore intimacy between the burial and the humans undertaking it. To return to the example of my family's cats, each has been buried within environmental sample containers, normally used for taking soil samples. The practical reason behind this was the need to transport the bodies to their final resting place, a journey that often took place some time after death. Like the cist from Silchester the containers protect the bodies of the cats, but also required acts of personal intimacy with each one as the body was positioned within the container. These acts were driven by emotion and mourning, as perhaps the creation of the cist and these other examples were as well.

NOTES

First, thank you to Margo DeMello for her hard work, patience, and understanding in putting together this volume. Thanks to Michael Fulford for permission to use the Silchester cat cist photo, Duncan Sayer for conversations on death and burial that inspired some of this work, and Rick Peterson for discussions on memory. As always thank you to Justine Biddle for her comments, continued support, and allowing our experiences with Tango, Greebo, Pepsi, and Henry to be shared. All errors remain my own.

1. For discussions on the development of zooarchaeology, see Nicky Milner and Dorian Q. Fuller, "Contending with Animal Bones," *Archaeological Review from Cambridge* 16 (1999): 1–12; Elizabeth J. Reitz and Elizabeth S. Wing, *Zooarchaeology* (Cambridge: Cambridge University Press, 1999), 11–31.
2. Claude Lévi-Strauss, *Le Totémisme aujourd'hui* (Paris: Presses Universitaires de France, 1962), 89.
3. Social zooarchaeology could be seen as an attempt to move away from the purely economic interpretations that dominate the field. See for example Nerissa Russell, *Social Zooarchaeology: Humans and Animals in Prehistory* (Cambridge: Cambridge University Press, 2012); Arkadiusz Marciniak, *Placing Animals in the Neolithic: Social Zooarchaeology of Prehistoric Farming Communities* (London: UCL Press, 2005); Naomi Sykes, *Beastly Questions: Animal Answers to Archaeological Issues* (London: Bloomsbury, 2014).
4. See Annie Grant, "Animal Husbandry," in *Danebury: An Iron Age Hillfort in Hampshire*, vol. 2, *The Excavations, 1969–1978: The Finds*, ed. Barry W. Cunliffe (London: Council for British Archaeology, 1984), 496–548.
5. Hermann Behrens, *Die Neolithisch-frühmetallzeitlichen Tierskelettfunde der alten Welt: Studien zu ihrer Wesensdeutung und historischen Problematik* (Berlin: Deutscher verlag der Wissenschaften, 1964).
6. Behrens, *Die Neolithisch-frühmetallzeitlichen Tierskelettfunde der alten Welt*, 81–82.
7. L. Gabałówna, "Pochówki bydlęce kultury amfor kulistych ze stanowiska 4 w Brześciu Kujawskim w świetle podobnych znalezisk kultur środkowoeuropejskich" [Bovine Burials of the Globular

Culture at Station 4 in Brześciu Kujawskim, in Light of Similar Finds Form Central Europe], *Prace i Materiały Łódź* 3 (1958): 63–108.

8. Particular exceptions are Sarah Tarlow, "The Archaeology of Emotion and Affect," *Annual Review of Anthropology* 41 (2012): 169–85; Oliver Harris, "Emotional and Mnemonic Geographies at Hambledon Hill: Texturing Neolithic Places with Bodies and Bones," *Cambridge Archaeological Journal* 20 (2010): 357–71; Oliver Harris and Tim Flohr Sørensen, "Rethinking Emotion and Material Culture," *Archaeological Dialogues* 17 (2010): 145–63; Rick Peterson, "Social Memory and Ritual Performance," *Journal of Social Archaeology* 13 (2013): 266–83.

9. Per Lagerås, "Burial Rituals Inferred from Palynological Evidence: Results from a Late Neolithic Stone Cist in Southern Sweden," *Vegetation History and Archaeobotany* 9 (2000): 169–73; Richard Tipping, "'Ritual' Floral Tributes in the Scottish Bronze Age: Palynological Evidence," *Journal of Archaeological Science* 21 (1994): 133–39.

10. Peterson, "Social Memory and Ritual Performance."

11. The articulated nature would suggest the animals were pets, although articulated remains resulting from consumption and skinning activities have been uncovered in the archaeological record. Rosemary M. Luff and Marta Moreno García, "Killing Cats in the Medieval Period: An Unusual Episode in the History of Cambridge, England," *Archaeofauna* 4 (1995): 93–114; Terry O'Connor, *Bones from Anglo-Scandinavian Levels at 16–22 Coppergate*, fasc. 3 of *The Archaeology of York*, vol. 15, *The Animal Bones* (York: Council for British Archaeology, 1989).

12. Once epiphyseal fusion is complete, aging relies on degradation, such as wear on the teeth, which can only give wide age ranges (adult, old adult, etc.).

13. For use of stable isotope analyses in zooarchaeology, see for example Elizabeth J. Reitz and Myra Shackley, *Environmental Archaeology* (New York: Springer, 2012), 423–67; Richard Madgwick et al., "Fallow Deer (*Dama dama dama*) Management in Roman South-East Britain," *Archaeological and Anthropological Sciences* 5 (2013): 111–22.

14. Mark Maltby, *The Animal Bones from the Excavations at Owslebury, Hants., an Iron Age and Early Romano-British Settlement* (Portsmouth: English Heritage, Ancient Monuments Laboratory Report 6/87, 1989). His opinion is now very different; see for example Mark Maltby, "Sheep Foundation Burials in Roman Winchester," in *The Ritual Killing and Burial of Animals: European Perspectives*, ed. Aleksander Pluskowski (Oxford: Oxbow, 2012), 152–63.

15. James Morris, *Investigating Animal Burials: Ritual, Mundane and Beyond* (Oxford: Archaeopress, 2011), 8.

16. A. Grant, "Animals and Ritual in Early Britain: The Visible and the Invisible," in *Animal et pratiques religieuses: Les manifestations matérielles; Actes du colloque international de Compiègne, 11–13 novembre 1988*, ed. Patrice Méniel (Paris: Association L'Homme et l'animal, 1989), 79–86; Patrice Méniel, *Les Sacrifices d'animaux chez les Gaulois* (Paris: Editions Errance, 1992); J. D. Hill, *Ritual and Rubbish in the Iron Age of Wessex: A Study on the Formation of a Specific Archaeological Record* (Oxford: Tempus Reparatum, 1995).

17. Michael Fulford, "Links with the Past: Pervasive 'Ritual' Behaviour in Roman Britain," *Britannia* 32 (2001): 199–218; Helena Hamerow, "'Special Deposits' in Anglo-Saxon Settlements," *Medieval Archaeology* 50 (2006): 1–30.

18. James Morris, "Associated Bone Groups: One Archaeologist's Rubbish Is Another's Ritual Deposition," in *Changing Perspectives on the First Millennium BC: Proceedings of the Iron Age Research Student Seminar 2006,* ed. Oliver Davis, Niall Sharples, and Kate Waddington (Oxford: Oxbow, 2008), 83–98; James Morris and Ben Jervis, "What's So Special? A Reinterpretaion of Anglo-Saxon 'Special Deposits,'" *Medieval Archaeology* 55 (2011): 66–81.

19. Morris, *Investigating Animal Burials*.
20. In this case the data comes from published excavations in the counties of Dorset, Hampshire, and Wiltshire. See Morris, *Investigating Animal Burials*.
21. L. V. Grinsell, *Dorset Barrows* (Dorchester: Dorset Natural History and Archaeological Society, 1959), 142.
22. Morris, *Investigating Animal Burials*, 34.
23. For further information on barrows, see Ann Woodward, *British Barrows: A Matter of Life and Death* (Stroud: Tempus, 2000).
24. Mark Maltby, "The Animal Bone from a Romano-British Well at Oakridge II, Basingstoke, Hampshire," *Proceedings of the Hampshire Field Club and Archaeological Society* 49 (1994): 47–76.
25. Richard Thomas, "Perceptions versus Reality: Changing Attitudes towards Pets in Medieval and Post-Medieval England," in *Just Skin and Bones? New Perspectives on Human–Animal Relations in the Historical Past*, ed. Aleksander Pluskowski (Oxford: Archaeopress, 2005), 95–105.
26. Alek Pluskowski, "The Dragon's Skull: How Can Zooarchaeologists Contribute to Our Understanding of Otherness in the Middle Ages?," in *Animals and Otherness in the Middle Ages: Perspectives across Disciplines*, ed. Francisco de Asis García García, Mónica Ann Walker-Vadillo, and María Victoria Chico Picaza (Oxford: Archaeopress, 2013), 109–24.
27. Richard Bradley, "Darkness and Light in the Design of Megalithic Tombs," *Oxford Journal of Archaeology* 8 (1989): 251–59.
28. James Morris, "Animal 'Ritual' Killing: From Remains to Meanings," in Pluskowski, *Ritual Killing and Burial of Animals*, 8–21.
29. For a detailed description of this approach, see Morris, *Investigating Animal Burials*, 167–72.
30. M. Maltby, "The Animal Bones," in *The Prehistoric Settlement at Winnall Down, Winchester: Excavations of MARC 3 Site R17 in 1976 and 1977*, ed. P. J. Fasham (Winchester, UK: Hampshire Field Club, 1985), 97–125.
31. Hill, *Ritual and Rubbish*, 127.
32. Morris, *Investigating Animal Burials*, 179.
33. Morris, *Investigating Animal Burials*, 180.
34. Jocelyn Toynbee, *Animals in Roman Life and Art* (Ithaca, NY: Cornell University Press, 1973), 110.
35. James Gossip, *Excavations at York Road Leicester (NGR SK 585039)* (Leicester: University of Leicester Archaeological Services, Report 99/111, 1999).
36. Ian L. Baxter, "A Dwarf Hound Skeleton from a Romano-British Grave at York Road, Leicester, England, UK, with a Discussion of Other Roman Small Dog Types and Speculation Regarding Their Respective Aetiologies," in *Dogs and People in Social, Working, Economic or Symbolic Interaction: Proceedings of the 9th Conference of the International Council of Archaeozoology, Durham, August 2002*, ed. Lynn M. Snyder and Elizabeth A. Moore (Oxford: Oxbow, 2006), 12–23.
37. R. A. Harcourt, "The Dog in Prehistoric and Early Historic Britain," *Journal of Archaeological Science* 1 (1974): 151–75.
38. Baxter, "A Dwarf Hound Skeleton."
39. Michael Fulford et al., "Silchester: Excavations at the North Gate, on the North Walls, and in the Northern Suburbs 1988 and 1991–3," *Britannia* 28 (1997): 87–168.
40. Morris, "Animal 'Ritual' Killing."
41. Peterson, "Social Memory and Ritual Performance."

Horses, Mourning
Interspecies Embodiment, Belonging, and Bereavement in the Past and Present

GALA ARGENT

When we are alive, you are my wings.
When we are dead, we have one grief.

—LINES FROM AN ALTAIC EPIC POEM ON THE
RELATIONSHIP BETWEEN HUMANS AND HORSES.

SOME 2400 YEARS AGO, PEOPLE BELONGING TO THE IRON AGE PAZYRYK ARCHAEOlogical culture gathered together to lay their dead to rest in burial mounds in the remote Inner Asian Altai Mountains. At these funerals, they sacrificed elaborately costumed riding horses and carefully buried them alongside the deceased (figure 1). While typical burials of this age present only metal and bone for analysis, here the graves subsequently froze in permafrost, preserving wood, leather, fabric, and often the entire bodies of the humans and horses. These unusual burials thus provide an excellent opportunity for exploring the particular connections between these people and horses.

My concern here is with the sacrifice of the horses and what meanings the Pazyryk might have attributed to both their killing and their loss. Initial interpretations of these issues viewed the horses as grave goods, objects of material culture no more or less relevant in the end than a clay pot or an iron cauldron.[1] I take a different, relational, approach, one that considers the intersocial connections between horses and humans from both sides of these relationships. To do this, I apply two distinct research frameworks. The first is ethnoethology, which explores the "interactive relational system that links humans and non-humans . . . [granting] all living beings the status of relational beings, that is, agents interacting on the phenomenon of 'culture' that was hitherto reserved for human beings."[2] Here I draw upon ethological studies of horses, and an inside autoethnographic strategy using my position within the context of those I shall term "working riders"—riders possessing the ability and knowledge to school horses to be ridden. I also apply an ethnozooarchaeological strategy, which rests upon similarities in dealings between humans and other animals in the past and present. Through these lenses and based upon artifactual fieldwork at the Russian Federation's Hermitage Museum I address the following questions: What types of relationships

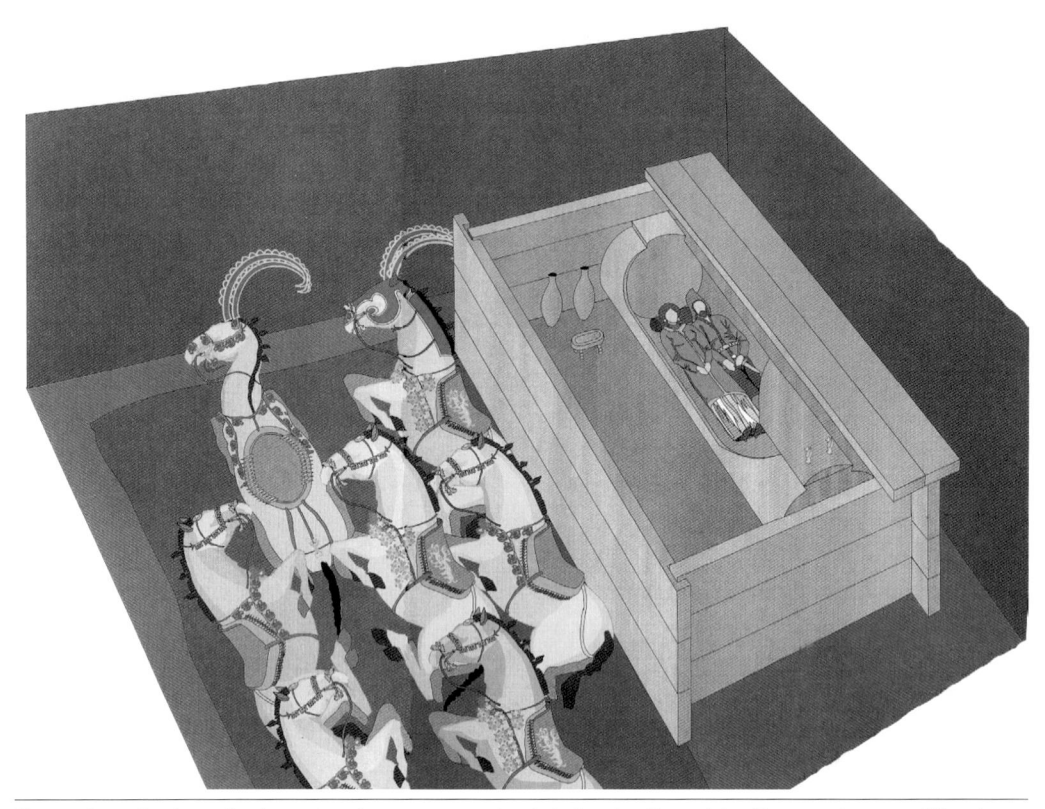

Figure 1. Pazyryk culture, Berel cemetery, kurgan 11, reconstructed, showing the variety of horse costumes and the placement of the buried horses within the burial mound. (After Z. Samashev, G. Bazarbaeva, G. Zhumabekova, and S. Sungatai, Beryl [Almaty, Kazakhstan: O.F. Beryl, 2000], 13.)

can develop between riders and horses, and how are they possible? What does the archaeological evidence imply about the horse-human interface within this particular community? And, how might these horse people have conceived of the act of sacrificing their horses, and their loss?

EMBODIMENT, BELONGING, AND INTERSPECIES INTERSOCIALITY

I begin with the continuities shared by humans and horses from a biosocial perspective. Humans are hardwired to seek connections with others. Because living in relational networks is more advantageous than tackling life alone, "the human brain is designed to assume that it is embedded within a relatively predictable social network characterized by familiarity, joint attention, shared goals, and interdependence."[3] Belonging within social networks is our human default, and it is telling that we term one of our most destructive psychological maladies antisocial personality disorder.

Like humans, horses are social animals—evolved to belong. In the wild, they exist embedded within communities of families, friends, bands, and herds. They live in bands consisting of a stallion, several mares, and their offspring, within which they are gregarious and highly cooperative. They form intense bonds and have "preferred partners" with whom they spend extra time, follow, and cogroom, and these best friends can be members of other species.[4] Horses are not only capable of such motives; as social beings they, like humans, *require* these needs to be met in order to be psychologically healthy. These similarities in ways of social being mean that humans and horses can understand a bit about each other, and the needs for belonging can be met by members of one species for the other.

This sense of mutual belonging is manifestly heightened through the embodied act of riding. Riding can be understood experientially not only as a tangible, shared space, "a spatiality of position," but also as "a spatiality of situation."[5] Riding takes place in the zone of intimate space that is reserved in both species for friends and lovers. For both comfort and safety, horse and rider must move together as one, in rhythm and synchrony, and horses can actively participate in this.[6] This funds recursive interrelatedness and care because from an evolutionary perspective such physical synchronization "is precisely where empathy and sympathy start."[7] Through riding both beings entrain to one another, fostering feelings of connection, boundary loss, and joined identity.[8] This strengthens the human-horse bond and creates a mutually apprehended and cocreated lifeworld. Within this situational space, horses can come to adopt a "protective, possessive attitude toward the rider" that motivates them to "think well and bravely"[9]—they will disadvantage themselves to help their riders. Riders and well-treated horses take care of one another.

Despret has noted, "What makes us 'one of us' for beings of one species will, like a proposition, overlap with what will become 'one of us' for beings of another species."[10] Horses, like humans, recognize other horses and humans as individuals.[11] Today where multiple horses and riders live or work together all will know one other as distinct beings. All will know generic things about each other's species and will come through time to understand others as individuals with strengths and weaknesses, likes and dislikes, moods and peccadillos. All will experience an intersubjective, interspecies community, enmeshed through shared needs for belonging and embodied experience. Although certainly humans and horses have changed over time, might something similar have been present in Pazyryk lives?

THE PAZYRYK BURIALS

The Pazyryk-era (ca. 600 to 300 BCE) burial monuments dot numerous high mountain plateaus where present-day Siberia, Kazakhstan, Mongolia, and China touch. In these raised, stone-covered mounds lie between one and twenty-two riding horses, sacrificed and buried with their gear and elaborate costumes (figure 2). Of concern within these incredibly rich and fascinating burials are three aspects of burial patterning that inform the nature of these human-horse connections.

First, the Eurasian Bronze Age (ca. 2500 to 700 BCE), which saw herding economies emerge, transitions to the Iron Age (800 BCE to 100 CE) with several key features, all driven by the horse. These sociocultural changes include the completion of the nascent shift from pastoral-agricultural economies to fully nomadic pastoralism and a refinement of horse-riding technology. In the Altai Mountains this transitional period saw intense experimentation in producing bits and bridles, with considerable thought and effort spent finding functional designs. This is evidenced by the extreme variability—no less than thirty-seven variants—of

Figure 2. Reconstruction of a Pazyryk horse's outfit from kurgan 11, Berel cemetery, Kazakhstan. (After Chang and Guroff, *Of Gold and Grass*, vi.)

bits found from this period.[12] These jointed bits are similar in all regards to snaffle bits used today. Although any bit can be used harshly, snaffles are understood today as one of the mildest bits, used not to inflict pain but as communication devices.[13] Apparently Altai bridle-makers were astute observers of equine biomechanics and behavior and were seeking designs that fostered rapport rather than domination. By the seventh century BCE, Altai bit-makers had fixed upon one style, implying this goal was satisfactorily achieved (figure 3).

Second, the period leading into the Pazyryk era also saw a significant shift in burial style. While during the Bronze Age parts of horse bodies and/or horse equipment had been buried *near* humans, by the Pazyryk era we see entire horses brought *into* the human graves. Bringing the horses into the burial mounds can be seen to accompany an increased perception of the importance of the horse and of human-horse bonds. The horses were now woven into and through this human society in ways that no animal had been before, and this is reflected materially—they were brought *closer*, in death as in life.

Third, although the horses were killed by blows with a battle-ax to the midforehead, I saw no presacrifice injuries on the Pazyryk horse bodies I examined (figure 4). All were well groomed, with clipped manes and tails. This holds significance because

> [mutual] grooming has become an end in itself, a gesture of "belonging" and a symbol of the bond between the equine companions. Because of this, the grooming of horses by their human owners has a viral significance. . . . In the horse's mind, [it is] an indication that its human companion is a close friend.[14]

The physical contact in grooming acts upon humans in a similar fashion. The "affectional interaction" in grooming is pleasurable and stress reducing, decreasing heart rates for horses *and* humans, promoting a "deep rapport, intimacy, and mutual understanding" between the two.[15] The horse costumes were well used and mended, indicating that such bidirectional

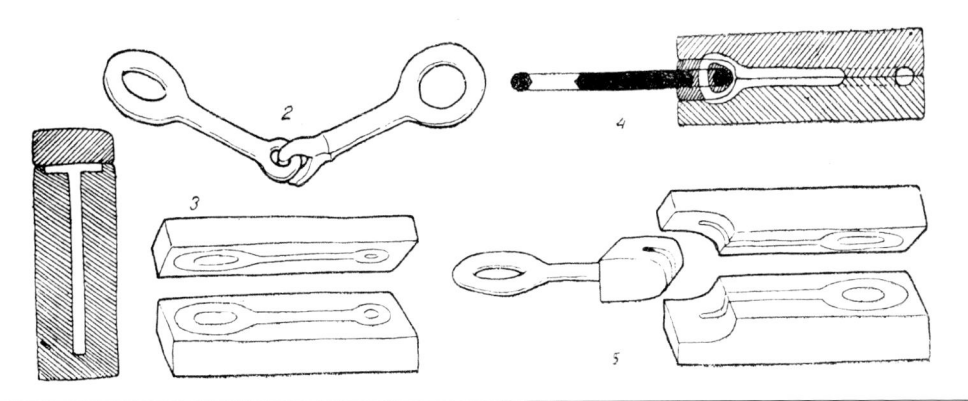

Figure 3. Pazyryk bit-casting process. (After Gryaznov, *Pervyi Pazyrykskii Kurgan*, fig. 18.)

Figure 4. Pazyryk horse showing the position of the lethal battle-ax wounds.

affection-inducing grooming was commonplace. Current ethological studies show that positive interactions with humans lead to lasting positive memories in horses,[16] and it is likely the Pazyryks knew this as well. As with the attention spent developing mild bits, these people apparently listened to what their horses told them. Here it seems the horses, at least to some degree, taught the Pazyryk people how they wished to be treated—gently and with kindness.

These archaeological details show that within this interspecies community horses were valued subjects and that relationships of mutual emotional closeness and cooperation were wanted, developed, and nurtured. The Pazyryk people subsisted through hunting, fishing, foraging, and herding, and they appear to have utilized horsepower to the fullest in these endeavors. We can envision them living with and on their horses, spending great amounts of time riding and developing equine-related skills. The Pazyryk humans and horses would have spent years working and facing dangers together. They would have traversed the landscape as known individuals within a socialscape of interspecies belonging and community, sharing both everyday embodied rhythms of life and epic adventures, their bonds confirmed by patterns of movement, touch, and time and dependent on trust and mutual care.

SACRIFICE AND GRIEF

Then why kill them? It is unlikely they were sacrificed because they were expendable—quite the opposite it seems. They were invaluable in death as in life. Jacobson notes of these burials, "in all cases it is apparent that the animals were understood to be in some manner essential either to the passage of the dead person's soul to the next realm or to that person's life when he arrived there."[17] But might there be more to it than this? Might also aspects of the tight interspecies relationships I have presented—and the social characteristics of both species allowing and underlying them—have contributed to the reasons for the sacrifices and the feelings engendered by the act?

Horses, through time, have been regarded as sensitive and responsive to the deaths of their people. Caesar's horse is said to have "shed tears for two days before the hero's death,"[18] and Patroclus's horses' sorrow upon his death was noted by Homer in the Iliad: "Therefore, these two horses stand here and grieve, and their manes are swept along the ground as they stand with hearts full of sorrow. They both refuse to move, saddled down with grief."[19] Recent neuroscientific studies show these narratives might not merely represent anthropomorphized hyperbole. We now know that the anatomical and chemical brain mechanisms that reflect separation distress for social mammals and birds are analogous to those that mediate the type of sadness that arises from social loss—grief—in humans.[20] When important social bonds are broken, many horses exhibit "classical signs of clinical depression" and can fall into an "exaggerated depth of depression [that] can present with physical problems."[21] Bereavement in horses is now treated in the same ways as for grieving humans, with antianxiety (e.g., Valium) and antidepressant (e.g., Prozac) drugs.[22] Horses grieve, although today many negate the magnitude of these feelings through depersonalizing language, qualitatively differentiating human grief from animal "separation distress,"[23] or demeaning it as speculative through the use of scare quotes, that is, horse "grief."

Certainly, as anyone living with horses has, the Pazyryk witnessed their horses' bereavement following the loss of a foal or a cobonded horse or a human friend.

If the Pazyryk people considered that horses mourned the loss of human and horse friends it is unlikely they viewed horse grief as distinct from human grief, as is common today, but rather understood it as a state shared among all within the close ties of this interspecies community. From this perspective, the reasons for the sacrifice of horses could have included not only the need for their services on the way to or in the otherworld, but also a belief that the emotional weight of the bidirectional bonds of loyalty between rider and horse were indissoluble, unrepeatable, and untransferable to others and should be maintained in death as in life. It is notable that although the horses were violently killed, the battle-ax blows fell at precisely just the point where today we are told to shoot an injured or dying horse should other options be unavailable, in order to provide the quickest and least painful death. This implies an attempt at providing respectful deaths. With this in mind, the sacrifice of the horses might have been comprehended by the Pazyryk as an act of empathetic kindness, much in tune with beliefs held today by some pet caretakers who call for the euthanasia of their pets upon their death, fearing they will be distraught at their loss.[24] Perhaps, for the Pazyryk, the belief in an afterlife for their human and equine compatriots alike helped soothe—as it does for many people today—the loss of both.

Materialized within these burials there appears a belief that we come from and go to the same place, a place where the human-nonhuman boundary seems more permeable than it is generally constructed in Euro-American thought today, a place where the divide between human and nonhuman animals, and life and death, seems less of a schism. The Pazyryk appear to have valorized not human-horse differences, but rather "those traits we obviously share with other lives—we are finite, interdependent, embodied, capable of pleasure and pain, vulnerable, born to, and one day will, die."[25] To tie this back to notions of embodied interspecies intersociality, for Stanescu,

> Vulnerability is the basis of sociality, the basis of community. If we were immortal and capable of being entirely sustainable individuals, there would be no need for society or culture. It is our very ability to be wounded, our very dependency, that brings us together. Mourning is a testament to such a shared embodiment, which is the source of its paradoxical productivity. It can bring us together in monuments, in rituals, in shared stories and memories, and sometimes in collective action.[26]

As close as these humans and horses were, members of both species would have grieved the loss of both human and horse individuals. In their placing of the bodies within the burial monuments, we can envision a ritual honoring both deceased humans and horses. We can imagine the Pazyryk sitting around their campfires, as today horse people sit around kitchen tables, sharing stories and memories of those who were gone. These narratives of belonging honored the brave actions not only of their deceased human comrades, but also of the horses who belonged with these people, because the two functioned together and cannot be untangled. The people around the fires recall the horses and people who took care of each other, horses and people alike who thought well and bravely. They speak of these horses' heart, loyalty, and courage; they call their actions honorable and perhaps even divine, and they do so without putting metaphorical scare quotes around the words. They do so because they comprehend that we are cut from the same fabric, we and these horses. And in that shared generosity—in the midst of the monumental messiness of daily life and in spite of bloody endings—there is indeed honor, and perhaps a type of divinity as well.

CONCLUSION AND IMPLICATIONS

Certainly justifications for sacrifice can be seen to be culturally determined. Yet in this case study I have argued that horses' abilities and behaviors played a crucial role in how they were conceptualized and treated, as evidenced archaeologically. If this is so, then some Pazyryk meanings about horses seem not entirely arbitrary, not entirely culturally constructed, but rather based in part upon iconic, inherent characteristics of horses. I may be wrong, but I suspect that statements such as these might be off-putting to my colleagues who focus solely on the human aspects of human-nonhuman junctures, and consider our relations with animals entirely culturally constructed (by humans). But this need not be the case. Perhaps I might be forgiven for what we might term critical essentializing if we can agree that evolutionary explanations of facilitating mechanisms (e.g. shared social needs that may be fundamentally evolutionarily based) exist, but are mediated within the social, historical, and ecological contexts of worlds shared between species. Correspondingly, the ethnozooarchaeological project rests on similarities in dealings between humans and other animals in the past and present, while at the same time acknowledging the multitude of ways these connections could have been structured.

Were I concerned with foregrounding the negative aspects of unequal power relations imposed upon horses when humans approach them with domination in mind, I might have focused upon these sacrifices as indicative of the subjugated nature of these horses. Certainly this could be argued. However, because this is not the only way humans and horses come together, I have intentionally avoided this well-trodden theme used by scholars of the human-horse intersection.[27] In highlighting horses' natural history and biosocial characteristics, my concern has been with the pro-social commonalities shared by both species as social animals with social needs—family, belonging, community, affection, loyalty, and grief. These aspects would be missed in narrow, anthropocentric analyses framed solely within human domination/equine submission. In acknowledging equine agency, the relational approach enlightens how smaller-scale interspecies connections can be seen to fund larger-scale social structures.

Finally, considering interpretations of interspecies relationships as materialized in the archaeologically visible past allows us to step outside of current Euro-American paradigms. This can reflect back on our understandings of human-nonhuman intersections today, broadening our views of the potentialities of these relationships in the present. Tacking back and forth between the past and present, humans and horses, and the biological and cultural, here both have informed, and been informed by, the bidirectional nature of human-horse relationships—and by horses' mourning.

NOTES

1. Mikail Gryaznov, *Pervyi Pazyrykskii Kurgan* [First Pazyryk Kurgan] (St. Petersburg: Hermitage, 1950).
2. Dominique Lestel, Florence Brunois, and Florence Gaunet, "Etho-ethnology and Ethno-ethology," *Social Science Information* 45, no. 2 (2006): 168.
3. Lane Beckes and James A. Coan, "Social Baseline Theory: The Role of Social Proximity in

Emotion and Economy of Action," *Social and Personality Psychology Compass* 5, no. 12 (2011): 976–77.

4. Claudia Feh, "Relationships and Communication in Socially Natural Horse Herds," in *The Domestic Horse: The Origins, Developments, and Management of its Behaviour*, ed. D. S. Mills and S. M. McDonnell (Cambridge: Cambridge University Press, 2005), 86. Matcheld C. Matcheld van Dierendonck and Debbie Goodwin, "Social Contact in Horses: Implications for Human-–Horse Interactions," in *The Importance of Social Relationships in Horses*, ed. M. C. van. Dierendonck (Utrecht: Proefschrift Universitat Utrecht, 2006), 28–44, 30.
5. Maurice Merleau-Ponty, *Phenomenology of Perception* (London: Routledge, 1962), 115.
6. Gala Argent, "Toward a Privileging of the Nonverbal: Communication, Corporeal Synchrony and Transcendence in Humans and Horses," in *Experiencing Animal Minds: An Anthology of Animal-Human Encounters*, ed. Julie A. Smith and Robert W. Mitchell (New York: Columbia University Press, 2012), 111–28.
7. Frans de Waal, *The Age of Empathy: Nature's Lessons for a Kinder Society* (New York: Harmony Books, 2009), 4.
8. See Argent, "Toward a Privileging of the Nonverbal"; also Ann Game, "Riding: Embodying the Centaur," *Body & Society* 7, no. 4 (2001): 1–12.
9. Vicki Hearne, *Adam's Task: Calling Animals by Name* (New York: Skyhorse, 2007), 149.
10. Vinciane Despret, "The Becomings of Subjectivity in Animal Worlds," *Subjectivity* 23 (2008): 128–29.
11. Leanne Proops, Karen McComb, David Reby, and Jeanne Altmann, "Cross-modal Individual Recognition in Domestic Horses (*Equus caballus*)," *Proceedings of the National Academy of Sciences* 106, no. 3 (2009): 947–51; Sherril Stone, "Human Facial Discrimination in Horses: Can They Tell Us Apart?," *Animal Cognition* 13, no. 1 (2010): 51–61.
12. Nikolai A. Bokovenko, "The Origins of Horse Riding and the Development of Ancient Central Asian Nomadic Riding Harness," in *Kurgans, Ritual Sites, and Settlements: Eurasian Bronze and Iron Age*, ed. Jeannine Davis-Kimball et al. (Oxford: Archaeopress, 2000), 304–10.
13. The common assumption that bits are used to "control" horses is fallacious, as anyone who has sat a runaway horse can attest.
14. Desmond Morris, *Horsewatching* (New York: Crown, 1988), 56.
15. Haruyo Hama, Masao Yogo, and Yoshinori Matsuyama, "Effects of Stroking Horses on Both Humans' and Horses' Heart Rate Responses," *Japanese Psychological Research* 38, no. 2 (1996): 66; Jan Yorke, Cindy Adams, and Nick Coady, "Therapeutic Value of Equine-Human Bonding in Recovery from Trauma," *Anthrozoös* 21, no. 1 (2008): 19.
16. Carol Sankey et al., "Positive Interactions Lead to Lasting Positive Memories in Horses, *Equus caballus*," *Animal Behaviour* 79, no. 4 (2010): 869–75.
17. Esther Jacobson, "The Issyk Headdress: Symbol and Meaning in the Iron Age Nomadic Culture," in *Of Gold and Grass: Nomads of Kazakhstan*, ed. Claudia Chang and Katharine S. Guroff (Bethesda: Foundation for International Arts and Education, 2007), 65.
18. Elizabeth Atwood Lawrence, "The Centaur: Its History and Meaning in Human Culture," *Journal of Popular Culture* 27, no. 4 (1994): 64.
19. Homer, *The Iliad*, trans. Robert Fagles (New York: Penguin, 1986), 283–84.
20. Jaak Panksepp and Lucy Biven, eds., *The Archaeology of Mind: Neuroevolutionary Origins of Human Emotions* (New York: W. W. Norton, 2012), 312.
21. Kenneth Marcella, "Managing Grief Responses: Bereavement Could Deteriorate the Health of Your Horses," *DVM 360 Magazine*, October 1, 2004.

22. Marcella, "Managing Grief Responses."
23. See Teja Brooks Pribac, "Animal Grief," *Animal Studies Journal* 2, no. 2 (2013): 67–90.
24. See Gerry W. Beyer, "Pet Animals: What Happens When Their Humans Die?," *Santa Clara Law Review* 40, no. 3 (2000): 661; also Diane Mapes, "When I Die, So Does My Dog: Some Pet Owners Take Animals to Their Graves," *MSNBC News*, November 30, 2010.
25. James Stanescu, "Species Trouble: Judith Butler, Mourning, and the Precarious Lives of Animals," *Hypatia* 27, no. 3 (2012): 569–70.
26. Stanescu, "Species Trouble," 577–78.
27. See, for example, Natalie Hansen, "Embodied Communication: The Poetics and Politics of Riding," in *Sport, Animals, and Society*, ed. James Gillett and Michelle Gilbert (New York: Routledge, 2014), 251–67; Paul Patton, "Language, Power, and the Training of Horses," in *Zoontologies: The Question of the Animal*, ed. Cary Wolfe (Minneapolis: University of Minnesota Press, 2003), 83–99.

The Issue of Animals' Souls within the Anglican Debate in the Eighteenth to Nineteenth Centuries

ALMA MASSARO

THE DEBATE ON ANIMAL SOULS AND THE PROBLEM OF THEODICY WITH RESPECT TO animal suffering, a discussion that has been a feature of European thought since the seventeenth century, became the perfect pillar for those philosophies that were born in the wake of scientific discoveries and that aimed to assert the unreasonableness of Christianity. Such philosophies questioned how a good and almighty God could let innocent animals undergo all the evils they endure daily. One solution was to deny to animals feelings and reason; for instance, Descartes's theory of the animal-machine suggested that animals were unable to feel pleasure and pain,[1] thus safeguarding God as both good and almighty. But alongside this theory alternative solutions were proposed, basically in opposition. Put in these terms, it clearly emerges that this debate arose from a need to redefine the human and not from a real interest in the lives of animals.

EIGHTEENTH- AND NINETEENTH-CENTURY ENGLAND

Even if this debate originated primarily in human concerns over the metaphysical structure of reality, it was in the wake of this discussion that reflection on the *status* of animals was born in eighteenth- and nineteenth-century England and led to social and legal renovation.[2] During this time period, attention shifted from the human to the animal plane, and this led to the development of an ethics inclusive of nonhuman animals, which were previously considered "outside the terms of moral reference."[3] This work will focus on four books published between 1742 and 1838 that trace the rise of Christian animal ethics. However, first, it is worth noting the cultural milieu in which these texts were written.[4]

The new focus on sentience, the new view of pain as something to avoid and not merely to accept, the new humanitarian sensibility, scientific discoveries, the birth of the urban middle class, and new attention to animals in poetry and children's literature all led to a redefinition of the human–animal relationship.[5] From the early decades of 1700 onward, numerous philosophical essays, children novels, and poems focused on the ethical consequences of human–animal proximity. But all of these changes would not have been so dramatic without

JOHN HILDROP

Published in London in 1742, *Free Thoughts upon the Brute Creation* "appears to be the earliest example in Britain of a book devoted almost entirely to the subject of humankind's relationship with animals."[7] Here the author, John Hildrop (1682–1756), denounced the absurdities of the work of French Jesuit Guillaume Hyacinthe Bougeant, who, in order to oppose the Cartesian theory and, at the same time, to find a solution to the problems of theodicy raised by animal suffering, developed an original theory in his *Amusement Philosophique sur les Langages des Bêtes*.[8] In this text, the French Jesuit suggests that animals will be vivified by the souls of rebel angels destined to eternal damnation;[9] therefore, the evils to which animals are exposed now is nothing compared to the eternal fire awaiting them. While the English clergyman shared Bougeant's opposition to the Cartesian theory, he denounced the absurdities of this work. Drawing from both common experience and the Bible, he argued that animals are innocent creatures, destined to a better future, and cruelty to them is a sin.

Appealing to both reason and revelation, Hildrop confutes Bougeant and Descartes. If experience is enough to recognize that animals possess a certain degree of understanding, then the notion of instinct appears to be only a philosophical stratagem to explain animal agency without granting them an immaterial and immortal soul.[10] In fact, if animals have reason and thought, it is necessary to recognize in them an immaterial and spiritual principle to which all these faculties inhere and from which they are directed—"Understanding without a Soul, a Soul that is not a Spirit, appears quite as absurd as Light without Flame, or Flame without Fire."[11]

And not only experience, but also the scriptures confirm the afterlife of the animal soul. In the light of the Pauline epistles, Hildrop interprets death and evil as direct consequences of original sin (Rom. 5:12). From this he infers that in the original divine plan all creatures, beasts included, took part in human immortality.[12] Therefore the evil we all suffer at present is a *preternatural* condition, which will not last forever.[13] Furthermore, if everything God has created is good, how is it possible to conciliate these truths with the threat of annihilation to which philosophy exposes each living being who is not human? "Does it not seem to imply Inconstancy and Mutability in God, that the same infinite Wisdom that made every Creature beautiful, useful, and good for certain Ends and Purposes, should destroy, or annihilate any thing that he has made, and thereby defeat the Wisdom of his own Counsel, and the Ends of his Providence?"[14] The idea of annihilation is absurd and contrary to revelation. God's original project is immutable—God is the same yesterday, today, and forever (Heb. 13:8). Therefore, what looks to us to be subject to alteration will appear, indeed, at the proper time, in its proper place in order to answer to the ends for which it has been originally created;[15] the same infinite wisdom that created them "will not fail to dispose of them here after in the most proper Manner, to answer the original Purposes of their Creation."[16]

RICHARD DEAN

In 1767, twenty-five years after the first publication of Hildrop's *Free Thoughts*, *An Essay on the Future Life of Brute Creatures* by Richard Dean (1726/27–78) was published in Manchester.[17] If on the one side the *Essay* is similar to Hildrop's work—since it aims to show the existence of an afterlife for nonhuman animals, in contrast with those who view them as mere instruments to achieve human pleasure—on the other it represents an evolution. In fact, as Rod Preece puts it, "While many before had commented on animal pain and suffering, Dean was perhaps the first to make it the focal point of his thesis."[18]

The work is twofold: the part dedicated to animal afterlife follows a study on the nature and origin of natural evil. In this first part, Dean shows how pain and death are "incidental Phaenomena, foreign to the original Constitution of the World"[19] and following from human sin. He suggests that nonhuman animals somehow have contracted human sin and that through the redemption of human beings all nature will be included in the salvation process.[20] The second part is divided into seven propositions where the author adds to the scriptures quotes from some ancient and modern authors and observations of animal behavior. Here he affirms that animals cannot be treated "as stocks, or stones, or things" since they "have sensibility, they are capable of pain, feel every bang, and cut, and stab," as much as a human being.[21] They also "have an intelligent principle" from which their actions originate.[22] Furthermore, there is evidence in the scriptures of animal immortality (Rom. 8:19–22).[23] Certainly humans are endowed with a major blessing in that their reason surpasses animals' faculties; nevertheless, even animal souls will enjoy a postexistence.

If animals are something more than mere Cartesian machines, possess an intelligent principle guiding their actions, and are able to feel pain as much as humans, they cannot be treated as insensitive instruments.[24] "Surely this principle of Sensibility in Brutes, entitles them to a milder Treatment, than they usually meet with from hard, and unthinking Wretches, as the Miseries it makes them liable to, give them a Claim to some Returns from a just and Benevolent Being, in another State."[25] In opposition to the skeptic and cruel attitudes promoted by the animal-machine theory, Dean infers, from the very fact that animals are under human governance and from the privileged position of human beings, the necessity of caring for them: in the Day of Judgment, in fact, we will have to answer for any cruelty committed against them.[26]

HUMPHREY PRIMATT

Nine years later, in 1776, Humphrey Primatt (1735–76/77) published *A Dissertation on the Duty of Mercy and Sin of Cruelty to Brute Animals*, "a founding work of the animal advocacy movement of the early nineteenth-century."[27] Primatt, in the light of a careful analysis of biblical sources, "plead the cause of the Dumb Creatures on the Principles of Natural Religion, Justice, Honour, and Humanity."[28] Moving from an analysis of the idea of *justice*, Primatt elaborates "a vision of universal emancipation";[29] notwithstanding the fact that humans profess different religions, the Holy Scriptures teach that *justice* is a universal law, valid for everybody, and originating in God.[30] God has manifested his wisdom in creating the whole universe and its inhabitants, with all their differences. And since differences among humans do not give the right to oppress other humans, in the same way interspecific differences do not justify the cruelty of one species to another.[31] Physical differences, furthermore, are mitigated by a common origin: modeled by the same ground and enlivened by the same divine breath, we all have in God the same father (see Mal. 2:10)—we are "breathing Dust."[32]

On the moral level, adds Primatt, the differences between humans and animals are annihilated by the common ability to perceive *pain*, as Dean had already pointed out and Bentham would ratify some years later.[33] Our love and mercy must include all that is embraced in God's love and mercy. Holy Scriptures, in fact, attest that on the Day of Judgment God will require from humans—the superior creature—a report of their behavior to other creatures and will judge each act of cruelty and oppression. The fact that human beings have a privileged *status* makes their responsibility greater.[34]

An important innovation of the *Dissertation* is Primatt's view of animal souls. Rather than following the path of his predecessors and looking for arguments to support the idea of an animal afterlife, he asserts animal sentience and analyzes the consequences of the opposite theory: animal nonfuture life.[35] If one assumes that animals do not possess a future life, he observes, there is no reparation for animal cruelty; therefore, "cruelty to a brute is an injury irreparable."[36] And he pushes the argument further: animals, even more than humans, have a right to happiness in this world, since this is their only condition of existence.[37] This hypothesis, rather than justifying human exploitation of animals, demonstrates that *brutal cruelty* is even worse than *human cruelty*. The belief in an animal afterlife is, for Primatt, a matter of belief, but it cannot affect our duties toward them—our ethics should be based on their sentience.

WILLIAM H. DRUMMOND

The path traced by these three books led to *The Rights of Animals and Man's Obligation to Treat Them with Humanity* by William H. Drummond (1772–1865), published in London in 1838.[38] The years between the publication of Primatt's and Drummond's works were particularly fruitful for animal ethics. In 1822 the first law for the protection of animals was passed in the UK;[39] in 1824 the first organization for animal protection was established, the Society for Prevention of Cruelty to Animals (SPCA);[40] and in 1835 animal fighting was declared illegal.[41]

Drummond explains that the duty to be compassionate to inferior creatures originates, as all the other moral obligations, in God's will. Religion, in fact, and not human nature, is the solid base on which mercy for humans and animals is based: "Benevolence, pity, mercy, compassion, are all moral virtues taught by reason, inculcated by religion."[42] The example offered by "the Great Teacher," who said "Blessed are the merciful, for they shall obtain mercy," should teach humans their duty to be merciful.[43] Drummond believed that legislators, in his day, seemed to have understood their duty to behave as God, that is, by extending mercy to each order of existence, using their power to prevent, rather than increase, cruelty. Yet the change on the legislative level was not able to control the manifold forms of abuse toward animals. For this reason, "Humanity must appeal to a higher tribunal for redress: she must invoke Religion to raise her solemn voice."[44]

Concerning the future life of animals, Drummond explains that some Christians (such as Bougeant) view animals as enlivened by rebel spirits, but others (such as Wesley) attribute to animals immortal souls; others call them machines. Drummond does not take a stand on any of these positions but, following Primatt, affirms that "Come to what conclusion we may on these subjects, if, as religion teaches, every man must hereafter give an account of the deeds done in the body, cruelty to animals is a crime that will not escape due chastisement; and whether reason be granted or refused to brutes, it will scarcely be denied that they can *feel*: for feeling does not depend on intellect."[45] As for Primatt, and so also for Drummond, the discourse should not be focused on the immortal souls of animals. But while the focus for Primatt was on human duties to animals, for Drummond the focus was animal rights. Drummond clearly affirmed the existence of some rights allocated to animals by their Creator that could not be violated with impunity.

CONCLUSION

The debate on animal souls during the eighteenth and nineteenth centuries lies initially within the wider debate on the metaphysical structure of reality and is only later about human morality. As we have seen, Hildrop's work, the first English work entirely devoted to animal ethics, is focused on the future life of animals as the foremost argument for supporting their respect. With Dean there is a progressive and gradual development: he is the first to affirm that animal sentience is the root of our duty to treat them kindly; nevertheless, he proceeds to argue for an animal afterlife in order to affirm respect for them. Primatt is the first to completely comprehend the argument about pain and the revolutionary significance of sentience: in his work his attention to sensibility delineates a new way to think about animal–human interaction that now does not need any providential justification.[46] For this reason, he can transform the traditional argument used to affirm the human right to exploit animals into a valid argument to assess human duties to treat them kindly. And from human duties to animal rights the step is short: as we have already seen, Rev. Drummond takes this step, explaining animal rights as something not limited to a humane treatment but extended to all that God has prepared for them.

The discussion of the afterlife of animals during the eighteenth and nineteenth centuries moves from assertions about the future life of animals to the acknowledgment of their right, independent from, but not opposed to, their future life. In ensuing years the necessity to show similarities between humans and animals becomes less urgent, thanks to the scientific discoveries that progressively show there does not exist a sharp distinction between humans and other animals, but rather that the passage from animals to humans is gradual. In this horizon the discussion about an animal afterlife loses its centrality and becomes a matter of faith, while human ethics develops on the concept of sentience.

NOTES

1. See Keith Thomas, *Man and the Natural World: Changing Attitudes in England, 1500–1800* (London: Penguin Books, 1984), 35. For Descartes's theory, see also iii, 33–35, and Richard D. Ryder, *Animal Revolution: Changing Attitudes towards Speciesism* (Oxford: Berg, 2000), 51–53.

2. See Ryder, *Animal Revolution*, 55–76. See also Thomas, *Man and the Natural World*, 173–81.
3. Thomas, *Man and the Natural World*, 148. As Harwood puts it: "This was a man's world," in *Dix Harwood's Love for Animals and How It Developed in Great Britain, 1928*, ed. Rod Preece and David Fraser (Lewiston, NY: Edwin Mellen Press, 2002), 66.
4. See Ryder, *Animal Revolution*, 147–61, and James Turner, *Reckoning with the Beast: Animals, Pain, and Humanity in the Victorian Mind* (Baltimore: Johns Hopkins University Press, 1980), 122–37.
5. *Dix Harwood's Love for Animals*, 137, 141. Poets who wrote about animals in this period include Christopher Smart, William Cowper, Samuel Taylor Coleridge, and William Blake; see Rod Preece, ed., *Awe for the Tiger, Love for the Lamb: A Chronicle of Sensibility to Animals* (London: Routledge, 2002), 156. See also Ryder, *Animal Revolution*, 127–89; Thomas, *Man and the Natural World*, 149; and especially *Dix Harwood's Love for Animals*, 361–410. On children's literature, see *Dix Harwood's Love for Animals*, 266–75. See Turner, *Reckoning with the Beast*, 80–82 (on pain), 6 (on humanitarian sensibility); as Harwood explains about animal fighting, "Compared to what men were made to suffer, the persecution of a captive bull or bear seems almost pardonable and at least comprehensible," in *Dix Harwood's Love for Animals*, 44–45. Thomas, *Man and the Natural World*, 177 (on sentience).
6. Turner, *Reckoning with the Beast*, 5–9. See Thomas, *Man and the Natural World*, 156, 173, on stewardship.
7. Ryder, *Animal Revolution*, 60. John Hildrop, *Free Thoughts upon the Brute Creation; or, an Examination of Father Bougeant's Philosophical Amusement &c. in Two Letters to a Lady* (London: R. Minors Bookseller and Stationer, 1742), 62.
8. Guillaume Hyacinthe Bougeant, *Amusement Philosophique sur les Langages des Bêtes* (Paris: Gissey, 1739).
9. See Umberto Eco, "Sull'anima delle bestie," in *Animalia*, ed. Ivano Dionigi (Milano: Bur, 2012), 67–86.
10. See Hildrop, *Free Thoughts*, 16.
11. Hildrop, *Free Thoughts*, 14.
12. See Hildrop, *Free Thoughts*, 105.
13. See Hildrop, *Free Thoughts*, 140.
14. Hildrop, *Free Thoughts*, 110.
15. See Hildrop, *Free Thoughts*, 110.
16. Hildrop, *Free Thoughts*, 61. See also 116–17, 141.
17. Richard Dean, *An Essay on the Future Life of Brutes, Introduced with Observations upon Evil, Its Nature, and Origin*, 2 vols. (Manchester: J. Harrop, 1767).
18. Preece, *Awe for the Tiger, Love for the Lamb*, 62.
19. Dean, *An Essay*, 1:57.
20. See Aaron V. Garrett, ed., *Animal Rights and Souls in the Eighteenth Century*, 6 vols. (Bristol: Thoemmes Press, 2000), 1:xviii–xix.
21. Dean, *An Essay*, 2:106–7.
22. Dean, *An Essay*, 2:62, 104. See Aaron V. Garrett, "Animals and Ethics in the History of Modern Philosophy," in *The Oxford Handbook of Animal Ethics*, ed. Thomas Beauchamp and Ray Frey (New York: Oxford University Press, 2011), 61–87.
23. See Dean, *An Essay*, 2:3–45.
24. Dean, *An Essay*, 2:104–6.
25. Dean, *An Essay*, 2:108–9.
26. Dean, *An Essay*, 2:111.

27. Garrett, "Animals and Ethics," 79. Humphrey Primatt, *A Dissertation on the Duty of Mercy and Sin of Cruelty to Brute Animals* (London: R. Hett, 1776).
28. Primatt, *A Dissertation*, 74.
29. Vasu Murti, *They Shall Not Hurt or Destroy: Animal Rights and Vegetarianism in the Western Religious Traditions* (Cleveland: Vegetarian Advocates, 2003), 101.
30. See Primatt, *A Dissertation*, i–iv.
31. Primatt, *A Dissertation*, 18. For the analogies Primatt draws between racism and animal oppression, see also Ryder, *Animal Revolution*, 62.
32. Primatt, *A Dissertation*, 101.
33. Garrett, "Animals and Ethics," 79.
34. Primatt, *A Dissertation*, 47.
35. The negation of an animal afterlife appears to be more a hypothesis rather than Primatt's credo. He clearly affirms that this is a supposition: "However, as we have no authority to declare, and no testimony from heaven to assure us, that there is a state of recompence for suffering Brutality, we will suppose there is none; and from this very supposition, we rationally infer that cruelty to a brute is an injury irreparable," *A Dissertation*, 42–43. Other authors believe the contrary, e.g. Harwood in *Dix Harwood's Love for Animals*, 176–77.
36. Primatt, *A Dissertation*, 43.
37. Primatt, *A Dissertation*, 43–44. Cf. also Garrett, "Animals and Ethics," 79–80.
38. William H. Drummond, *The Rights of Animals, and Man's Obligation to Treat Them with Humanity* (London: John Mardon, 1838).
39. Ryder, *Animal Revolution*, 82.
40. Harriet Ritvo, *The Animal Estate: The English and Other Creatures in the Victorian Age* (Cambridge, MA: Harvard University Press, 1987), 127–35.
41. Ryder, *Animal Revolution*, 84.
42. Drummond, *The Rights of Animals*, 5.
43. Drummond, *The Rights of Animals*, 6.
44. Drummond, *The Rights of Animals*, 8–9.
45. See Drummond, *The Rights of Animals*, 205.
46. As Garrett, "Animal and Ethics," 79, points out, "Primatt's novelty was due to the fact that his core arguments, as above, needed no providentialist justification. Pain is pain whoever experiences it, and that alone is sufficient for moral obligation and legislation."

Hartsdale Pet Cemetery

LIZA WALLIS MARGULIES

Despite living most of my life within a fifteen-minute drive of the country's oldest pet cemetery, it wasn't until a brisk late-winter afternoon that I visited there for the first time. I had just said a final goodbye to my bonhomous black lab, Ben, and brought him to the crematory on the grounds of the cemetery. The arrestingly cheerful woman behind the desk invited me to walk around the place while he was being cremated. She said it would take roughly two hours. In the end I would leave with a container of ashes.

This is the first example of what makes a pet cemetery so special and so different from the human equivalent. One might think that a heart-wrenchingly sad occasion like this wouldn't be conducive to strolling through a cemetery, but it was. It was the perfect tonic for my sadness—therapeutic even. While stones in human cemeteries tend to mark little more than birth and death, the stones at this pet cemetery tell stories of love, laughter, and companionship and pay tribute to the personalities, behaviors, quirks, and memorable misdeeds of the pet buried there. These marble or granite tributes almost seem to invite interaction with the people walking by. I always have a camera with me, and this day was no exception. By the time I headed back to the office to pick up Ben's ashes I had easily a hundred photos. All of them touched some emotion deep inside of me. All of them struck a chord of recognition. All of them made me smile. They still do.

The second difference is the lack of uniformity, regimentation, and religious division at the Hartsdale Cemetery. There are large graves and small, simple and ornate, and those carved with a variety of religious symbols. There are stones shaped like books, dog houses, and hearts, to name just a few. Some stones bear photos or etchings of the pet; some are plain. If you have ever loved or shared your home with a pet, as you walk through this cemetery you're likely to nod in recognition of the love, loyalty, nuttiness, and magic these furred, winged, and hooved creatures add to our lives. Perhaps you'll think back on the time your dog ate your sofa down to the bare wood (as Ben had—twice), your cat clawed through and unraveled a fresh roll of toilet paper, you rode your horse like the wind, or your parrot sung opera as you tried desperately to get some sleep. You will remember all that and more, and if you're like me, you'll realize that mourning an animal is different. The pain cuts deep but memories of the warmth, humor, and unpredictability of these companions are the salve ready to comfort and carry us through our tears.

Since that first visit eight years ago, I've returned to the Hartsdale Pet Cemetery a few more times and almost always with my camera. I never know what I'll find among those memorial stones, but each visit brings new stories. Each time I leave smiling and am reminded of how much fuller, richer, and funnier my life is thanks to the furry critters with whom I have shared my home.

Liza Margulies, *Algernon*. (From the series "Hartsdale Pet Cemetery." Photos courtesy Liza Wallis Margulies and Hartsdale Pet Cemetery.)

Liza Margulies, *Graves*. (From the series "Hartsdale Pet Cemetery.")

Liza Margulies, *Bébé*. (From the series "Hartsdale Pet Cemetery.")

Liza Margulies, *Danny*. (From the series "Hartsdale Pet Cemetery.")

Liza Margulies, *Sydney*. (From the series "Hartsdale Pet Cemetery.")

Liza Margulies, *Honeybunch*. (From the series "Hartsdale Pet Cemetery.")

Liza Margulies, *Grumpy*. (From the series "Hartsdale Pet Cemetery.")

Liza Margulies, *Duke*. (From the series "Hartsdale Pet Cemetery.")

PART 2

Companion Animals: Those We Love

All the World and a Little Bit More
Pet Cemetery Practices and Contemporary Relations between Humans and Their Companion Animals

MICHAŁ PIOTR PRĘGOWSKI

BURYING COMPANION ANIMALS HAD BEEN PRACTICED BY HUMANS AS EARLY AS 16,500 years BP, as recent archeological findings from the Epipaleolithic cemetery of Uyun al-Hammam suggest.[1] During the Early Neolithic (ca. 8000 BP) the burials of dogs who accompanied hunter-gatherers were already common.[2] Despite having a significant history, mortuary practices related to companion animals gained social significance not so long ago—in the nineteenth century, following industrialization, urbanization, as well as the rise of the middle class. At that time, purebred dogs ceased to dwell mostly in upper-class estates and became a fixture in the confined spaces of European and American cities. Spatial limitations, as well as societal aspirations and emotional needs, were the key factors in the emergence of the contemporary pet cemetery. Not surprisingly, the first official establishments of this kind were created on the outskirts of two bustling metropolises of the world—New York (Hartsdale Pet Cemetery, est. 1896) and Paris (Cimetière des Chiens et Autres Animaux Domestiques, est. 1899).

After the Second World War, however, pet cemeteries sprang up around the United States and Western Europe, especially in the 1970s and 1980s.[3] Other countries followed, for example due to a new pet boom, as witnessed by 1990s Japan, where nowadays more than nine hundred pet cemeteries exist,[4] or due to large-scale sociopolitical changes, as was the case of Poland after the fall of communism. Restoration of democracy and readoption of a market economy in 1989 prompted Poles to adopt numerous social practices of Western capitalism; burying deceased companion animals in pet cemeteries turned out to be one of them.[5]

Contemporary pet cemeteries are compelling, yet little-researched, sources of information about our relationships with companion animals. By looking at the graves of the deceased animals—that is, by analyzing the surroundings of the graves, accompanying objects, as well as tombstone inscriptions—we are allowed a look into the intimate world humans share with their nonhuman friends. This interspecies bond is multidimensional: on the one hand individual and undoubtedly unique, and on the other, clearly recurrent and experienced across cultures around the world.

Companion animals can be commemorated in many ways: as representatives of their species or breeds, as beloved pets, as best friends or surrogate children. One may choose to highlight their virtues, compose a poem in their honor, or focus on expressing one's own grief and longing. The last goodbye, a lasting written record carved in wood or stone, can also express faith in the immortality of a former companion's soul and in a future reunion in heaven or another sacred place.

The research discussed below consisted of three field trips (2012–14) to Psi Los pet cemetery, located in Konik Nowy, on the outskirts of the Polish capital city of Warsaw. A set of almost one thousand pictures of companion animal graves and tombstones was collected and studied. The description is divided into two major categories: general pet cemetery symbolism and its aesthetics, and the meaning of gravestone inscriptions.

PET CEMETERY SYMBOLISM

Psi Los (in English, "Dog's life," literally "Dog's fate") was established in 1991 and as such is the oldest pet cemetery in Poland. It is the resting place of roughly twelve thousand companion animals, making it the biggest Polish pet cemetery so far.[6] Psi Los was founded when Mr. Witold Wojda, owner of the grounds on which the cemetery lies, read a story in a local newspaper story: an elderly lady was cheated by men who promised to bury her deceased dog but, upon payment, threw the body in the garbage. Disturbed by the extreme insensitivity of the crooks and by the trauma suffered by the lady who eventually found out the truth, Mr. Wojda concluded that animal lovers in Poland should be able to say goodbye to their nonhuman friends with dignity, in an organized way—and decided to facilitate that.[7]

Situated on the edge of a serene, deciduous mixed forest, Psi Los reminds one of a human cemetery, although the graves are understandably smaller and the space between them is more confined. In many cases the main decorative element is a granite tombstone or a distinctive boulder, where basic information about the deceased animal—and sometimes about his or her human guardians as well—is inscribed. Some tombstones are more adorned, including those made from marble. Aside from natural aging processes and occasional negligence, gravestones from the early 1990s do not differ

Figure 1. Mourners at Psi Los, the oldest and largest pet cemetery in Poland. (Photo courtesy of Michał Piotr Pręgowski.)

significantly from the most contemporary ones. The cemetery is home to animals of numerous species—overwhelmingly dogs, but also cats, rats, rabbits, guinea pigs, hamsters, mice, ferrets, chinchillas, canary birds, turtles, and at least one iguana. The most conspicuous tombstone, heart-shaped, made from marble, and almost the size of a man, is dedicated to the memory of a rabbit named Kicuś. Although the vast majority of the last goodbyes are written in Polish, inscriptions in English, French, Spanish, Turkish, German, or Japanese remind us that Psi Los also served bereaved foreigners, including a former U.S. ambassador to Poland.[8]

Pet cemetery symbolism and aesthetics largely derive from contemporary human burial practices. This, at least, is the case of Psi Los, as well as of the historically significant Hartsdale Pet Cemetery, as reported by Brandes, and the Cimetière des Chiens et Autres Animaux Domestiques, as described by Gaillemin.[9]

Similarities between human and nonhuman cemeteries start with how the tombstones are constructed; stones like granite, marble, terrazzo, or limestone are the same as those used for deceased humans. This notion may seem obvious, but it is not—the use of the same type of the material and the way it is shaped indicate the absence of a certain taboo on the aesthetic level. Nika the cat can therefore rest in peace under a stylish, heart-shaped terrazzo tombstone strikingly similar to that seen elsewhere on a grave of a deceased child. At times, though, pet tombstones receive species-related contours, of which a bone-shaped granite tombstone of Rektor, a French bulldog, is a very good example.

Inscriptions on nonhuman tombstones are laid out in a very similar way to those known from human cemeteries. A basic, minimalist message one will encounter in both types of cemeteries is one that states the name of the deceased and his or her birth and death dates. Even though many graves at Psi Los lack detailed information on these dates—many indicate only the years—they also reveal more information about the departed and their survivors than human cemeteries.

A typical fixture on human graves in Poland is a photographic portrait of the departed; many animal gravestones at Psi Los also include photographs, predominantly portraits as well.[10] Most pictures are black and white or in sepia, matching the aesthetics typical for human cemeteries. Additionally, some tombstones in Konik Nowy are accompanied by statues of animals, reminiscent of a slightly passé trend of erecting monuments and sculptures by the graves of human relatives. The statues in question are usually on the small side and predominantly depict dogs.

Significant similarities can also be observed in social practices. In the predominantly Catholic Poland, All Saints' Day (November 1) is mirrored by the informal Pet Memorial Day, held at Psi Los and other local pet cemeteries on the first Sunday of October after World Animal Day (October 4). On this day, the animal guardians flock to Psi Los to visit their departed companion animals. A frequent view is that of a whole family paying a visit, often in the company of their present dog companions. Psi Los is very egalitarian—on Pet Memorial Day the differences in social status of visitors are particularly visible, even striking (such as when the newest model of Mercedes, driven by a busy executive, parks next to a run-down, twenty-year-old car of a poor pensioner couple in their eighties). Needless to say, social stratification has no negative effect on the pensive but very cordial atmosphere of the event.

The ways of commemorating beloved companion animals mirror those typical for human cemeteries in Poland: lighting candles (safely set in glass containers) and placing fresh and artificial flowers, as well as funeral posies, on graves. This form of showing love and dedication is practiced throughout the year.

Some pet cemetery practices seem distinctive. Leaving the belongings of the animals at their graves is the most striking: Kong toys, stuffed animals, catnip-infused rings, squeaky toys, tennis balls, collars, and favorite snacks can all be found beside animal graves. The same custom can be observed in pet cemeteries in France and in the United States.[11] Brandes suggests that bringing toys and goods to the graves indicates the emerging status of companion animals as surrogate offspring.[12] Even though in some countries grieving parents indeed leave toys on the graves of their children, this is not customary in Poland, making this practice distinctive to local pet cemeteries.

Many pet accessories found at Psi Los appear to be new or nearly new. Caregivers bring them to the graves on relevant occasions, such as anniversaries or Pet Memorial Day, often many years after the death of their companion animals. Purchasing new objects for the deceased seems to carry a very similar meaning to lighting candles; it is a declaration of remembrance and a testament to the significance of the human–companion animal relationship.

Among the items readily brought to the graves, the rainbow pinwheel deserves particular attention. While ubiquitous at Psi Los (and other pet cemeteries in Poland as well as abroad), it is obviously not a toy or a belonging of the departed. Instead, it is a symbol and a representation. To many frequenters it symbolizes the metaphorical Rainbow Bridge, the heaven-like place to which companion animals go upon their death, eventually to be reunited with their people. The rainbow pinwheel can therefore be seen as a symbol of hope and transcendence, as well as the indication of belief in animal immortality. In Konik Nowy, however, the rainbow pinwheel may also represent the Christian cross. Many graves in Hartsdale, especially ones from the 1980s onward, are endowed with religious symbols, especially the cross and the Star of David.[13] This matches my observations from a field trip to a rural Sheabel Pet Cemetery near Richmond, Kentucky, taken in September 2013. In contrast, sacred symbols and verses are sporadic at Psi Los, and no religious mortuary rites are officially available. Because Poland is predominantly Catholic, it can be hypothesized that the rainbow pinwheel serves as a representation of the cross for some animal guardians who do not feel comfortable using the symbol of their faith.[14]

GRAVESTONE INSCRIPTIONS

As Brandes aptly put it, pet cemeteries are rich repositories of information about contemporary attitudes toward some animals.[15] A companion animal's death and subsequent burial can be seen as an inevitable culmination of a significant, long-lasting relationship between a human and a nonhuman who is considered a friend or a family member. One good way of understanding the intimacy of human–animal relationships is through analyzing the last goodbyes in the form of inscriptions chosen to commemorate the departed in an ultimate and permanent way.

Some inscriptions at Konik Nowy are very laconic, and only include the name of the animal, dates of birth and death (or just the latter), and sometimes the species or breed if a memorial photograph is absent (e.g. "Tajfun 05.1996–27.02.2009"; "Gucio, canary, 2007"; "Charlie the rabbit, 1999–2005"; "Sznaps, pointer, 2001–2014").[16] However, many of them contain additional information about the departed and his or her relationship with grieving humans. A few particularly recurrent ways of commemorating companion animals are the following:

- praising them and expressing their virtues
- declaring dedication and love
- vowing to remember the animals forever
- writing poems in memory of the companions
- sharing testimonies of the interspecies bond
- inscribing highly personal messages for departed companions

Although dogs account for 90 percent of all creatures resting in peace at the cemetery,[17] there are few significant cross-species differences in the inscriptions. In other words, the Rainbow Bridge is equally accessible to dogs and members of other species buried in Konik Nowy. Dogs are, however, praised significantly more readily than other species for their virtues; these include faithfulness and dedication (e.g., "Max—beloved, faithful friend"), intelligence ("Beloved, wise Zuzia, XII.2008"), as well as vigilance and courage (e.g., "Prot 1995–2008. Brave, vigilant, and devoted. Bye, Prot!"), among other characteristics. Usually a few traits are mentioned, as in the cases of Alfik ("Alfik, 1996–2010, you were smart, faithful, and lovable") and Bąbelek ("Small body, yet a great spirit. Bąbelek, 9.IX.1986–13.XI.2001. Brave, courageous, gallant, reliable").

Regardless of their species and above all else, animals of Psi Los are beloved. Declarations of love are very commonly inscribed on the gravestones and, despite a general similarity, may vary in form, as these examples show:

- Our most beloved rabbit Tosiu
- Beloved Bianeczka 1999–2007. You were our joy and happiness. We love you, Darling
- Our beloved cats: Pirka 1990–2006, Franek 2006–2013
- Olo 5.X.1995–18.X.2005. We love you and we miss you
- Diana. 1983–1999. Our big love. Forever in our hearts
- Duduś, bullterrier. 10.01.2006–31.08.2010. With love, Ania and Edwin
- Misiu, [who] lived 17 years, 1990–2007. You loved me / I loved you / Forever you will stay / In my heart

Bereaved human guardians of Psi Los also vow to remember their companion animals forever or at least until their own final days:

- To my beloved friend Onyx. 1997–2006. I will never forget you.
- Mała. 1996–2001. You live in our hearts.
- Negra, 31.VIII.2002. Cuddly bear: you will be in our hearts forever.
- yganek. 24.01.1995–03.03.2012. . . . You will always be our biggest love, joy, and source of happiness. Wait for us—we'll see you again.
- Miki. 1987–2005. You gave us tons of joy and happiness, you will stay in our hearts forever

Until recently, such declarations were reserved either for kin or for great compatriots revered for their achievements. However, when Gucio's people state "We will always love you, friend," they in fact declare dedication shown to kin, not friends, as the Polish equivalent of "love" (*miłość*) has a more intimate and rather exclusive meaning than in English.

Some inscriptions take the form of poems (often not very good) or maxims. A good example of the latter is inscribed on the grave of Dina the rescue dog (1994–2006): "When our

Best Friend departs, we are left with Hope that beyond the Rainbow Bridge he is as happy as he always was." Another inscription, this time in English and dedicated to Tosia and Misia, states: "To the world you are a rat. To me you are the world."

Declarations of the meaningful interspecies relationship can also take the form of a testimony. It then aims at describing the bond that a nonhuman and his or her humans shared. Such testimonies are usually addressed directly to the animal and can be quite elaborate. In the case of Kicuś the rabbit, seven years in his company are described by his guardians as their "happiest days"; they also express their belief in otherworldly reunion. Leszek, Edyta, and Agnieszka, guardians of a dog named Giza (2000–2006), address her in these words: "We want to thank you for all the years we spent together, for this otherness you brought to our lives. . . . We thank you for everything. And remember, there will never be a dog like you and we will not forget you, our faithful friend."

However, some of the most intimate testimonies take a very minimal, one-sentence-long form:

- Dwight. 1989–2004. My life
- Ralf. All the world and a little bit more
- Ben. 1991–2005. Thank you for being there for me, my only friend
- Sonia, you were the only one who loved me. 1999–13.III.2012
- Axel. 1996–2005. Beloved friend, it is so hard to live without you

Witnessing gravestone inscriptions as touching as these leaves little room for wondering whether companion animals are "friends" or "family." Even though Axel's human calls the dog a "beloved friend," he or she clearly struggles without him. Do we really mourn our human friends this dramatically?

The answer may sound obvious, but in Polish it is uncommon to describe companion animals as members of the family. The examples from Psi Los unveil the reality of social practices, in which nonhumans *are* family to some Polish people, but this is not backed by the language. Whereas in Anglo-Saxon cultures animal guardians readily call themselves "moms," "dads," "parents," or "family" and their deceased companions "children," this is atypical for Poland. The human–companion animal relationship at Psi Los is therefore rarely described in terms of surrogate parenthood. Nonhumans are rather friends, even if often best ("Mars, our best friend. 1996"), beloved ("Gienio the cat. 2003–2008. Our beloved friend"), or loyal and faithful ones ("Skay 1997–2006. Our loyal friend"). Words such as "mom," "dad," or "parent" hardly ever occur. However, some guardians do define themselves as family of the animals ("Fucha. Plain good soul. Wise, faithful. . . . Thank you, we love you, and we miss you. The family") and sporadically call them sons or daughters ("Hektor, 1994–2004. Sleep tight, [our] beloved sonny"), although at times these words are also put in quotes ("Perełka. 1996–2005. My 'daughter'"), as if the guardians wanted to ensure others that they know the difference between human children and nonhumans. Another rare-but-present practice is providing the animal with the family surname, thereby converting them symbolically into relatives.[18] Considering that Maxio Litwiński, Pimpuś Branicki, Fruzia Kazimierska, and Pyza Banaszek left their humans in grief fairly recently, it may be an indication of a new, slowly forming trend.

As Shakespeare famously urged in *Macbeth*, "Give sorrow words; the grief that does not speak knits up the o'er wrought heart and bids it break."[19] The sheer fact of burying a beloved animal at a pet cemetery, commemorating him or her with a gravestone, and returning to

Figure 2. Grave for Zenuś the dog at Psi Los. "Endless love. Thank you for 9 years of happiness." (Photo courtesy of Michał Piotr Pręgowski.)

pay respects to his or her memory is socially significant. Social practices are independent from changes in the discourse and often precede them, and the Polish habit of defining the relationship with companion animals as friendship seems to be a good example of this. The broader context suggests that animals at Psi Los are called friends, but are considered family members. Humans cherish their friendships; having said that, friends very rarely mean "all the world and a little bit more." Ralf the dog, however, meant this much to his bereaved guardian.

NOTES

Part of the research from 2012, dedicated exclusively to canines, was previously used in an article published in Polish in the book *Pies też człowiek? Relacje ludzi i psów we współczesnej Polsce* (A Dog's Life? On Humans and Canines in Contemporary Poland) (Gdańsk: WN Katedra, 2014). I would like to thank Iwona Jakubowska-Branicka who first told me about Psi Los in 2011, as well as Robert W. Mitchell for his insight and invaluable comments.

1. Lisa A. Maher et al., "A Unique Human-Fox Burial from a Pre-Natufian Cemetery in the Levant (Jordan)," *PLoS ONE* 6, no. 1 (2011): e15815, doi:10.1371/journal.pone.0015815.
2. Robert J. Losey et al., "Burying Dogs in Ancient Cis-Baikal, Siberia: Temporal Trends and Relationships with Human Diet and Subsistence Practices," *PLoS ONE* 8, no. 5 (2013): e63740, doi: 10.1371/journal.pone.0063740.

3. Adrian Franklin, *Animals and Modern Cultures: A Sociology of Human–Animal Relations in Modernity* (London: Sage, 1999).
4. Barbara R. Ambros, *Bones of Contention: Animals and Religion in Modern Japan* (Honolulu: University of Hawai'i Press, 2012).
5. While pet cemeteries become gradually more and more recognized in Poland, it must be noted that, as of 2014, only eleven officially registered facilities offered cremation and/or burial of companion animals. However, as is the case of other countries, numerous people in the suburbs and in rural regions bury pets on the grounds of their properties.
6. For comparison, Hartsdale Pet Cemetery, established ninety-five years earlier, is home to more than seventy thousand deceased animals (for more information see: Stanley Brandes, "The Meaning of American Pet Cemetery Gravestones," *Ethnology* 48, no. 2 (2009): 102).
7. As described in Polish on the official website of the cemetery at http://psi-los.com.
8. As relayed to the author by Witold Wojda (July 7, 2014).
9. Brandes, "The Meaning of American Pet Cemetery Gravestones"; Bérénice Gaillemin, "Vivre et construire la mort des animaux: Le cimetière d'Asnières," *Ethnologie française* 39, no. 3 (2009): 495–507.
10. These are sometimes replaced by situational pictures, such as animals sleeping on couches and dogs on walks.
11. Gaillemin, "Vivre et construire la mort des animaux," 499; Brandes, "The Meaning of American Pet Cemetery Gravestones," 113.
12. Brandes, "The Meaning of American Pet Cemetery Gravestones," 113.
13. Brandes, "The Meaning of American Pet Cemetery Gravestones," 108–9.
14. One can hypothesize what such omissions, and reasons for such omissions, mean in a predominantly Catholic society; perhaps some choose not to use religious symbols out of fear of disturbing their brothers and sisters in faith. Such hesitation is somewhat reinforced by the caretaker of the cemetery, who claims he's not looking for unnecessary attention from local Catholic Church authorities, perhaps not very supportive of the pet cemetery concept (personal communication with Witold Wojda, July 7, 2014).
15. Brandes, "The Meaning of American Pet Cemetery Gravestones," 102.
16. Inscriptions from Psi Los were translated by the author unless stated otherwise.
17. According to Witold Wojda, the proprietor of Psi Los (July 7, 2014).
18. Brandes, "The Meaning of American Pet Cemetery Gravestones," 107.
19. William Shakespeare, *Macbeth* (New York: Simon & Schuster, 2014), act 4, scene 3, 155, lines 246–47.

To All That Fly or Crawl
A Recent History of Mourning for Animals in Korea

ELMER VELDKAMP

IN RESIDENTIAL NEIGHBORHOODS IN KOREA UP UNTIL THE 1980S, DOG BUYERS would roam the area calling out "Sell your dogs, sell your dogs!," indicating their willingness to pay for privately kept dogs as a source of meat. For many, the divide between pets and non-pets was not a clear-cut line, and the death of dogs, cats, and other animals was not considered something to mourn for.

On October 30, 2014, news came out that a seventeen-year-old high school student had taken her own life. In her final communication with other students, she stated that she felt guilty about her participation in a school club involved in the breeding and killing of mice to be sold to zoos as feed for other animals.[1] This incident illustrates the rapid developments that have occurred in the perception of animals in Korea in the last two decades. Increased intimacy and empathy felt for animals has also raised animal death as a matter of importance. There are two cultural practices in particular where such sentiments are expressed: pet funerals and animal memorial services.

FROM EATING TO CUDDLING

In traditional Korean culture, perceptions of animals are diverse. The Confucian tradition of the elite has handed down stories of dogs, horses, and cows as exemplary defenders of virtue, in particular of loyalty toward one's master.[2] In the "Precious Mirror of Eastern Medicine"[3] of 1613, dog meat is attributed medicinal qualities that are beneficial to diverse physical ailments, an interpretation that remains strong today.[4] On the other hand, in some regions the folk perception of consuming dog meat entails taboo and misfortune.[5]

The debate on dog meat plays a crucial role in the valuation of animal death in Korea, as it symbolizes the changing cultural boundaries of which animals are good to kill and which are not. From the 1970s, the consumption of dog meat came to be criticized by certain Western countries. The regulation of slaughter and selling of dog meat began with the designation of dogs as livestock under the Act on Processing Livestock in 1975. When Korea was selected as the location for the 1988 Summer Olympics in 1981, the consumption of dog meat became the main focus point of foreign awareness about animal issues in Korea.[6] Similarly, before the 2002 soccer World Cup in Japan and Korea, FIFA president Sepp Blatter expressed his concerns about the issue in a letter to Vice President Chŏng Mong-chun in 2001, and debate flared up. All in all, the foreign image of Korea is often that of an animal-unfriendly nation.

The last two decades have seen a rapid increase in the popularity and presence of pet animals among Korean people. The current popularity in Korea of pets originates in the early 2000s, following a period of economic malaise from 1997 (the "IMF era"). The Korean pet market has shown an enormous growth, from 500 billion won (approximately US$461,000) in 1995 to 1.8 trillion won (approximately US$1.66 billion) in 2010, and is expected to continue growing due to the effects of the aging society and the increase of one-person households.[7]

The early 2000s saw a revitalization of the pet shop district around T'oegye-ro in central Seoul and the opening of pet hypermarkets.[8] Accompanying this pet boom was a great increase in the variety of commodities and services that became available for pets. These developments have helped to promote the image of pets as an intimate presence among parts of the Korean population, resulting in heightened concern for the animal afterlife as well.

PET CREMATION IN KOREA

The first pet funeral companies were established around 1999, but it was not until a revision of the Animal Protection Law in 2008 that they would be acknowledged legally. Before that time, pet cemeteries existed in the margins, with regard both to the law and to their geographical location. Two companies to claim a pioneering role in this—Arongi Ch'ŏn'guk (Arongi Heaven) and Pet Nara (Pet Land)—started out with an office in Seoul, while maintaining an incinerator and ossuary (figure 1) outside the city borders to evade environmental regulations. Operating in a grey zone in their initial years (due to the absence of legislation allowing or prohibiting the cremation of animals), these companies depended on personal connections to animal hospitals and mouth-to-mouth advertising for publicity.

Both owner-directors of the above two companies utilize a personal narrative to account for the establishment of their pet funeral company: the death of their own pet. This made them aware that there was no proper way to dispose of the body other than have it collected as combustible household waste.[9] These stories also function to create rapport with potential customers and are presented prominently on the respective websites.[10]

Compared to Japan, where Buddhist temples have traditionally been involved in prayer for nonhuman beings,[11] there is no such tradition to fall back on in Korea. Due to the absence of this cultural foundation, pet funeral pioneers looked outside Korea (Japan and the United States) for inspiration. Combined with elements from Korean human funeral custom and personal creativity, they shaped a Korean ceremonial space and time for bereaved pet owners. Some of the basic equipment, such as a truck-mounted mobile incinerator from Japan, was obtained from outside Korea, while pet-sized caskets are custom ordered locally.

One typically Korean aspect of pet funerals is the way the body is treated before it is cremated. In Korean funeral custom, the body of the deceased is washed and dressed with a shroud of hemp or silk (Kor. *suŭi* or "longevity garment"), and these are provided for pets as well (figure 2). Another aspect that emphasizes the Korean context is the ceremonial space and

Figure 1. Locker-style ossuary with offerings and gifts for the deceased pets at Pet Nara (Pet Land), Seoul. (Photo courtesy of Elmer Veldkamp.)

altar design. About half of the Korean population claim to be religious, with 30 percent being Christian or Catholic and about 23 percent being Buddhist.[12]

This is addressed in different ways. The company World Pet offers separate caskets in Christian and Buddhist styles, while Pet Nara maintains separate ceremonial rooms for each religion.[13] Pet Sky in Seoul, on the other hand, takes an integral approach with an altar featuring statues of Buddha, Jesus, and Mother Mary (figure 3). Pet funerals in Korea reflect changing relationships with animals as much as they mimic the religious segregation witnessed in human funeral practice.

"THANK YOU FOR YOUR SACRIFICE": MEMORIAL SERVICES FOR ANIMALS

Before the pet funerals arrived, a select group of people was already professionally involved in posthumous care for animals through the observance of animal memorial services or *tongmul wiryŏngje*. Together with the increasing public attention to animals and animal death, this preexisting form of mourning for animals has become more visible to the general public as well.

Memorial services for animals are conducted primarily at research institutes and universities

Figure 2. Shrouds for pets at Arongi Ch'ŏn'guk (Arongi Heaven), Kwangju, Kyŏnggi province. (Photo courtesy of Elmer Veldkamp.)

Figure 3. Altar for deceased pets with statues of Buddha, Jesus, and Mother Mary at Pet Sky, Seoul. (Photo courtesy of Elmer Veldkamp.)

involved in animal testing, but monuments are present at zoos and other institutions that deal with animals, such as slaughterhouses, as well. More recently, Buddhist temples have adopted animal services (*tongmul ch'ŏndojae*), and memorial ceremonies have become a way to express changing attitudes toward animals in Korea.

The majority of life science research institutes, veterinary university departments, and other locations involved in animal experiments in Korea possess a stone monument or conduct ceremonies dedicated to the souls of animals sacrificed for science. The oldest remaining monuments are located at the Seoul National University Museum of Medical History in Seoul (dated 1922), at the National Veterinary and Quarantine Service in Pusan (dated 1922), and at the Korea Food and Drug Administration (KFDA) in Seoul (dated 1929).

Each of the above institutes has its origins in the period of Japanese occupation (1910–45), and the monuments were erected by Japanese during that period. In Japan, providing posthumous prayer for the successful rebirth of the animal soul is a widespread phenomenon. It was adapted to the modern context of animal experiments, and Japanese scientists and researchers brought this spiritual take on the utilization of animals for human purposes with them when they moved to Korea.[14]

In Korea, these very specific historical circumstances are not widely acknowledged. One news article covering the KFDA memorial service for animals of 2008 literally states, "From its start in 1929, this event welcomed its 80th anniversary this year,"[15] even though none of the research institutes have hosted ceremonies continuously for such a long time. After 1945, very few services were continued by Koreans on a regular basis, and it was not until the 1970s that some of the major institutes started to conduct them again.

Since there was limited preexisting terminology or vocabulary to express the sentiments contained in these ceremonies, the early adopters in the 1970s were also innovators in shaping these ceremonies and the accompanying ceremonial address. One of the first animal monuments to have been built by Koreans is located at the National Veterinary Research & Quarantine Service in Anyang. Erected in 1969, it is titled *Ch'ukhonbi* ("Monument for Souls of Cattle"), a reference to the service's involvement with livestock. The following text is inscribed on the monument:

> In order to gain ten lives
> The sacrifice of your single life will shine brightly
> Dear souls, rest peacefully
> October 20, 1969

This monument was constructed on the initiative of Park Kŭn-shik (1934–), a cattle pathology research veteran who started working at the Animal Health Research Institute in Anyang in 1966. His personal experiences with taking blood samples from live animals and killing them afterward led him to conduct short prayers before commencing his work. The suggestion to express his state of mind through a monument and ceremonies came from a Japanese researcher who had been responsible for animal health research during the occupation period.[16]

Another early example of a Korean-built monument is the Monument for Beastly Souls (*Suhonbi*) located at the Seoul National University (SNU) College of Veterinary Medicine, which is dated 1978. The following poem is inscribed on the back:

To all beasts and birds,

although our looks differ we both enjoy life.

Your pitiful lives did not evade a virtuous death.

Please do not bear a grudge against Heaven, and do not bear a grudge against people—it was for the sake of human welfare and the health of your fellow beasts and birds.

We pray in silence for your sad souls and wish for your happy afterlife, so you may be born into this world again and live eternally.

National institutes such as SNU have functioned (and still do) as a point of reference in the adaptive and innovative process that accommodated the spread of memorial services for animals across the nation. This is illustrated by the fact that slightly altered versions of this text are found in ceremonies at other locations as well. Former head of Laboratory Animal Resources at the KFDA Cho Chŏng-shik is very clear about her role in initiating the annual ceremony from the mid-1970s, when she states: "This is not tradition, I came up with it myself."[17] Still, she too eventually adopted the SNU text because it suited the purpose of the ceremony better.

Ceremonies of more recent origin frequently utilize the event or monument to convey a particular message to the outside world. For example, the inscription of the monument at the Samsung Biomedical Research Center in Seoul (dated 1997) and the ceremonial address at SNU's College of Medicine make explicit mention of the concept of "3R" (replace, reduce, refine) in animal experiments,[18] and at Hallym University in Ch'unch'ŏn, the monument and ceremony for laboratory animals marked the development of an educational program on animal experiment ethics in 2001.

At present, the phenomenon of animal memorial services has outgrown the specific context of animal research institutes and found its way to the general public as a way to express regret and compassion or empathy for instances of animal death. The most significant developments are cooperation between animal protection groups and Buddhist temples, and the appearance of animal memorials in times of disaster (often also with involvement of these two parties).

Priest Hyŏnjong of Hyŏndŏksa temple in Kangnŭng, a pioneer in the Buddhist appropriation of these ceremonies, has been conducting annual memorials for roadkill since 1999. In his teachings, he emphasizes environmental issues and compassion for animals, and the tenth anniversary of the ceremony for animals in 2008 gathered hundreds of visitors in a ceremony of several hours with prayer, dance, and entertainment, concluded by food and drink for all attendants (figure 4). A similar event is organized on Kŏje, an island near Pusan, since 2007, where annual ceremonies for roadkill are held by the local branch of the nationwide Environmental Federation in cooperation with a local Buddhist temple, the priest of which is a federation member. These ceremonies are not only meant to pray for a safe journey to paradise for the animal souls, they are also positioned as "a place for repentance toward the wild animals that meet a gruesome death because of industrialization and technological development."[19]

The increasingly frequent valuation of animal death as a matter of concern to the general public has also produced gruesome and adverse side effects, one of them being the repeated use of violence toward animals as part of demonstrations. In May 2007, one such protest was held in front of the Ministry of National Defense in central Seoul to oppose the relocation of a special forces unit. As part of the performance, a live piglet was torn apart by the crowd. In reaction to the killing of the piglet, animal protection groups Coexistence of Animal Rights

Figure 4. Praying in front of the altar at a Buddhist service for roadkill, Hyŏndŏksa temple, Kangnŭng, Kangwon province, July 2008. (Photo courtesy of Elmer Veldkamp.)

on Earth (CARE) and the Korean Association for Animal Protection (KAAP) organized a counterprotest against animal cruelty to demand persecution of the people involved in killing the piglet.[20] In cooperation with Seoul-based Buddhist priest Chŏnggwang (who also happens to perform pet memorial services) a public "memorial service for the little pig" (*agi twaeji ch'ŏndojae*) was conducted on May 22, 2007.[21]

This utilization of memorial services to deal with animal death could also be seen following the outbreak of foot-and-mouth disease in Korea from late 2010.[22] In attempts to contain the outbreak as quickly as possible, officials were reported to bury the pigs alive because they had run out of euthanasia drugs, and this course of events evoked much criticism both in- and outside of the country.[23] In January 2011, it became clear that the Korean government had culled over one million swine. Following this news, numerous temples across the country conducted public memorial services for the sacrificed livestock, which included prayer for a swift ending of the epidemic.[24]

Together with the increase of Buddhist temples catering to pet owners by conducting annual pet memorials, this application of Buddhist services to animals has become a new way for temples to garner interest from the public. Whereas the origins of memorial services for animals in Korea are situated within the highly specialized context of animal testing and research, they have now gained a place in the cultural repertoire for reacting to the death of all sorts of animals, from pets to cattle and from zoo animals to laboratory mice, and are a key component of "mourning for animals" in Korea.

CONCLUSION

Mourning for animals in Korea is multilayered and heterogeneous. The ceremonies mentioned here are not just a fourth R for "remembering" added to the 3R of animal experimentation,[25] nor are they merely the continuation of a particular Eastern way of thinking. Instead, posthumous care for animals comprises a complex collection of practices that have emerged from specific historical, social, and cultural circumstances in the last decades.

This chapter has charted some of the complex developments and innovations that take place in Korea today. We may conclude that mourning for animals is not a universal practice, but a cultural construct that develops under specific historical and sociocultural circumstances. For animal death to become real as an event of sadness, compassion, and mourning, a particular ideological setting and empathic perception of animals need to be established. The occurrence of similar practices in adjacent regions does not guarantee a universality or common sense, as illustrated by the late arrival of Korean Buddhism to the social treatment of animal death in comparison to the long tradition it has in Japan.

In Korea, ceremonies expressing compassion or empathy with animal death have appeared as a common ground between animal protection, pet culture and cremation, and memorial services for animals. These are all components of a story of change with regard to Korean attitudes toward animals and nature. These attitudes comprise an interconnected web of practices and perspectives that are adopted and habitualized into the ever-changing circumstances of everyday life. Through a selective and historical process, the innovative aspects of this adaptation of formerly unknown customs expresses changing sentiments toward the nonhuman animal among the Korean public.

NOTES

1. "'Out of guilt for killing and selling animals . . .': Turmoil about Last Notes of High School Student Who Committed Suicide" [in Korean], *JTBC / Joongang Ilbo*, October 30, 2014.
2. Elmer Veldkamp, "Densetsu no inu ga yomigaetta toki—kōhi no gugenka wo tōshite miru Kankokujin no shizenkan" [When a Legendary Dog Comes Back to Life: Korean Views of Nature Seen through the Concretization of Oral Literature], in *Sekaiisanjidai no minzokugaku* [Folkloristics in the Age of World Heritage], ed. Iwamoto Michiya (Tokyo: Fūkyōsha 2013), 349–77. Yi Shin-sŏng, *Han'guk kojŏnmunhak kyojaeyŏn'gu* [Research on Teaching Materials for Korean Classic Literature] (Seoul: Bogosa Books, 2004).
3. Kor. *Tongŭi Pogam*, a series of volumes on traditional medicine published by Hŏ Chun (1539–1615). Registered as UNESCO Memory of the World since 2009.
4. Anthony L. Podberscek, "Good to Pet and Eat: The Keeping and Consuming of Dogs and Cats in South Korea," *Journal of Social Issues* 65, no. 3 (2009): 615–32. Boudewijn Walraven, "Bardot Soup and Confucians' Meat: Food and Korean Identity in Global Context," in *Asian Food: The Global and the Local*, ed. Katarzyna Cwiertka and Boudewijn Walraven (Richmond: Curzon 2002), 95–115.
5. Elmer Veldkamp, "Aiganken to shokuyōken no aida: Kankoku no inuronsō ni kansuru ikkōsatsu" [Between Pet Dogs and Food Dogs: On the Dog Debate in Modern Korean Society], in *Higashi Ajia kara no jinruigaku: kokka, kaihatsu, shimin* [Anthropology from East Asia: Nation,

Development, Citizens], ed. Editorial Board for the Festschrift of Professor Ito Abito (Tokyo: Fūkyōsha 2006), 181–93.
6. In 1974, one column in a national newspaper lashed out at critics by comparing the consumption of dog soup in Korea to France, where people would dump pet dogs before going on vacation. "The 'Vacation Crisis' of French Dogs" [in Korean], *Chosun Ilbo*, July 25, 1974.
7. "New Family, Companion Animals" [in Korean], National Statistical Office blog, February 24, 2014, http://hikostat.kr/2250.
8. Byun Duk-kun, "Asia's Biggest Pet Store, Mega Pet, to Open in July," *Korea Times*, January 29, 2003.
9. Chang Hyo-hyŏn (owner-director of *Arongi Ch'ŏn'guk*) and Park Yŏng-ok (owner-director of Pet Nara), personal communication, 2005.
10. The pet crematories mentioned here can be found at http://arong.co.kr and http://www.petnara.co.kr.
11. Elmer Veldkamp, "The Emergence of 'Pets as Family' and the Socio-Historical Development of Pet Funerals in Japan," *Anthrozoös* 22, no. 4 (2009): 333–46.
12. "Population per Gender/Age/Religion 2005," *Statistics Korea*, http://kostat.go.kr.
13. World Pet was established in 2003 in Kimp'o, Kyŏnggi Province; Pet Nara was established in 1999 in Kimp'o, Kyŏnggi Province.
14. Elmer Veldkamp, "Commemoration of Dead Animals in Contemporary Korea: Emergence and Development of *Dongmul Wiryeongje* as Modern Folklore," *Review of Korean Studies* 11, no. 3 (2008): 149–69.
15. "The 'Vacation Crisis,'" October 30, 2008.
16. Park Kŭn-shik, personal communication, 2009.
17. Cho Chŏng-shik, personal communication, 2007.
18. The concept of 3R was originally introduced in W. M. S. Russel and R. L. Burch, *The Principles of Humane Experimental Technique* (London: Methuen, 1959).
19. As stated on the federation's website announcement for the 2008 ceremony, http://www.kojefem.or.kr.
20. CARE (Korean: Tongmul sarang shilch'ŏn hyŏphoe) was established in 2002, http://www.careanimalrights.org/. KAAP (Korean: Han'guk tongmul poho hyŏphoe) was established in 1999, http://www.kaap.or.kr.
21. "We Are Sorry, Little Pig! Memorial Service Held" [in Korean], *Han'guk Kyŏngje*, May 28, 2007.
22. Evan Ramstad and Jaeyeon Woo, "Foot-and-Mouth Disease Roils Farms," *Wall Street Journal*, January 11, 2011.
23. Allen Wagner, "S. Korea Foot-and-Mouth: Over a Million Animals Culled," *Time*, January 18, 2011.
24. "Prayer for Rebirth in Paradise of Sacrificed Livestock: Memorial Services for Animals with Foot-and-Mouth Disease All over the Country" [in Korean], *Maeil Chonggyo Shinmun*, January 12, 2011.
25. Susan A. Iliff, "An Additional 'R': Remembering the Animals," *ILAR Journal* 43, no. 1 (2002): 38–47.

Freeze-Drying Fido
The Uncanny Aesthetics of Modern Taxidermy

CHRISTINA M. COLVIN

TWO FORMS OF TAXIDERMY PREDOMINATE IN THE POPULAR IMAGINATION: THE TYPE specimen in the natural history museum and the severed-head-style hunting trophy. In the case of the museum specimen, taxidermic animals stand in for their species; single animals serve as representatives of whole populations. In the tradition of the "Father of Modern Taxidermy" Carl Akeley, the aesthetic of the museum specimen minimizes differences between individuals (such as bullet wounds and other surface blemishes) to maximize an animal's emblematic power; according to Donna Haraway, such taxidermy makes "nature true to type."[1] In the case of hunting trophies, taxidermic animals represent the achievements of the humans who killed them. As Garry Marvin explains, hunting trophies do not memorialize how an animal lived; rather, they celebrate "the process of how the hunter was able to bring about its [an animal's] death."[2] In both cases, taxidermists mount these animals with an eye toward maintaining "realism": they reproduce postures, musculatures, facial expressions, and other visually attractive features. More important, however, is the particular relationship suggested by both the specimen and the trophy: human dominance over animals. In the natural history museum, perfectly reconstructed, idealized animal bodies imply scientific knowledge and a mastery of forms, and in the trophy room, animal mounts hung on walls commemorate the power of the hunter to pursue, outwit, and "take" his quarry.

Because these forms of taxidermy are recognizable and ubiquitous, both the public and animal studies scholars have often read taxidermy as evidence of human dominance and control over animals. Neither the specimen animal nor the trophy animal represents itself or participates in the process of its own representation. In contrast to this view, several forms of modern taxidermy, including taxidermy in new media, televised taxidermy, and in particular, pet taxidermy, suggest and portray relationships between humans and animals irreducible to narratives of dominance or mastery. Instead of representing humans dominating animals, performances of modern taxidermy show humans *with* animals, engaged in the taxidermic process as a way to work through and even critique several of the paradigms through which humans typically engage with animals. Rather than forget or efface the lives of animals, then, modern taxidermy can facilitate the work of memory by emphasizing an animal's death and the particularity of the animal who died. Further, by revealing the particular rather than the representative animal, taxidermy has the potential to establish animals as subjects of grief.

More so, perhaps, than all other forms of media, the Internet has been responsible for the recent surge of public fascination with taxidermy. "Bad" taxidermy enjoys particular popularity; these mounted creatures recall Steve Baker's term "botched taxidermy," or "recent art practice where things . . . appear to have *gone wrong* with the animal . . . but where it still *holds together*."[3] As a Twitter account with, at the time of this writing, over 145,000 followers, @CrapTaxidermy posts daily photographs of mangled, misshapen, decayed, or awkwardly posed taxidermic animals. Images from @CrapTaxidermy were recently collected into a book, *Much Ado about Stuffing*, available for purchase in the United States and the United Kingdom.[4] Public interest in bad, amateur, and premodern taxidermy suggests a shift from regarding taxidermy as evidence of human dominance over animals; reproduction of animals' forms as they were in life presents itself as a challenge poorly met by many people who attempt taxidermy.[5] Public interest in unskilled or amateur mounts extends to the practice of taxidermy as well. Experienced taxidermists offer workshops for first-time taxidermists in major cultural hubs such as Brooklyn and London, classes that attract mostly women to a practice historically dominated by men.[6] Moreover, taxidermy supply sites such as McKenzie Taxidermy Supply include extensive catalogs of taxidermy supplies for online ordering. Far from the exclusive product of museum preservationists or professionals, the wide availability of supplies has democratized the practice of taxidermy and multiplied its practitioners. These websites offer for purchase everything from premolded plaster casts of commonly hunted species such as white-tailed deer and endangered animals such as tigers, to substitute ears and tongues, glass eyes, and various kinds of specialized knives, scissors, needles, groomers, and other such products to aid in flensing, fleshing, cleansing, sewing, and mounting.[7] The strange, uncanny, or awkward forms of many examples of amateur mounts call attention to their own poor construction and therefore question any simple claim that taxidermy unambiguously demonstrates the mastery of the human over the animal.

In contrast to traditional taxidermy, which strives to produce lifelike animal mounts that efface the taxidermists' own labor, modern taxidermy emphasizes the procedures involved in making taxidermy mounts. The shift in popular representations of taxidermy and taxidermists to include the processes of taxidermy necessitates we expand the definition of modern taxidermy to include not simply the finished products themselves—the mounted animals—but also the human–animal relationships and potentially collaborative labor of humans and animals that produces the mounts. In particular, televised taxidermy and shows featuring taxidermists have furthered and capitalized on taxidermy's popularity during the last several years. These shows highlight a shift away from models of taxidermy as displays of human dominance over animals to focus instead on taxidermy's artificiality and the labor involved in making dead animals appear lifelike.

Prior to the February 14, 2013, debut of *Immortalized*, a reality television series that challenges taxidermists to fashion animal mounts in response to an assigned theme, the network AMC released a series of commercials to promote its new show.[8] Rather than offer a glimpse of the competitive taxidermy to take place during the series, the ads stage encounters between taxidermic animals. By perverting the snapshots of "nature" offered by the habitat dioramas common in natural history museums, the ads show a variety of dead, stuffed animals without a familiar or legitimating context. Motionless fish hang in empty space against a painted river backdrop, and the head of an antelope floats in a flat, dimensionless desert. Without a diorama's reproduction of a habitat setting, these animals look suspended in meaningless voids. As camera shots alternate between mounts and species, the commercials culminate with a taxidermist's artful intervention. Camera close-ups reveal gloved, human hands modifying the mounted creatures, and when the ads cut to a wide shot, the products of the taxidermists' work are revealed: a fox sports sunglasses, a bear wears a salmon for a tie and carries a suitcase made of fish, and a desk lamp replaces the head of a hen and light bulbs the heads of her two chicks. Twice reconstructed, these dead animals do not offer an image of the "natural world" but rather a parody of traditional taxidermy. For the stuffed animals in natural history museums, the aesthetic of the specimen provides the narrative that "justifies" the animals' deaths, skinning, and stuffing: these few emblematic animals become stand-ins for entire species. In this way, animals once doomed to decay and decomposition become *found*, rescued from meaninglessness by human language and their appropriation as cultural objects. The clever trick of the *Immortalized* ads, then, reveals itself in the way taxidermic animals can resist such a narrative. In the ads, a bear who accessorizes with fish and baby chickens with light bulb heads baffle far more than they explain, educate, or even epitomize all bears and all chickens. These animals do not represent their species; rather, they present themselves as human-made animal-things. The logic that guides the aesthetic of the specimen—that a single dead animal can stand in for many animals—is violated by the mounts' own highly visible construction.

Televised taxidermy's accentuation of the processes involved in the creation of lifelike dead animals emphasizes the fact of animal mounts' constructedness as well as the invasive processes involved in creating taxidermy. Visual depictions of the labor of taxidermists suggest not that animals submit readily to manipulation as if passive subjects, but that in order to represent these animals, much of what made them living beings must be discarded. As Dave Madden explains, the taxidermist begins his or her work by making "a small incision to start, choosing a spot on the body that'll be hidden on its final pose. . . . Through this incision he removes all the internal organs: the heart and liver and lungs and stomach and intestines," as these parts contain toxins that could mar the appearance of the animal over an extended period of time. Further, "eyeballs are all water," so the taxidermist cuts them out. "Then he runs a drill up into the skull cavity and scatters the brains." Brains are "more of a grease product than anything else," one taxidermist explains.[9] In televised taxidermy, the visual demonstration of the taxidermic process reveals not only the violent evisceration of animals, but also the parts of the animal taxidermists must remove and discard for the sake of preservation.

Questions surrounding what parts of animals taxidermists preserve and discard are particularly important for a consideration of pet taxidermy. That a particular individual's skin is preserved through taxidermy is a fact essential to this industry, and by taking pet taxidermy seriously, taxidermy may emerge as a way for animals and pets in particular to be directly involved in their own representation. As a method of preserving the bodies of dead pets popular during England's Victorian period, pet taxidermy has experienced a resurgence in public interest in contemporary American culture, although said interest does not imply approval or admiration. Such renewed interest is owed in part to the sophisticated technologies of pet taxidermy: unlike most other modern methods of stuffing animals that rely primarily on premolded plaster casts around which animal skins are arranged, pet taxidermists increasingly use freeze dryers to remove excess moisture from animals' hollowed-out bodies. The procedure for preserving a pet also requires a significant amount of advanced planning on the part of the dying or deceased pet's owner; most preservationists recommend inserting a newly dead pet into a plastic bag and then into a traditional freezer as soon as possible. Once the corpse arrives at the taxidermist's, it is prepared for the freeze dryer: the taxidermist removes all organs prone to acidification, then poses the corpse with wire and pins and stuffs it with straw.

For Jane Desmond, pet taxidermy remains, like the display of dead human family members, "unthinkable for most of us" due to pet taxidermy's preservation of a "particular, individualized, humanized animal" as opposed to an anonymous wild one.[10] Because of our familiarity with these humanized animals, we understand the invasive processes of taxidermy as violations to pets' bodily integrity. Even more potentially disturbing about pet taxidermy is our familiarity with pets' personalities and, by extension, the seeming absence of said personality in the still, taxidermic body. Unlike the unknown or unknowable personalities possessed by wild animals, pets are intimately known to us; by living closely with them, we come to recognize their quirks, tendencies, dislikes, and preferences. Rachel Poliquin critiques the practice of pet taxidermy on the grounds that owners of preserved pets do not miss what is absent in their mounts, namely, the pets' animating, individuating insides. She asserts, "We remember departed companions because of their spirit, their charisma and personality. Once dead, this liveliness departs, and all that remains is a husk. Preserving that husk and claiming that it is still the creature is a disturbing confusion of corporeality for presence, or worse: it suggests that what has departed is not particularly missed."[11] I suggest that dismissals of pet taxidermy as an acceptable response to the death of a loved animal may establish an uncritical precedent whereby unfamiliar animals, especially wildlife, warrant more violent treatment due to our not recognizing their individuality as we recognize the individuality of companion animals. Further, dismissals of pet taxidermy assume that grief for lost animals must replicate the same rituals and procedures as grief for lost humans. Even when we keep in mind that pets represent "humanized animals," must we grieve them as we grieve humans for that grief to be valid? Or might pet taxidermy offer a possibility for grief work particular to the experience of losing a beloved companion animal?

To address these questions, I briefly turn to another reality television show featuring taxidermy and taxidermists: *American Stuffers*. After it premiered on Animal Planet in 2012, *American Stuffers* aired for a mere five episodes before the network canceled it due to low ratings, a result attributable, perhaps, to the mixture of taxidermic procedure, family values, and human–pet intimacy the show offered. Episodes follow taxidermist Daniel Ross, his wife LaDawn, and their three children as they maintain the family business: a taxidermy shop that specializes in freeze-dried pets. In one episode, Ross demonstrates for his new, inexperienced assistant how to carve open the tiny body of a customer's dead Chihuahua. Moving from a shot of the dog's soft, upturned belly to the assistant's face, the camera shows her shuddering and retching as Ross cuts into the animal with a scalpel. The episode also depicts the taxidermists removing the dog's eyes and replacing them with glass replicas. Finally, before entering the freeze dryer already packed with rows of dead animals, Ross stuffs the little dog's body with straw and arranges it on a flat platform, pinning down its limbs for stability.[12] The Chihuahua's limp, bloodied body haunts the clean, still, posed form of the mounted Chihuahua presented to its weepy owner at the conclusion of the episode. Televised taxidermy shows how the invasive processes of taxidermic preservation may linger over every dramatic reveal of the finished, mounted product.

The processes of taxidermic reconstruction *American Stuffers* makes visible again differentiate modern taxidermy from the traditional practices that efface the deaths of animals with unblemished, idealized mounts. Further, because of taxidermy's invasive techniques, it may be tempting to read preserved pets as innocent, passive victims of human violence. Less immediately apparent, perhaps, is the human vulnerability and dependence on animals suggested by stuffed pets. Letters from owners of preserved pets describe the feelings of emptiness alleviated by the choice to mount dead companion animals. In a letter to the pet preservationists at Anthony Eddy's Wildlife Studio, a taxidermy business located in Slater, Missouri, "John K."

writes of the "void" left behind after the death of his cat. Once the taxidermists returned the cat's freeze-dried body to him, however, John enjoyed a "permanently . . . good feeling." "His fur is just as silky as ever," John writes of the stuffed cat, "and he looks exactly like he used to. And even though I can never again hear his 'cordlike' voice or his frequent purring, it's good to know that at least his vocal chords and mechanisms . . . are still there."[13] John's praise for the appearance of his cat, the softness of his fur, and the preservation of his vocal cords shows the importance of the animal's body to the human–pet relationship. In addition to keeping the pet's body from decaying, taxidermy enables common forms of interaction between humans and pets such as touching, holding, and looking at to continue after the pet's death.

More than any other medium of representation, taxidermy emphasizes how an animal's body reflects a particular existence. "Kathleen," owner of the freeze-dried basset hound Peanut, stresses the importance of her pet's body to her understanding of the animal's individuality. In her letter to Anthony Eddy's, Kathleen praises the freeze dryer's ability to make animals appear as if they had not "passed from this life." She notes that visitors to her home respond with praise after glimpsing her preserved dog: "Everyone who has been here to see her have all had the same reaction and the same words; 'she looks so natural.' And in that lies the beauty of your work. I so much appreciate your small touches that mean so much to me; the wrinkles of skin between her ears and eyes, and especially her little tuft of fluffy fur by her tail."[14] Kathleen covets the details specific to her pet, details that her familiarity with an animal enables her to recognize. These details distinguish the dead dog *as* Peanut both before and after death: that is, the dog's wrinkles and tuft of fluffy fur shape what makes Peanut, Peanut. Perhaps most importantly, Kathleen's recognition of Peanut's unique and irreplaceable body establish the dog as a grievable individual. No other dog or animal will ever substitute for Peanut with her wrinkles and fluffy tuft, features captured and treasured through taxidermy.

Rogue taxidermy, the artistic, imaginative re-creation of dead animals as well as the assembly of taxidermic, hybrid creatures without real-life counterparts, provides my final challenge to the suggestion that taxidermy reflects only human mastery over animals. As a combination of pet taxidermy and rogue taxidermy and, for many, undeniable evidence that taxidermy represents disrespect for animals, the "Orvillecopter" is a taxidermic cat with a staring, wide-eyed face, four outreached limbs, an engine in its belly, and a propeller on each paw so it can take flight.[15] Visually arresting, the Orvillecopter confronts onlookers with its unnaturally posed body and the uncanny familiarity of a dead, preserved, and animate pet-animal. After his cat was struck and killed by a car, Dutch artist Bart Jansen decided to have his cat Orville "preserved." Enlisting the help of a taxidermist friend, Jansen had Orville stuffed. The artist then attached the paw-propellers and installed a remote-controlled engine inside the dead animal's stomach. This dead cat-machine makes no attempt to hide its own artifice, and the manner of the Orvillecopter's presentation insists on the recognition of the taxidermist's labor. As a result, Orville the cat presents itself as a body acted upon and formed into a strange shape. Even so, through Orville's outstretched body we glimpse a jarring disjunction between life and death, that is, between the cat who stalked the ground in life and the body of the animal who hovers above in death. Further, the Orvillecopter exposes how our perception of an animal's humanlike qualities directly influences what we think can acceptably be done to their bodies: pets are not supposed to go through the process of taxidermy due to their "more-than-animal" status. At the same time, however, Orville the cat's animal qualities are not effaced: rather, they *insist*. Confronted with the Orvillecopter, we recognize simultaneously that we are encountering a cat and that we are encountering a cat transformed. As a cat, too—a companion animal rather than an anonymous wild creature—this piece of taxidermy is haunted by the individuality of a pet: the cat's habits, likes and dislikes, personality, and unique way of being. As an echo of the cat's former life, the Orvillecopter calls attention to Orville's unique existence, albeit unconventionally represented. The Orvillecopter makes the unsubstitutability of this animal's particular existence immediate and visceral.

Because humans living in industrialized societies most frequently encounter animals as abstractions, especially through the catch-all term "meat," taxidermy is uniquely positioned to make animal deaths and bodies present and visible in their material particularity. By thinking through mourning practices such as freeze-drying pets, not to mention forms of modern taxidermy that challenge traditional modes of effacing the lives and deaths of animals, we might recover taxidermy's potential to represent a broad range of human–animal relationships. Taking this possibility seriously, we might also consider revisiting those animals in natural history museums and trophy rooms to ask if their unique bodies and forms may similarly guide us toward understanding them, as well as the whole range of their wild cousins, as grievable subjects rather than passive participants in the processes of representation.

NOTES

1. Donna Haraway, "Teddy Bear Patriarchy: Taxidermy in the Garden of Eden, New York City, 1908–1936," in *Primate Visions: Gender, Race, and Nature in the World of Modern Science* (New York: Routledge, 1989), 38.
2. Garry Marvin, "Enlivened through Memory: Hunters and Hunting Trophies," in *The Afterlives of Animals: A Museum Menagerie,* ed. Samuel J. M. M. Alberti (Charlottesville: University of Virginia Press, 2011), 203.
3. Steve Baker, *The Postmodern Animal* (London: Reaktion, 2000), 55–56.
4. Adam Cornish, *Much Ado about Stuffing: The Best and Worst of @CrapTaxidermy* (Kansas City, MO: Andrews McMeel Publishing, 2014).
5. By "premodern" I refer to mounts that, as was often the case, only vaguely resemble their live counterparts due to the taxidermists' unfamiliarity with the species and accurate "look" of the animals they mounted.
6. Such workshops have received coverage in such popular news outlets as *The Atlantic* and the *New York Times*, further suggesting the range of taxidermy enthusiasts as well as the association between taxidermy and a seemingly aberrant preoccupation with death.
7. McKenzie Taxidermy Supply, http://www.mckenziesp.com.
8. Juniper Jones, "Immortalized," Vimeo video.
9. Dave Madden, *The Authentic Animal: Inside the Odd and Obsessive World of Taxidermy* (New York: St. Martin's Press, 2011), 22.
10. Jane Desmond, "Displaying Death, Animating Life: Changing Fictions of 'Liveness' from Taxidermy to Animatronics," in *Representing Animals*, ed. Nigel Rothfels (Bloomington: University of Indiana Press, 2002), 167.
11. Rachel Poliquin, *The Breathless Zoo: Taxidermy and the Cultures of Longing* (University Park: Pennsylvania State University Press, 2012), 208.
12. "How to Preserve Your Pet Forever," *American Stuffers*, http://www.animalplanet.com/tv-shows/american-stuffers/videos/how-to-preserve-your-pet-forever/.

13. "Customer Letters," Anthony Eddy's Wildlife Studio, http://www.pet-animalpreservation.com.
14. "Customer Letters," Anthony Eddy's Wildlife Studio.
15. "Half Cat, Half Machine: Dutch Artist Turns Dead Cat Orville into the Orvillecopter," *The Telegraph*, June 4, 2012.

Clutching at Straws
Dogs, Death, and Frozen Semen

CHRISSIE WANNER

ONE SUMMER MORNING IN 2013, I RECEIVED A CALL FROM A VET WHO HAD BEEN assisting me in my research on the ethics of pedigree dog breeding. She asked me to meet her at her canine reproduction clinic because she had been contacted by a client whose three-year-old male dog, Jake, had just been diagnosed with terminal cancer and was not expected to see the end of the summer. The owner had been given the diagnosis the previous day, and the clinic was her first port of call. The vet did not offer any hope of a cure for the dog, nor did she provide any form of treatment intended to relieve his suffering. What she offered instead was hope for the owner who, faced with the prospect of losing her dog so soon and unexpectedly, was seeking comfort and solace in the thought that all was not lost: although Jake would soon be gone, his semen would be deep-frozen in a tank of liquid nitrogen, with the prospect that his owner could, at some point in the future, choose to be reunited with him in the form of his offspring.

METHODOLOGY

This article is based on data collected between 2011 and 2013 over eighteen months of participant observation with pedigree dog breeders in the UK. As part of this research, I volunteered regularly at two clinics that specialize in canine reproduction. At the time, there were at least six clinics in the UK staffed by vets trained in the use of reproductive technologies. Of the two facilities at which I conducted my research, one had been running for twelve years, the other for fifteen, and in an average week both provided services to between three and seven clients. Most of these clients had heard about the clinics by word-of-mouth, and in both cases around two-thirds of the clients were breeders of either show or working dogs, while the rest were a mix of commercial breeders and pet owners. Quotations throughout this chapter come from interviews and informal conversations with the veterinarians and their clients at these clinics.

CRYOPRESERVATION OF SEMEN

The most popular service on offer at both clinics was the cryopreservation of semen, a process by which semen is divided into doses, sealed into plastic straws, and deep-frozen for later use in artificial insemination. Semen could be stored on behalf of the dog's owner or sold and shipped to other breeders worldwide.[1] Cryopreservation of various bodily tissues and substances has emerged in recent decades as a technological method that provides hope—if not a guarantee—that an individual can be regenerated after death, most famously, perhaps, by means of cloning.[2] In the reproduction clinics, however, cryopreservation was promoted as a method of preserving the reproductive potential of young, fertile male dogs, because semen collected in the early years of a dog's life could be stored indefinitely, retaining potency and vitality while the dog continued to age. Interestingly, however, many clients were using cryopreservation to preserve the semen of old or ill dogs in the hope that the process might enable the genetic revival or regeneration of their dying pets, and as my research progressed, it soon emerged that this reproductive technology had the potential to play an important role at both the beginning and the end of a dog's life.

A GESTURE OF MOURNING

The majority of clients at the two clinics spoke of their definite intentions to breed a litter from the semen they were preserving. A few had very specific ideas as to how and when this would be done. "We'll buy a bitch puppy," one client had decided, "and when she is old enough, we'll have her inseminated, using [the deceased dog's] semen. My husband thinks it's daft. He thinks we should just buy another dog, but I don't want another dog. I want to keep the one I have." The vets were often privately skeptical in such cases, one telling me that "things rarely work out the way people plan. They might buy a female with the intention of producing another 'Benji' down the line, but after a year or so has passed and they've come to terms with it, they tend to be happy enough just to get on with life with their new bitch."

This is not to say that all clients were then happy to let go of the stored semen. Both facilities I worked at had numerous straws of frozen semen that had been in storage for ten years or more. "People might not have any intention of using [the semen]," one of the vets explained, "but it is something that most find very hard to get rid of." One such client who had been storing his deceased dog's semen for the past twelve years admitted that "at the time we thought we would use it [the semen] at some point to breed our own litter. Looking back, it wasn't ever going to happen, but it was our first dog and losing him was a difficult time." I asked whether he felt it was a worthwhile thing to do. "Yes," he told me, "because it helped us. Gave us something to focus on." And now? "He's still there—or *it's* still there, I should say—in the clinic. They phone us every so often to see if we still want to keep it. I suppose there isn't much point, but it's sort of a little memorial to him. It would feel a bit like tearing down your granny's gravestone to get rid of it."

The cryopreservation of semen, then, constituted an initial gesture of mourning as owners sought a means to extend the life of their dogs by preserving their reproductive potential. Over time, however, the straws of frozen semen gained further significance as physical memorials to deceased dogs, that is, as objects in their own right. In this dual role, frozen semen had the potential to be both subject and object in ways that other physical memorials did not, a potential that appeared particularly effective in allowing grief-stricken dog owners to focus on future hopes rather than on past losses. And while the "him" of the deceased dog and the "it" of the frozen semen may have become distinct and separate over time, the potential for reunification—of both subject and object, and dog and owner—remained ever present.

In this sense, semen—arguably more than any other body part or substance—embodied the essence of the dog and did so in both practical and figurative terms. This double view reflected wider cultural perspectives on semen[3] as well as the clients' personal experience of the clinical process, particularly the use of imaging technologies, namely an electron microscope that enabled clients to view magnified images of sperm moving about. This viewing process seemed to encourage clients to think of sperm as lively subjects, as was evident in the words of one client who spoke of the comfort it provided: "It's comforting to think of the sperm swimming about, so active. I picture them in my head as little puppies running around. Now they're all sleeping at the clinic, waiting to be woken up." Other clients spoke of the careful "chilling down" of semen as a gentle "putting to sleep" of the sperm, which, rather poignantly, is a phrase often used to describe the euthanasia of animals. Unlike the dogs themselves, however, the sperm, clients imagined, would be stored in a comfortable state of inertia from which it could later be "woken up."

TECHNOLOGIES OF HOPE

As both a reproductive substance and a memorial object, the material and affective qualities of semen—in concert with the technologies and authority of veterinary science—offered grieving owners a particularly effective form of hope by focusing on future breeding plans. As has been well established, hope is often an important aspect of interventions in human reproduction, and in some cases reproductive procedures are said to have become an end in themselves.[4] More than once, this appeared to be the case in the reproduction clinics I visited. As one client told me when I asked her why she had decided to preserve the semen of her dying dog, "I think this will make it easier—to let him go, I mean." This supports Sarah Franklin's suggestion that reproductive technologies are "not entirely *about* the deliverables [but] the investment is about hope." The appeal of reproductive procedures, Franklin claims, is not always or only the expectation that they will work "but the occasion for hope."[5] Following Franklin, Tiffany Romain has argued that the use of cryopreservation creates hope by "holding off known and looming possibilities for the future."[6] For many of the grieving dog owners who frequented the clinics, cryopreservation had the potential to forestall the finality of death by extending the life of the dog in the form of his semen. The apparent hopelessness of death was displaced by the hope of continued life that, whether or not clients would eventually put the possibility of future conception to the test, allowed them to envisage new futures for themselves and their dogs.

Of course, this only worked if a dog's semen was considered viable. While medical and veterinary clinicians alike are obliged to inform clients of major risks involved in any treatment, as Frances Price has observed, "how much a clinician should diagnose is left as a matter of clinical judgement. Clinicians are assumed to employ their medical expertise as agents of their patients in the attempt to maximise the benefits of treatment."[7] The clinic vets were mindful of the fact that, although semen collection offered little hope of improving the well-being of the dog, the procedure had potential to improve the well-being of the owner, and evaluation of semen was, the vets felt, an opportunity to maximize the benefits to the grieving human client.

Semen evaluation usually required little consideration when the sample in question was highly motile and low in defects, but when there were problems with a dog's semen, the vets were faced with the dilemma of what and how to tell the owner. As one vet told me, "You're dealing with people who are usually quite upset already. The last thing they need is more bad news. But I have to be honest—even when I know they'll probably never use the semen, I still have to tell the truth if it's rubbish. But there are ways to say things, and I try to leave them with as much hope as I reasonably can." This echoes Romain's point that, when it comes to reproductive interventions, hope often "depends on not knowing the specifics of things to come."[8] The value of not knowing was evident among clients who were quick to dismiss any information that might dampen hope. Although both vets routinely explained to dog owners that artificial insemination using frozen semen was not a particularly reliable method of impregnating a bitch, clients rarely responded with either interest or concern. Of the few responses this information did provoke, "Don't tell me that," was the most common, often followed by the insistence that "I don't want to know."

Despite the vet's warnings, most clients seemingly managed to remain optimistic and continued talking about "when" rather than "if" puppies would be born. Of those few who did seem to register the low chances of success, some speculated that this was due to other clients "not using the right bitch." Others reasoned that advances in biotechnology would no doubt have increased the odds of conception by the time they came to breed a litter using their dog's semen. In each case, clients' hope for the future relied on a reasonable certainty of success, which itself relied on their uncertainty when it came to the limits of the technology.

PEDIGREE DOGS

While the aforementioned examples reflect the experiences of the clinics' pet-owning clients, the majority who attended the clinics were breeders of pedigree show or working dogs. The death of a successful show or working dog was not only a loss to the owner, but was often also considered a loss to the wider breed. To the breeders who visited the clinic—and to the other breeders I encountered during my research—a pedigree dog was a bloodline incarnate. Influenced by what Mary Bouquet has termed "pedigree thinking,"[9] breeders spoke of the process of semen storage as a means to mitigate their grief at the loss of both a dog and his ancestors who "lived on" through successive incarnations of their bloodline. As one breeder explained, "When a special dog dies, it is not just that dog that you grieve for. It's all the other dogs that went before it that you miss, too. If a bloodline isn't carried on, you lose everything. That's a huge blow. Much harder to deal with, I think, than just losing one dog." Another client spoke of her grief at the thought of losing her current dog, who, she told me, was the son of a "once in a lifetime" show-winning bitch, "bred by one of the best breeders we've ever had in this breed." The client's current dog was the only remaining offspring of this celebrated bitch and had been, she told me, "the only thing that got me through losing her." Preserving the son's semen had become a priority for the breeder who worried that "if I lost him before he sired a litter, I don't know what I would do. At least if we have his semen stored . . . he can come back in some way, him and his mum."

As this breeder's words suggest, the bodies of pedigree dogs document the shared history of their human and canine forbearers and act as living testament to the skill of breeders past. Accordingly, many breeders bringing their dogs to the reproduction clinics were concerned to ensure that their dog's (and their own) place in the breed's history was established and their bloodline perpetuated. This required that the dog's reproductive potential was realized and his name immortalized in the pedigrees of his offspring and their descendants. Writing in the weekly *Dog World* newspaper, a well-known breeder explained that "they might be the most wonderful example of the breed ever—but if that animal does not breed on then there is little point in its existence."[10] In other words, genealogical continuity is vital, not only to commemorate the legacy of the individual dog but also to ensure the survival of the breed, and the privilege of owning a "good" show dog comes with the moral responsibility to breed from it. Unsurprisingly, then, many of those who brought aging and sickly male show dogs to the reproduction clinics cited both their personal attachment as owners and their wider responsibilities as breeders as reasons for preserving their dog's reproductive potential.

A GOOD LIFE AND A GOOD DEATH

Along with the duty they felt toward the breed, many clients felt it their duty to ensure that their dogs had led a "good" life, a good life being one in which a dog had fulfilled his potential as both a show dog and a sire. In cases in which reproduction did not occur during the life of the dog, cryopreservation provided breeders with hope that this potential might yet be realized. "A dog as good as him deserves to sire a litter," one client explained of a young show champion recently diagnosed with a terminal illness. "It's not fair to him if he doesn't." While it was preferable that a dog reproduce during his lifetime, if this had not been possible then cryopreservation allowed clients the peace of mind that it was still possible for the dog's life to be "made good" posthumously—he might still achieve full status as a successful sire and might still live on as an ancestor in the pedigrees of future generations.

Most importantly, whether the dogs were prized show-dogs or simply cherished pets, cryotechnology had the potential to make the end of a dog's life significantly easier for owner and dog alike. Cryopreservation had the potential to transform a dog's impending death into an at least partially positive process for both breeders and pet owners as, once life in the form of semen had been extracted and preserved, the dog could be peacefully released from his suffering. "Now I feel I can let him go," one client told me once her dog's semen had been collected. "It's time for him to rest." For this client, as for many others who brought their dogs to the clinic, cryopreservation was a preemptive gesture of mourning, part of the predeath grieving process that would enable her to make the final decision to have her dog put to sleep. For this client, then, as for many others, holding on to her dog's semen was an important step in the process of letting go of her dog.

CONCLUSION

For owners and breeders struggling to deal with the impending death of a dog, cryopreservation constituted the first gesture in a mourning process. As I hope to have shown, this gesture was often one of empowerment as well as surrender, as cryopreservation allowed owners to take control of their dog's reproductive lives at the same time as surrendering to the grievous inevitability of the animal's imminent death. So beyond its symbolic value, the preservation of semen provided a means of preserving and producing life when faced with the prospect of death. The use of cryogenic preservation in the mourning process challenged widely established notions of what mourning is and does, as mourning, in these cases, was no longer a process of letting go of someone who could never come back. In choosing to freeze their dog's semen, owners and breeders were challenging the finality of death, and in memorializing their dogs through cryogenically frozen sperm, they were keeping more than just memories alive.

By preserving semen, cryopreservation was also able to preserve hope. To quote Sarah Franklin, reproductive technology "can 'succeed' in providing this hope, even if it fails to deliver, as it were."[11] What we learn from the above examples of grieving dog owners and breeders is that the success of cryopreservation is perhaps best measured not only by the relatively low number of puppies eventually produced through artificial insemination, but also by its ability to cultivate hope and provide emotional relief. Regardless of whether or not its reproductive potential would ever be realized, the affective qualities of frozen semen contributed to its power as an active agent that provided hope in times of grief and allowed owners to let go of their dog, or rather, to let go of their dog in its current incarnation. This they could do in the comforting knowledge that, as one grieving owner put it, "part of him will still be here. And maybe I'll see him again."

NOTES

1. It should be noted that although I am focusing here on the use of cryopreservation in the UK, my informants were responding to the deployment of this technology and the discourses it had generated around the globe.
2. See Donna Haraway, *When Species Meet* (Minneapolis: University of Minnesota Press, 2008); Susan McHugh, "Bitches from Brazil: Cloning and Owning Dogs through the Missyplicity Project," in *Representing Animals*, ed. Nigel Rothfels (Bloomington: Indiana University Press, 2002), 180–98.
3. For a full discussion, see Emily Martin, "The Egg and the Sperm: How Science Has Constructed a Romance Based on Stereotypical Male–Female Roles," *Signs* 16, no. 3 (1991): 485–501.
4. See Sarah Franklin, *Embodied Progress: A Cultural Account of Assisted Conception* (London: Routledge, 1997). Also Gay Becker, *The Elusive Embryo: How Women and Men Approach New Reproductive Technology* (Berkeley: University of California Press, 2000); Tiffany Romain, "'Fertility. Freedom. Finally.': Cultivating Hope in the Face of Uncertain Futures among Egg-Freezing Women," in *The Anthropology of Ignorance: An Ethnographic Approach*, ed. Casey High, Ann H. Kelly, and Jonathan Mair (New York : Palgrave Macmillan, 2012), 189–216.
5. Franklin, *Embodied Progress*, 226.
6. Romain, "'Fertility. Freedom. Finally.,'" 190.

7. Frances Price, "Now You See It, Now You Don't: Mediating Science and Managing Uncertainty in Reproductive Medicine," in *Misunderstanding Science? The Public Reconstruction of Science and Technology*, ed. Alan Irwin and Brian Wynne (Cambridge: Cambridge University Press, 1996), 84–106.
8. Romain, "'Fertility. Freedom. Finally.,'" 191.
9. Mary Bouquet, *Reclaiming English Kinship: Portuguese Refractions of British Kinship Theory* (Manchester: Manchester University Press, 1993).
10. Sheila Atter, "Small Numbers, Big Responsibility," *Dog World*, February 15, 2013.
11. Franklin, *Embodied Progress*, 226.

I Remember Everything
Children, Companion Animals, and a Relational Pedagogy of Remembrance

JOSHUA RUSSELL

Memory is a complicated thing; a relative to truth, but not its twin.
—BARBARA KINGSOLVER, *ANIMAL DREAMS*, 1990

ON A COOL APRIL AFTERNOON IN 2012, I SAT DOWN TO INTERVIEW SIX-YEAR-OLD Oscar at his family's kitchen counter in their semidetached home in Toronto. I asked Oscar if it was okay to turn on the audio recording device during our conversation. He said yes, and I showed him how to turn it on. He agreed to be in charge of the recorder during the interview, a task that many children seem to enjoy. After waiting for the red recording light to appear, I showed Oscar a piece of paper with a short list of interview guidelines and matters of consent.[1] I told him that I would be asking him a series of questions about a difficult topic—the death of his family's dog, Sneakers—and that I needed his permission not only to interview him, but to analyze that interview and write about his experiences for a variety of audiences. Oscar nonchalantly agreed to participate. Next, I suggested that we come up with a series of rules or guidelines for the interview, in case he wanted to stop, change the topic, or avoid answering a particular question. We practiced a few short, fun scenarios to help Oscar feel more at ease with his role and to feel a sense of control over the process. At the very end, before starting into my suggested list of questions, I assured Oscar that if he did not know the answer to a question or if he forgot something, that he should say so and we could move on to something else. At that point Oscar interrupted me, emphatically stating, "I remember everything about Sneaks."

There are many ways of interpreting Oscar's response above. On the one hand, I interpret his comments as a desire to maintain a connection with his beloved dog, Sneakers. On the other hand, it is possible that Oscar was trying to emphasize his legitimacy as a participant in response to my instructions. Maybe he was upset that I insinuated he could have forgotten something about Sneakers or some detail about their relationship. Regardless of the intention behind his comment, Oscar openly challenged my statement by asserting that he was capable of *total* recall. Oscar's desire to "remember everything" reveals a profound, underlying sense of responsibility for Sneakers's memory. In the course of our interview, Oscar shared various examples of his own acts of care toward Sneakers—feeding him, walking him, even comforting him during thunderstorms—as well as his parents' caring behaviors toward the dog. He expressed some frustration when he identified his younger sister as an unreliable or irresponsible caretaker. Remembering Sneakers after his death serves as Oscar's last caring act, an act that is significant in present contexts. Oscar's comment—understood within the rest of his interview as well as within the context of my analysis of other children's interviews and narratives—resonates with many who experience the death of another intimately known subject.

Using an ecological view of childhood, remembrance is an act that is shared between children and significant others—siblings, parents, guardians, grandparents—within the context of various kinds of living arrangements and spaces that may or may not be referred to as a "home." Children also work through memories with teachers and counselors. I also consider researchers as actors who are engaged participants in children's meaning-making processes. Engaging in memory work around lost objects may serve several ends for children, including working through the grieving process. Memory work also allows children to organize and explore their sense of self through time, connecting them with the living through the meaningful reconstruction of shared experiences.[2] Memorialization, as a set of activities engaged in for preserving the memory of other beings or of events, presents a significant opportunity to extend care and responsibility for others beyond the boundaries of life and into an ongoing connection between the living and the deceased. Given the highly relational contexts of children's lives, it makes sense that their acts of remembering are shared with various others, especially parents, caregivers, friends, siblings, teachers, and even qualitative researchers.[3] I suggest that remembering a deceased companion animal is a kind of intersubjective, pedagogical act.

Through the semistructured qualitative interview process, I encourage children like Oscar to think about, recall, and interpret past experiences with deceased companion animals, in this case Oscar's dog Sneakers. This process involves a good deal of trust, openness, and even courage. Interviewing children about difficult matters also requires what Max Van Manen refers to as "pedagogic tact." Pedagogy is a vital and yet ineffable aspect of educational and child-focused theory and research. It is also a core component of parent–child or caregiver–child relationships. Pedagogy entails a reflective, dialectic approach to education in a variety of contexts:

> Learning to understand the essence of pedagogy as it manifests itself in particular life circumstances contributes to a more hermeneutic type of competence: a pedagogic thoughtfulness and tact. And it is characteristic of pedagogic thoughtfulness and tact that it always operates in unpredictable and contingent situations of everyday living with children.[4]

My relationship with Oscar, however fleeting, was pedagogically challenging for several reasons. First, I was—at the time—uncertain about the accuracy of Oscar's recollections. To what extent was he accurately reconstructing the past in his narratives and anecdotes? Second, I was concerned about any potential stress that Oscar might experience throughout the course of our interview about his dead dog, Sneaks. Finally, I wanted to maintain a focus on Oscar's own thoughts, sensations, feelings, and experiences, without steering him in any particular direction. Yet as an educator and researcher, my own interpretation of this pedagogic moment—sharing stories about a deceased pet—shifted away from concerns with accuracy or "validity" and toward an aim for mutual understanding and meaningful interpretations.

The ongoing research project I am drawing upon throughout this chapter examines children's relationships with companion animals, including guinea pigs, hamsters, dogs, cats, rabbits, hermit crabs, and tropical fish. Like the children with whom they live, these nonhuman animals share actively in the coconstruction of domestic spaces.[5] Insofar as is possible, given that many of the companion animals in this chapter are no longer living, I attempt to acknowledge and respect those animals' voices, subjectivities, and points of view. Indeed, the children in this study help me to work through the difficult politics and ethics of representing nonhuman subjects—living and deceased—by their attentive and thoughtful responses to my questions or in their drawings and authored works.

THE RELATIONAL CONTEXTS OF CHILDREN AND PETS

For many children, family life within the home space is the most significant context or background of their lived experiences. Blending historical research with cultural and literary analyses, Erica Fudge draws out several of the ways in which the human decision to live with pets has resulted in significant shifts around the concepts of domesticity, family, and even community. Borrowing from Jacques Derrida and Claude Lévi-Strauss, Fudge proposes that not only are pets "good to think with," but that pets are, "as many of the households that include non-humans tell us, good to live with."[6] Statistics around children and pets bear this out, as "the majority of pet owners are families with children," suggesting that families place children and pets firmly together within the sphere of domestic life.[7]

In many ways, children and companion animals share in the coconstruction of domestic space, while also serving as central figures in discourses around vulnerability, innocence, maturity, and development. Some of the children and parents I speak with talk about the constant presence of animals in their homes, and in fact, all of the children I have interviewed about pet death still have pets at home. In a significant way, children and pets have become companions in intergenerational family narratives, or family "trees," that may stretch back into the deep past. In recent work, Leesa Fawcett suggests that children's experiences with and narratives of nonhuman animals form the basis for what she calls a "kinship imaginary," an interspecies ethics built upon the kinds of curiosities that emerge from shared experiences as described above.[8] Such research takes the experiences and ideas of children seriously and makes them central to theoretical explorations of life in multispecies communities. In my own work, children and pets become the central figures in meaningful narratives of "home" as a multispecies, intergenerational space.

ON MEMORY AND FORGETTING

Paul Ricoeur describes memory as having two kinds of relation to the past: "a relation of *knowledge* . . . and a relation of *action*."[9] As a relation of knowledge, memory is an attempt to claim some truths about the past: we might describe memories as either accurate or inaccurate because we hope to develop a coherent, singular view of particular events for personal or historical reasons. As Barbara Kingsolver notes in the epigraph, memory is a complicated phenomenon when we consider the problem of validity, truth, or accuracy. On the one hand, memory describes a cognitive capacity to recall information, past events, even sensations and affects.[10] Many synonyms for memory utilize the prefix *re-*, meaning "back to the original place; again, anew, once more," but what we recall, remember, or retain is often just an impression, a picture or snapshot with a partial view. As a result, memory is imperfect at best and fallible or completely inaccurate at worst.[11]

Subjective awareness of the incompleteness or even failures of memory may cause some individuals to experience anxiety. The French existentialist Jean-Paul Sartre alludes to this anxious condition regarding memory. He suggests that for human beings, the past is an existential problem:

> The past, it is said, is no longer. From this point of view it seems that being is to be attributed to the present alone. This ontological presupposition has engendered the famous theory of cerebral impressions. Since the past is no more, since it has melted away into nothingness, if the memory continues to exist, it must be by virtue of a *present* modification of our being. . . . Thus everything is present: the body, the present perception, and the past as a present impression in the body—all is *actuality*.[12]

Sartre's insight provides a challenging starting point for an inquiry into children's memories of their deceased companion animals. Does recalling a potentially traumatic event bring emotions from the past into the present? Furthermore, if the past remains present to us, in what ways do the body, mind, and/or spirit of deceased loved ones dwell within living beings? I believe these are significant ethical, emotional, and pedagogical questions.

The second point that Ricoeur makes about memory is that it is a relation of action. When we remember, we are "*doing* things, not only with words, but with our minds; in remembering or recollecting we are exercising our memory, which is a kind of action."[13] One significant act of remembrance, especially within the context of loss and death, is memorialization. The children I interviewed described a range of memorial practices and rituals, including religious rites, burial rites, cremation and display of cremains, the creation of photo albums, making tombstones, writing letters or poems, and even creating artistic pieces in tribute to their pets. Many of these acts occurred directly after the death of a pet, but some took place up to a year later; in fact, ten-year-old Adele suggested to me that it was common knowledge that you had a year within which to memorialize your deceased loved ones with a tombstone or sculpture. These actions often coincide with telling stories about the lost pet, a narrative act that persists long after the pet's death and even after the period of bereavement that children described as temporally limited.

Through the shared act of remembering, children and I discussed and explored past relationships with pets while illuminating their various meanings and interpretations of those experiences with death. Over the course of an interview, we crafted a larger narrative of children's experiences of living with a pet, witnessing that pet's death, and grieving the pet's loss. In the course of my analysis, I have become cognizant of how the children I interviewed recalled and represented their relationships with their companion animals. Most children readily provided coherent stories about the past, while some spoke in more poetic, metaphorical ways.

A few children displayed an embodied sense of the past, such as when ten-year-old Adele described her recently deceased cat, Harley:

INTERVIEWER: And what did Harley look like?
ADELE: Um, she was this big, this tall (*indicating with her hands*), she was about this long, and she was uh, what's it, tortoise-shell tabby.

Adele indicated the dimensions of her cat's body, indicating her height from the floor and sweeping her hand through the space between us along the presumed length of Harley's body before stopping to describe her color. Adele's kinesthetic description arose from her own embodied memory of touching and being with Harley, who was no longer physically there. Such physical enactments, examined together, provide additional nonverbal insights into children's lifeworlds and their experience of memory.[14]

The ongoing use of storytelling to remember a lost loved one is perhaps the most significant, recurring example of memory as action. Despite some legitimate concerns that psychological researchers raise about the validity of children's memories, I suggest that children's memories are better understood by considering the *present* meanings that are given to past events, whether personally remembered or shared with us by others. Shared memories become important through repetition over time, and as we connect meanings to particular experiences throughout our own lives—or through analysis of others' lives—they are given greater and lesser degrees of validity based on their continuity, reflection, and interpretation. Sharing the work of remembering provides an opportunity for children to reach back into the past for a sense of understanding that is relevant to the present. Remembering is a social process that children learn. By reaching back into the deep past, even further than one's own sense of self or cognitive awareness, those meanings are given deeper roots and the self is given a sense of continuity within particular social structures, such as the family.[15] Through others, children also come to know of significant events and relationships from their own deep past, events they may not recall on their own. In a sense, the question shifts from children's accuracy regarding past events toward a curiosity about what their memories of the past reveal about present meanings and relationships.

As Sartre suggests, the past is "no longer," and so memory serves as a (re-)creative medium by which those who survive the dead move forward in life with new meanings or understandings of their relationships; all is *actuality*.[16] I care about animals because of various experiences with animals in my lifetime. Those feelings and values become strengthened when I consider that significant others in my life—my parents, my siblings, or my friends—not only share those values but also actively share in the recollection of those meaningful experiences.

PEDAGOGICAL RELATIONS AND COAUTHORING THE PAST

Memory, though often a personal experience, emerges within a variety of intersubjective contexts.[17] I suggest that the shared act of remembering—what might be called memory work—is a pedagogical activity that children engage in with various prominent "others" in their lives, including both human and nonhuman animals. Research on children's storytelling suggests that relationships with parents or caregivers, for example, are key to narrative development, as these significant adults both model and help children to shape narrative components—plot, sequence, characters, setting—into a culturally significant form.[18]

Anna: And what happens every time the sand cherry tree blooms, what do we say?
Sister: (indecipherable)
Mac: Suri is coming back, I don't know.
Anna: Mmhmm.
Interviewer: Oh yeah?
Anna: We say "Hello Suri" and there she is!

The social process of remembering is not necessarily just about accuracy of content. In the excerpt above, Mac's mother, Anna, utilizes a seasonal event—the blooming of a cherry tree where some of the dog's ashes were scattered—to prompt her children's recollection of their deceased dog, Suri. While a more positivist or reductionist approach to qualitative research would suggest that the data was made useless by Anna's interruption and manipulation of the interview, I found it a useful, firsthand opportunity to witness what may be taking place within parent–child interactions more privately. On the one hand, Anna may have wanted to help Mac answer "correctly" for the benefit of my research or to account accurately for Suri's behavior in order to maintain a truthful depiction of her personality. On another level, we might see this sharing of events as Anna actively reminiscing about the dog *with* Mac.

Parents and caregivers like Anna use memory work and storytelling about shared events pedagogically. Anna's interventions are shaping not only the content of Mac's memory but his evolving ideas about animals, values, and himself, all the while strengthening his relationship with his mother through shared experiences. Such interventions and clarifications can be seen as pedagogical in myriad ways. First, they help to prioritize particular details and events that are central in one's own life and in social or communal living. In a related manner, they work to exclude superfluous or undesirable memories. Finally, sharing memories and working through them can help children to negotiate or reflect upon their own values, emotional responses, and ethical priorities in relation to others.

The sharing of memories over time also presents an opportunity to articulate the family's moral values regarding animals, or the emotional significance given to relationships with their pets. While talking about her deceased guinea pig, Cotton, Lily, age nine, briefly hinted at the importance of such sharing:

Interviewer: When you talked to your parents about it, what kinds of things did they say?
Lily: Um, (pp) they were (p) they loved Cotton and (p) they had good memories of her as well.
Interviewer: Yeah (p) well that's good.
Lily: So, they kind of felt the same way as I did.

I interpret this passage as a prime example of what Van Manen refers to as "pedagogical competence . . . a kind of thoughtfulness, a form of praxis (thoughtful action: action full of thought and thought full of action)" where those adults who are living with and caring for children work to engage fully and thoughtfully with those children's concrete lives, relationships, activities, and situations.[19] Whether Lily's parents loved Cotton or felt the same as her is not important in this sense; for Lily, she has learned that her own feelings and memories are validated through the sharing of those affects with her parents. As vital parts of her developing sense of self, Lily's parents have clearly taken on the responsibility of fostering not only their own sense of the value of animals' lives, but encouraged her in formulating and articulating her own thoughts, ideas, feelings, and memories.

Memory is spatial, embodied, and perhaps most of all, relational. Gaston Bachelard writes at length about the phenomenology of memory in *The Poetics of Space* and *The Poetics of Reverie*, suggesting that poetic language in particular provides deep insights into adults' reconstruction of their own childhood.[20] Bachelard alludes to the centrality of relationships in our remembering of the past, especially our childhood:

> When, all alone and dreaming on rather at length, we go far from the present to relive the times of the first life, several child faces come to meet us. We were several in the trial life (*la vie essayée*), in our primitive life. Only through the accounts of others have we come to know of our unity. On the thread of our history as told by the others, year by year, we end up resembling ourselves. We gather all our beings around the unity of our name.[21]

Bachelard was interested in the geography of memory and the role of space in our recollections of the past. Yet, whether through the imaginative engagement of one's own past self or through an active engagement with others, he acknowledges the role of relationality within the act of reverie, or daydreaming. Mikhail Bakhtin draws a similar conclusion about the roles of others in establishing an overarching unity within individual histories, a process he refers to as "consummation."[22] We coauthor our life stories with the help of others and their reflections upon ourselves and the events of our pasts. Such coauthorship is perhaps especially vital for children. Within my analysis of interview data, I found several examples indicating the importance of human others—notably primary caregivers and family members—within children's acts of remembering nonhuman others.

Children's experience of remembering their pets is a largely relational phenomenon. My observations and interpretations of children's reliance upon others—particularly caregivers, siblings, other pets, and even myself in the role of researcher—suggests that memory is a highly social experience; but why is this relationality significant in a study seeking to understand the meaning of a companion animal's death? Coauthored experiences are meaningful for a variety of reasons, both ethical and emotional. Life is given partial meaning through the recognition, re-creation, and repetition of narratives lived with others and shared with others.[23] I suggest that this recounting of the past intimately involves the agencies and communicative contributions of nonhuman and human beings alike. For children, as for adults, the presence of others impacts the stories we tell, the details we incorporate, and the overall messages our narratives convey.

Returning to Ricoeur's dual sense of memory—as a kind of knowledge and a kind of action—provides a further point of reflection here. I asked children to describe past events, feelings, stories, and perceptions in order to develop a descriptive account of what it was like for them to experience both living with their pet and the death of their pet. My initial expectation, my hope as a researcher, was that children would remember the past as accurately as possible, a desire that is perhaps traceable to my early academic training in quantitative psychological research. I have learned, however, that there is no guarantee of the veracity of memory, quite the contrary in fact. As a result, I am less interested in children's accurate *knowledge* of the past and more intrigued by memory as an *active* process whereby children engage with others in the world. Memories are often incomplete or inaccurate, but the meanings that are tied to a past experience illuminate the present moment. In addition, memory is composed of various presences: the others who surround us and share in our experience of the world, as well as the places in which we find ourselves. Children's ongoing recollection and memorialization of a companion animal's death is significant for their present and future relationships with human and nonhuman animal others, and as such, death becomes an experience of great pedagogical importance in our interspecies world.

NOTES

1. While consent from parents or guardians is required for interviews involving minors, many progressive researchers working with children have worked hard to establish children as capable participants whose consent or "assent" should be honored.
2. Sigmund Freud, *On Murder, Mourning, and Melancholia*, trans. Shaun Whiteside (London: Penguin Classics, 2005).
3. Erica Burman, *Deconstructing Developmental Psychology* (New York: Routledge, 1993).
4. Max Van Manen, *Researching Lived Experience: Human Science for an Action Sensitive Pedagogy* (London, ON: Althouse Press, 1990), 143.
5. Erica Fudge, *Pets* (Stocksfield: Acumen, 2008).
6. Fudge, *Pets*, 13.
7. Ipsos-Reid, "Paws and Claws: A Syndicated Study on Canadian Pet Ownership," June 2001, 4, http://ocpm.qc.ca/sites/import.ocpm.aegirvps.net/files/pdf/P56/7a1a.pdf.
8. Leesa Fawcett, "Kinship Imaginaries: Children's Stories of Wild Friendships, Fear, and Freedom," in *Routledge Handbook of Human–Animal Studies*, ed. Garry Marvin and Susan McHugh (New York: Routledge, 2014), 259–74.
9. Paul Ricoeur, "Memory and Forgetting," in *Questioning Ethics: Contemporary Debates in Philosophy*, ed. Richard Kearney and Mark Dooley (New York: Routledge, 2002), 5–11.
10. Jan K. Coetzee and Asta Rau, "Narrating Trauma and Suffering: Towards Understanding Intersubjectively Constituted Memory," *Forum: Qualitative Social Research* 10, no. 2 (2009): art. 14.
11. Jens Rydgrens, "Shared Beliefs about the Past: A Cognitive Sociology of Intersubjective Memory," in *Frontiers of Sociology*, ed. Peter Hedstrom and Bjorn Wittrock (Leiden: Brill, 2009), 307–30.
12. Jean-Paul Sartre, *Being and Nothingness: An Essay on Phenomenological Ontology*, trans. Hazel E. Barnes3 (New York: Routledge, 1984), 160.
13. Ricoeur, "Memory and Forgetting," 5.
14. A lifeworld is the subjectively perceived world that is the source of a being's observations, sensations, feelings, and interpretations of their surroundings. Phenomenological researchers identify the essential characteristics of an experience or phenomenon by collecting relevant data from a diverse range of sources, including interviews, observations, memoirs, poetry, and even film or literature. These data can be interpreted and organized in different ways, but what remains key is a focus on the meanings inherent in the descriptions as they are articulated by an individual who has experienced the phenomenon in question. See Van Manen, *Researching Lived Experience*.
15. D. Jean Clandinin and F. Michael Connelly, *Narrative Inquiry: Experience and Story in Qualitative Research* (San Francisco: Jossey-Bass, 2000).
16. Sartre, *Being and Nothingness*.
17. Rydgrens, "Shared Beliefs about the Past."

18. Susan Engel, *The Stories Children Tell: Making Sense of the Narratives of Childhood* (New York: W. H. Freeman, 1995).
19. Van Manen, *Researching Lived Experience*, 159–60.
20. Chris Philo, "'To Go Back up the Side Hill': Memories, Imaginations, and Reveries of Childhood," *Children's Geographies* 1, no. 1 (2003): 7–23.
21. Gaston Bachelard, *The Poetics of Reverie: Childhood, Language, and the Cosmos* (Boston: Beacon Press, 1969), 99.
22. Mikhail Bakhtin, *Art and Answerability: Early Philosophical Essays* (Austin: University of Texas Press, 1990), 13.
23. Katherine Nelson, "Event Representations, Narrative Development, and Internal Working Models," *Attachment & Human Development* 1, no. 3 (1999): 239–52; Richard Kearney, *On Stories* (New York: Routledge, 2002).

On Cats and Contradictions
Mourning Animal Death in an English Community

BECKY TIPPER

Since time immemorial mankind has been plagued by the question, "What do you do with a dead cat?"

—SIMON BOND, *101 USES FOR A DEAD CAT*

WE LIVE AMONG NONHUMAN ANIMALS. EVEN IN CITIES AND SUBURBS, SPACES SEEMingly dominated and shaped by human intent, animals inhabit our homes and gardens (sometimes by invitation and sometimes not); their tracks and trails intersect with ours; their lives touch our own. For more than a year, I researched these ordinary encounters between the species. I focused on a neighborhood in a northern English city, and (following in a tradition of interpretive sociology) I employed an ethnographic approach to explore the ways that people made sense of their everyday engagements with the creatures who shared their neighborhood.[1]

In the course of my fieldwork, a well-known neighborhood cat, Vincent, was run over by a car. His death provoked a significant response within the local community. Vincent's story—a story both tragic and banal, remarkable and commonplace, moving and humorous—can, I suggest, illuminate what it means to mourn animals, and might begin to answer that seemingly frivolous (yet fraught and troubling) question of what it is we can *do* with a dead cat.

A LEGEND IN THESE PARTS: THE STORY OF VINCE

The first I heard of Vince's death was in an interview with local resident Cynthia, a warm, softspoken woman in her seventies. As she was telling me about various local cats she sometimes encountered, including one who had visited her regularly, she suddenly remembered some news she had recently heard.[2]

"Oh, but, I was quite sad about it!" she says, interrupting herself, "Brian [Cynthia's husband] only told me yesterday, but there was a cat—" here she pauses, and with a smile, pronounces his name precisely and comically, "called Vincent!"

We both laugh.

"Oh, but he was the most *friendly* cat," she continues. "Over where the road is over there, there's a seat, and sometimes I catch the bus there, and just as you walk past, he'd come up and then he'd set you to the stop!"

There is more laughter. "Aw," I say.

"And the postman, he used to follow him up the street to deliver the letters! You know, that's a cat you couldn't help but like!"

Cynthia chuckles for a moment, and then leans in close, her voice hushed as she recounts what she had heard. "Well, *unfortunately*, he got knocked down. I don't know whether it was Sunday . . . or Monday morning . . . but I know a lady down the road will be really upset, because she was always dashing out of her house and taking him back across the road because she was so frightened he'd get run over! And now it has done."

She recalls how she heard the news from Frank, a man who regularly sat with Vince on the bench at the corner of the street. "Well, it was Frank who told Brian that it'd been killed. And this lady called Olive, she'll be *devastated*. I'm sure she fed him and everything. So it's a shame."

"Was he called Vincent, or was that what people named him?" I ask.

"No, that was his name, or so Olive said. So I always called him Vincent! I'd say, 'Good morning, Vincent!'" She says this in a cheery tone of mock formality, and we both laugh again. "He *always* came to greet you. Everybody who came, he always came up and said, 'Hello!'"

As Cynthia indicated, news of Vince's demise flowed quickly through networks of neighborhood acquaintanceship as local people told one another. One person placed flowers at the bench where Vince had often sat, and other local residents followed suit. The bench was soon adorned with cards and flowers (figures 1 and 2). The cards carried messages to Vince, such as "Every time we passed, we checked to see if you were at the bench. We will miss you," and "In memory of my mate Vince, a legend in these parts." Several days later, a brass plaque in memory of Vince had been affixed to the bench (figure 3).

I subsequently spoke to the local couple, Naomi and Phil, with whom Vince had lived. They too remarked on Vince's prominent role in the neighborhood and observed that the plaque and many of the tributes had been left by people they did not know, but with whom Vince had independently been acquainted.[3]

As Naomi recalled: "That bench—that was *his* corner on the road. You know, that was his spot and he would just keep people company, and come and go, and go to the bus stop and wait for people getting off the bus or he'd walk them to the bus stop and wait till they got on the bus. . . . And there's a guy on the corner and . . . he basically goes to the corner most mornings unless it's pouring with rain and—he's a lovely man—and when Vince died, he basically referred to Vince as his guardian angel! . . . And Vince would just appear and be there for people, and I think that's just what Vince *did*."

WE WILL MISS YOU: MOURNING A NONHUMAN NEIGHBOR

In this somewhat remarkable response to the death of a local cat, there is much to unpack about the ordinary ways people might mourn the animal deaths that punctuate everyday life.

Figure 1. Tributes on the bench. (Photo courtesy of Becky Tipper.)

Figure 2. Card featuring a photograph of Vince. (Photo courtesy of Becky Tipper.)

Figure 3. "Everybody Loved Him" memorial plaque. (Photo courtesy of Becky Tipper.)

Mary Phillips, reflecting on the naming of nonhuman animals, observes that a name enables the "production of a biography" so that the story of an animal's life, and death, can be told. Consequently, a named animal's death might be perceived as "tragic" in a way that an unnamed animal's cannot since "tragedy belongs to the realm of narrative."[4] It did seem that knowledge of Vince's name (in contrast to unnamed stray or wild animals who also perish on roads) enabled the community to share the news of this animal's death and to tell a narrative of a tragic loss.

However, the tributes also indicated that people were mourning an individual with whom they had had a personal relationship—what mattered was not only that they had known his name, but that they had known *him*. This resonates with recent scholarship exploring how human relationships with companion animals can be understood as interactions between thinking, feeling individuals. As sociologist Leslie Irvine argues, animals "have a core self that becomes present to us through interaction with them."[5] In the case of Vince, we see how such insights are not limited to human engagements with their own pets; many local people had known, and grieved the loss of, this cat's distinctive "self." Vince was seen as an individual with a distinctive personality, described in the written tributes and people's talk as "friendly," "sweet," and "remarkable" and referred to by the personal pronouns "he" and "who" (rather than the impersonal terms "it" or "that" sometimes employed for animals).[6]

People knew Vince, yet it was notable that they also felt known *by* him: they recalled how he had greeted them, anticipated their routines, and recognized them.[7] As sociologist David Morgan observes, this "state of mutually admitted mutual knowing" is what defines (human) acquaintanceship—the slippery relationship between "stranger" and "intimate."[8] In fact, it was striking that the written tributes framed this interspecies relationship in terms usually reserved for human acquaintances of various types: Vince was called a "friend," a "mate," and a "neighbor."

Morgan further observes that "probably the most significant practice of acquaintanceship is conversation."[9] Interestingly, the tributes also suggested that people understood their encounters with Vince explicitly as conversational exchanges; they recalled regular "visits" from Vince, who had been "the first neighbor to introduce [himself]," and with whom they had enjoyed daily "chats."

As Nickie Charles and Charlotte Davies observe, people often consider their pets to be "family members" or "kin," breaking apart categories conventionally understood to refer only to *human* relationships.[10] And, as Donna Haraway writes, the mutuality and intimacy of dog–human engagements opens up theoretical space for destabilizing the boundary between "human" and "animal" and for reconceptualizing "kinship" to incorporate the nonhuman.[11] In the tributes to Vince, it appeared that not only kinship but also friendship and acquaintanceship were readily understood to incorporate more than human relationships.

The possibility that a cat could be considered a neighbor or acquaintance also recalls Donaldson and Kymlicka's proposal that animal "citizenship" offers a basis for fundamentally rethinking human ethical obligations to other species.[12] Just as citizenship might transcend humanity, for many philosophers, expanding the category of moral and legal "personhood" to include certain animals offers a framework for building more ethical interspecies relations. For instance, Mary Midgley argues that an animal with the capacity for "emotional fellowship" should be defined as a person.[13] Similarly, Carol Adams observes that personhood emerges in interspecies intimacies and that in human–companion animal relations we might witness "recognition of that animal's individuality, or, in a sense, that animal's personhood: Given a name, touched and caressed, a life that interacts and informs another's."[14] Such definitions of personhood seem particularly pertinent here: when Vince was killed, for many locals, *someone they knew*—a person whose life had informed their own—had died.

The implications are provocative and profound. In the responses to Vince's death, we seem to see an embodiment of the ethical ideals of animal personhood and citizenship and to glimpse a social world where affective relationships transcend the human and where people readily and openly mourn the death of a friend and neighbor who simply happens to belong to another species.

FOR A CAT? THE LIMITS OF MOURNING

However, although it seemed that in Vince's memorial the traditional human–animal boundary was queried, or even dissolved, other responses offered a more complicated and conflicted view. In the days following my meeting with Cynthia, events continued to unfold, and the media even took notice of Vince's memorial. A journalist for the national newspaper *The Independent* happened to see the tributes and wrote a personal column reflecting on Vince's demise.[15] The city's daily newspaper, *The Press*, also featured a full-page article on the neighborhood's response (figure 4).

In the online edition of the newspaper, this article generated numerous comments. Several commentators noted that they too had known Vince: "Very sad to hear Vincent has gone—he has walked me home many a night." They too expressed regret about his death: "He was a lovely puss, so sad," recalling, "Yes, remember him well. A real street cat."[16]

While such remarks underlined Vince's status as a neighborhood acquaintance, other

Figure 4. Article in the local newspaper on Vince's death, *The Press*, July 30, 2009. (Photo courtesy of Becky Tipper.)

commenters felt both the reportage and expressions of grief were inappropriate and absurd: "Why on earth has a cat's death got coverage in a paper?" asked one. Another drew attention to the fact that the oldest surviving World War I veteran had recently died, and "yet the cat receives column inches instead? Hang your heads in shame . . . this is just stupid." Others expressed profound contempt for cats: "Get a life you saddos all moggys [sic] should be shot or run over!!!!!!! P.S. what a stupid story. Anymore halfwits care to comment?" Another observed, "It's a cat ffs . . . people are killed every day on the roads and don't get this much coverage," to which another replied, "I agree, I saw the flowers last night, thought somebody had been killed at the junction." In stark contrast to the tributes left at the bench, here Vince's death was not a death to be marked and mourned; and for the writer who feared "somebody had been killed," the death of a cat was indisputably not the death of *somebody*.

Improvised street-side shrines—such as those established after terrorist attacks or traffic accidents—can be arresting, visual expressions of raw emotion.[17] Yet, as Judith Butler writes, while "some lives are grievable" through such public displays and obituaries, "others are not."[18] Although Butler's concern is with human deaths, it seemed that for some people, Vince's death was not legitimately "grievable" in this manner. Butler argues that denying individuals such public memorials dehumanizes them. Perhaps those critical of Vince's memorial were alert to the inverse implication of Butler's statement: that public mourning threatens to *humanize* the nonhuman.

Public memorials for dead animals are not unheard of. However, the spontaneous tributes to Vince had a distinctive character, closely resembling those for (human) victims of road accidents, a resemblance perhaps perceived by some as a disturbing transgression of the species boundary. As philosopher Raimond Gaita observes, attempts to mourn, or to extend, the lives of pets often face accusations of sentimentality, confronting the awkward question of how far one should go "for a *dog*."[19] Although the tributes hinted provocatively at an appreciation of animals as valued companions, whose deaths are potentially tragic, the online comments reflected a more traditional view of the species divide where human lives have an obvious, inherent value that animal lives do not; they seem to ask in exasperation, "for a *cat*?"

REST IN PUSS: IRONY AND ANIMAL DEATH

The online discussion and the written tributes illustrate starkly opposed perspectives on animal death, but it was not the case that all responses could be so categorized; some reflected a more slippery and complex view.

This is neatly illustrated by Cynthia's discussion of Vince's death, which was infused with laughter and apparent contradictions. Cynthia was sad about the death of a cat whom she knew by name and called "he," and yet also, at times, referred to as "it." When she spoke of meeting him, she recounted her playfully formal salutation, "Good morning, Vincent," which seemed to both acknowledge his personhood and at the same time to express amusement at the notion of greeting a cat with such a comical, quaintly human name. (While possessing a name can allow the articulation of a tragic narrative, here it seems equally to counteract the suggestion of tragedy.) Cynthia's account is subtle and ironic, telling of a death that seems at once serious and laughable.

Such contradictions were echoed in Naomi's account. Recalling Vince's penchant for meeting new neighborhood residents, she recalled how "If someone moved into the area, he was always the first person to go over," before laughing and correcting herself, seeming to search for a better term: "Well you know, not the first *person*! . . . But the first . . . well, you know. . . . the first *one* to go over and introduce himself!" Although reinforcing the idea that Vince was an individual who actively forged relationships (by "introducing himself") she was hesitant to call him, unequivocally, a person. And, while moved by the tributes left at the bench, she laughingly noted that the neighborhood's response was, perhaps, "a bit much for a cat."

A decidedly tongue-in-cheek tone was also evident in the local press coverage (figure 4). In contrast to the sadness of the tributes, the newspaper article embraced the comic potential of the story, incorporating puns such as the headline "Fur-well Vince" and the caption "Rest in Puss." The story was presented as moving and yet humorous, the jokes adding a levity that would be unthinkable in reportage of a human death.

This kind of ironic sympathy—a simultaneous expression of sadness and amusement—also emerged when I presented some of this data at academic conferences, where audience members reported being deeply moved by the story, and yet where photographs of the tributes were met with spontaneous laughter.

Such examples do not align tidily with either the earnest grief expressed in the memorial, or with the comments that mocked such concern for a cat. However, attending to these ironic and contradictory accounts is essential for understanding how people ordinarily respond to, and make sense of, animal death.

Anthropologist Nigel Rapport has written insightfully about the contradictory. He argues that while dominant anthropological traditions assume human cultures are driven by a desire to categorize and classify, we might usefully develop an "appreciation of the contradictory as a ubiquitous (and desired) cognitive practice and resort: the recognition of a conscious playing with, and denial of, symbolic classifications at the same time as such classifications are assumed true."[20] For Rapport, in moving beyond the "either/or" dichotomies of classificatory systems, we orient to the possibilities and "creative promise" of "both/and" thinking that does not seek to resolve contradictions but dwells in a plurality of possibilities that are understood as equally true. This state of both/and thinking is, he argues, a fundamental aspect of how humans make meaning.

The "conscious playing with . . . symbolic classifications" of "both/and" thinking outlined by Rapport seems an apt description of the above responses. Such ironic engagements seemed to suggest *both* that Vince's death was the death of a person *and* that it was not. They seem to assert that an animal's death might be *both* comical *and* tragic. The role of irony and humor in interspecies relations has often been overlooked, but it is a pervasive aspect of the ordinary ways that humans make sense of their encounters with animals.[21] Attending to the irony of Cynthia's and Naomi's comments and the newspaper's coverage is integral to understanding what the death and mourning of this cat *meant*.

Such both/and thinking not only can be seen as an individual orientation, but perhaps also offers a way to characterize a *cultural* attitude that is complex and about which we cannot make definitive statements: a culture that both embraces and contests the mourning of a cat, where a cat's death both matters profoundly and also does not.

A case study, by its nature, offers a detailed snapshot of a particular moment in a particular place. Certainly, in other circumstances, animals may be mourned differently or not at all, and the deaths of other animals in this ethnographic site went unmarked. However, what this case offers is a chance to examine the multifaceted and nuanced responses to a cat's death when it *is* mourned. This case is a flashpoint—a moment of intensity and controversy—that illuminates how people in this particular British context (and, perhaps by extension, the West) engage with, and make sense of, animal death. It shows how the boundaries between humans and animals are sometimes dissolved and provides a glimpse of how the world would be if we mourned the deaths of the animals whom we live alongside as we mourn our human neighbors and friends. And it illuminates how, just as quickly, such radical possibilities are eclipsed, how the mourning of animals is an as-yet-unfinished engagement with multiple, and often contradictory, possibilities.

NOTES

1. Becky Tipper, "Creaturely Encounters: An Ethnographic Study of Human–Animal Relations in a British Suburban Neighborhood" (PhD diss., University of Manchester, 2012). My research incorporated participant observation, media and documentary analysis, and in-depth, qualitative interviews with thirty local residents. I attended to a variety of engagements with a range of animals—including neighborhood pets (or companion animals), backyard and park wildlife, as well as those creatures generally defined as domestic and garden pests.
2. In general, interview participants' names have been anonymized. However, Naomi and Phil gave permission for their real names to be used in connection with their interview data, since the local newspaper article had already identified both them and Vince by name. All qualitative interviews were recorded and transcribed. They were subsequently annotated with contextual details such

as tones of voice and nonverbal information to produce a narrative, ethnographic account of the conversations.
3. As others have noted, the disappearance of a pet cat can expose a web of intricate social relationships that the cat's human caretakers were entirely unaware of. See Eric Laurier, Angus Whyte, and Kathy Buckner, "Neighbouring as an Occasioned Activity: 'Finding a Lost Cat,'" *Space and Culture* 5, no. 4 (2002): 346–67.
4. Mary T. Phillips, "Proper Names and the Social Construction of Biography: The Negative Case of Laboratory Animals," *Qualitative Sociology* 17, no. 2 (1994): 121.
5. Leslie Irvine, *If You Tame Me: Understanding Our Connection with Animals* (Philadelphia: Temple University Press, 2004), 3.
6. See Gaëtanelle Gilquin and George M. Jacobs, "Elephants Who Marry Mice Are Very Unusual: The Use of the Relative Pronoun Who with Nonhuman Animals," *Society & Animals* 14, no. 1 (2006): 79–105; Anthea Fraser Gupta, "Foxes, Hounds, and Horses: Who or Which?" *Society & Animals* 14, no. 1 (2006): 107–28.
7. Here, my focus is on how humans understood and described their relationships with Vince, rather than the thorny question of Vince's own perceptions (i.e., whether he "really did" recognize them). However, for a detailed exploration of animal subjectivity in human–animal relationships, see Irvine, *If You Tame Me*.
8. David Morgan, *Acquaintances: The Space between Strangers and Intimates* (Maidenhead: Open University Press, 2009), 10.
9. Morgan, *Acquaintances*, 110.
10. Nickie Charles and Charlotte Aull Davies, "My Family and Other Animals: Pets as Kin," *Sociological Research Online* 13, no. 5 (2008).
11. Donna Haraway, *The Companion Species Manifesto: Dogs, People and Significant Otherness* (Chicago: Prickly Paradigm Press, 2003).
12. Sue Donaldson and Will Kymlicka, *Zoopolis: A Political Theory of Animal Rights* (Oxford: Oxford University Press, 2011).
13. Mary Midgley, *Utopias, Dolphins and Computers: Problems in Philosophical Plumbing* (London: Routledge, 1996), 116.
14. Carol J. Adams, *Neither Man nor Beast: Feminism and the Defense of Animals* (New York: Continuum, 1995), 61.
15. Jonathon Brown, "Everybody Loved Vince: I Hope that When I Die, I'll Be as Fondly Remembered," *The Independent*, August 20, 2009.
16. All online comments are taken from the website of the York city newspaper *The Press*: http://www.yorkpress.co.uk, July 30, 2009. Note that some comments initially posted online in 2009 (and discussed in this chapter) have since been deleted.
17. See, for instance, Les Back, *The Art of Listening* (Oxford: Berg, 2007).
18. Judith Butler, *Precarious Life: The Powers of Mourning and Violence* (London: Verso, 2004), xiv.
19. Raimond Gaita, *The Philosopher's Dog* (London: Routledge, 2003), 21–38.
20. Nigel Rapport, "The 'Contrarieties' of Israel: An Essay on the Cognitive Importance and the Creative Promise of Both/And," *Journal of the Royal Anthropological Institute* 3, no. 4 (1997): 654.
21. This chapter addresses only adults' engagements with animals, although the role of the contradictory and ironic may be quite different for children, as I have discussed elsewhere: Becky Tipper, "'A Dog Who I Know Quite Well': Everyday Relationships between Children and Animals," *Children's Geographies* 9, no. 2 (2011): 145–65.

So Sorry for the Loss of Your Little Friend
Pets' Grievability in Condolence Cards for Humans Mourning Animals

DAVID REDMALM

IF A FRIEND OF YOURS LOSES A BELOVED COMPANION ANIMAL, WOULD YOU SEND HER or him a condolence card? Previous research suggests that, because of a widespread taboo on the display of grief for companion animals, it is doubtful that you would. The explanations for such a pet grief taboo converge around one main point: a human's grief for members of other species threatens humans' anthropocentric worldview.[1] Companion animals have a liminal position as they are regarded both as persons and as property, as subjects and objects, and to mourn such liminal persons would be to transgress the human/animal divide.[2] Nevertheless, there are a great number of condolence cards for bereaved pet keepers available on the market. Together with other numerous practices and services around pet loss, the cards challenge the notion of a taboo against mourning companion animals. The production and exchange of condolence cards for pet keepers aim at creating a shared cultural understanding of what it means to lose a beloved companion animal, partly in opposition to a conceived pet grief taboo. These cards are often less somber than the typical human condolence card, and also offer a greater variety of representations of loss, grief, and death. For example, it is unlikely that a human who has recently passed away would be referred to as one's "little friend," which is a phrase used in pet condolence cards. Rather than a ban on pet grief, there thus seems to be a set of complex rules structuring the way grief for a nonhuman being may be expressed.

THE DIFFERENTIAL ALLOCATION OF GRIEVABILITY

Judith Butler's writing on loss and grief is particularly helpful when studying the social rules and limits of grieving because of her focus on the border between grievable and ungrievable, or "lose-able," life.[3] Butler identifies a "differential allocation of grievability" in human societies according to which some beings are grieved when they pass away, while others are rendered ungrievable. The border between grievable and ungrievable is established and maintained by the way lives are framed discursively. Butler contends that the differential allocation of grievability generally discredits nonhuman animals; it "operates to produce and maintain certain exclusionary conceptions of who is normatively human."[4]

Butler discerns several phenomenological aspects of grief: I grieve someone when I conceive of that person as *irreplaceable*, when the power of grief is overwhelming and its effects are *unpredictable*, and when I can relate to the loss in question through *bodily empathy*. The lost being's grievability is challenged when one or several of these aspects are lacking in the discursive framing of that being.[5] Following Butler's perspective on grief, it becomes possible to critically scrutinize the differential allocation of grievability to map out the discourses compromising some beings' grievability and to understand how beings who are not normatively human nevertheless can be grieved. Accordingly, Butler has characterized her approach as "a non-anthropocentric framework for considering what makes life valuable."[6]

While Butler allows us to see the frames that make some lives grievable and others lose-able, the work of Giorgio Agamben reminds us that the fact that these frames lack tangibility simultaneously guarantees their efficiency and leaves room for a revision of these frames. Agamben has conceptualized the production of what is normatively human as an "anthropological machine." Agamben regards Homo sapiens as "an optical machine constructed of a series of mirrors in which man, looking at himself, sees his own image always already deformed in the features of an ape."[7] The idea of the human as an animal separate from all other animals is produced by a never-ending series of comparisons that are often vague and vary depending on context. It is exactly this evasive differentiation that makes the anthropological machine efficient. Whenever an alleged difference between humans and other animals is challenged, a new difference can be mobilized to secure human exceptionalism.[8] Human identity can thus be said to include an exclusion of "the animal." But this "inclusion of what is simultaneously pushed outside" is fundamentally insecure.[9] Irreplaceable human life may at any time be reduced to lose-able animal life, or, with Agamben's terms, *bios*, political life, and *zoē*, bare life; the comparison of some humans to animals has been used to justify, for example, colonization, slavery, and racism. Simultaneously, as the notion of the animal is a prerequisite in the mirroring act that is the anthropological machine, the fragility of human identity allows beings categorized as animals to at least partially leave their position as lose-able.[10] When read in accumulation, condolence cards for bereaved pet keepers expose the anthropological machine and consequently unsettle the distinction between humans and other animals.

Condolence cards for pet keepers are not readily available in any card store, but there are several smaller online suppliers of condolence cards for pet keepers. I have collected and analyzed about 350 cards from two online stores.[11] Most of the cards address cat and dog owners, but grievability is not restricted to these two species. I also found condolence cards for owners of horses, gerbils, rats, birds, and fishes. I will present the analysis of the cards in relation to the three aspects most central to Butler's conceptualization of grief—irreplaceability, unpredictability, and embodiment—and focus on how the aspects are mobilized in the cards, and to what extent the three aspects are challenged or left out.

IRREPLACEABILITY

For Butler grief is a phenomenon of interdependence. She points out that for someone to be grieved, that being has to be conceived of as irreplaceable. Our relations to others make us into who we are, and when we lose someone important to us, we must reconfigure the way we relate to ourselves, to others, and to the world around us.[12] Irreplaceability is also a persistent theme in the condolence cards, which repeatedly emphasize that the lost companion animal is a unique being who cannot be replaced. For instance, a card with a black Labrador puppy with a flower under her or his nose says: "[front:] Unconditional love . . . [inside:] How do you replace that?"

The cards repeatedly address the idea of a taboo against mourning animals and emphasize that it is always difficult to lose an animal companion, and that it is a loss similar to human loss—"dogs are people too!" as one of the cards points out. A black-and-white card with paw prints and a cat's face says: "[front:] Losing a pet is never easy [inside:] Please know that others understand your sense of loss and are thinking of you." One way the cards emphasize that pets are unique beings is by speaking of them as friends and family, with phrases such as "Pets are a special part of the family" and "It hurts to lose a little family friend." The epithet "little" is telling—it is recurring in the material in phrases such as "So sorry for the loss of your little friend." The word emphasizes pet keeping as a caring and loving practice, but it also points to the fact that humans always have the ultimate responsibility in the relationship. Pets' irreplaceability is also emphasized by the religiously themed cards that suggest that each animal has a unique, immortal soul: cards with cats and dogs with halos and angel wings, cards with texts saying things such as "All dogs go to heaven," and cards with biblical texts or the Christian "Rainbow Bridge" poem.

While irreplaceability is a central theme in the studied collection of cards, there is also a tendency to frame pets as replaceable. The very use of the word "pet" in a condolence card points to this dilemma.[13] Phrases such as "With Sympathy on the Loss of Your Pet" and "Sincere sympathy on the loss of your pet" are seemingly treating pet loss as any human loss; yet the fact that the cards mention the lost one as a "pet" also intimates that what has been lost is not a unique individual but someone fulfilling the role as pet. One card with an image of a cat articulates this tension between the word "pet" and the ascription of grievability: "They are more than a pet—they are a friend." The problematic use of "pet" is accentuated by a George Eliot quote used in two different cards: "Animals are such agreeable friends—they ask no questions, they pass no criticisms." Here, the idea of replacing unconditional love does not seem so strange: if animals fulfill this passive function in people's lives, it should be possible to replace one animal companion with another.

Finally, the use of generic images of animals in the cards highlights the lost pets' function or role in the life of its owner, rather than pays respect to the individual that has been lost. Many condolence cards for pet keepers depict cats and dogs in ways reminiscent of comic books or children's books to allow for the viewer to see not an individual being but a token cat or dog. Cheryce Kramer has suggested that viewers tend not to contextualize images of animals in the same way as those of humans, and animals are therefore more efficient "vehicles of emotion" in pictorial language.[14] Human condolence cards may display symbols of death or divinity, such as a cross, a flower arrangement, or a dove, but images of humans are extremely rare. In contrast, pet condolence cards display generic images of pets to acknowledge the grief for a specific pet, which renders the grieved pet at once replaceable and irreplaceable. This is characteristic for the cards in general: in various ways, they frame pets as both irreplaceable individuals and replaceable beings fulfilling the role of "pet."

UNPREDICTABILITY

Butler emphasizes that it is impossible to predict our reactions to a loss of someone important to us. We cannot know who we will be when a relationship ends that has defined us.[15] Along the lines of this reasoning, the condolence cards emphasize the impact of the grief for a pet—that the loss of a companion animal who has played a central role in one's life can make the pet keeper react in ways that are not easy to predict and manage. For example, a card with a generic light blue paw print says: "[front:] If not for the loss . . . [inside:] you wouldn't know the love." Although the card recognizes that the effects of the loss of a cat or a dog are unpredictable—it is not until you lose someone you can fully "know the love"— the card suggests that the bereaved owner should relate to the loss as something inevitable, as a natural aspect of having a pet. This is a contrast to relationships between humans, in which one's partner's imminent passing is not necessarily central to the experience of the relationship. The numerous cards that frame pet loss as something inevitable form a pattern that suggests that there is an expectation on pet keepers to be prepared for the demise of their pets. As many companion animals have a shorter life span than humans, these cards urge the recipient to memento mori and carpe diem, and stress that, as a dog card says, "in life, the best walks are always too brief."

One way by which a pet condolence card can frame pet loss as something inevitable is to suggest that the bereaved person thinks of the lost companion as one in a row of pets that come and go. One card perfectly summarizes the sinister condition of sharing one's life with a dog: "There is a cycle to life and death that shapes the lives of those who keep the company of dogs." The use of the word "dogs" in a general sense underscores that the card is not only addressing the individual animal who has just been lost, but also mediates a normative idea of how you should relate to the death of a companion animal.

Jokes are another way to defuse the impact of the grief for a pet. Joking about one's pet can for a pet keeper be a way to handle pets' ambivalent status as, on the one hand, friends and family members and, on the other hand, members of the category "animals" who are most often rendered ungrievable.[16] For example, a card says "It's just a dog's life! With sympathy," which can be read as the idiomatic expression here used as a euphemistic expression of sympathy, as well as a repetition of the normative inhibition of grieving one's pet—"It's just a dog." For the cat owner, there is a card with a crowd of stuffed toy animals attending a funeral for a cat, with the words "The only ones happy on this day were the mice."

An aspect of the relative predictability of pet loss is that many pet keepers make a decision to euthanize the pet to prevent the pet from experiencing too much of the pain of growing old. A card with two dogs and a cat curled up on a bed says: "[front:] Letting yours go was surely one of the hardest things you've ever done [inside:] And one of the most loving things you'll ever do." The normative implication of the cards is that pet keepers should prepare for the fact that one's pet will one day pass away and become used to a "cycle of life and death" to manage the impact of the loss. Instead of being overcome with the unpredictable force of grief, "the loving thing to do" is to plan one's pets' passing and make a decision to end their lives when the time is right.

EMBODIMENT

When people pass away, they leave us not only with a relational void, but also with a physical void. When we lose someone we are also reminded that life is fundamentally precarious and finite. Therefore, according to Butler, grievable loss is always an embodied experience.[17] As James Stanescu has pointed out, this is another reason why Butler's work on grief is nonanthropocentric: not only human life is finite and precarious.[18] When pets pass away, they leave not only a relational void, but also a physical one, because of the physical character of many personal human–animal relationships.[19] This physical void is a returning theme: an abandoned dog house, an empty dog or cat bed, a laid off collar, a ball or a leash left on the ground, paw tracks in sand. The embodied aspect of pet keeping is also regularly emphasized. For example, a card depicting rat paradise teems with rats, a sight that would set off any rat phobic person. Yet, for a rat owner the "teeming" is itself integral to the everyday, embodied experience of living with rats and is therefore something to which a bereaved rat owner can relate.

There is another crucial aspect to the embodied relation between pet and owner. The widespread practice of euthanizing elderly pets is not only a matter of making loss predictable, but also a matter of balancing between embodied empathy and distancing techniques. To see one's companion animal grow older can be particularly painful as pet keepers are generally expected to euthanize their pets when their bodies grow too weak. But at the same time, empathic pet keepers must be ready to read their pets' expressions as bodily signals telling the owners when it is time to end their pet's life.[20] This is accentuated by a card depicting a golden retriever lying with closed eyes on a bench in a pub. The exhausted posture and the facial expression suggest that the dog has had a long life and is now reaching the end of it. The card says "[front:] We may want them with us always, but they have a way of letting us know . . . [inside:] when it's their time to go sleep with the angels." Several cards similarly display drawings, paintings, and photos of cats and dogs lying down with closed eyes. Cards that in this way more or less directly address suffering and death can be a comfort for pet keepers who are faced with the choice of ending the life of a suffering companion animal. Yet images in this vein are also somewhat objectifying: a tired, weak, and inanimate body of an animal is made into a symbol for humans' difficulties when facing a euthanasia decision. It would be unsettling to see similar images of inanimate humans on condolence cards. The matter-of-fact stance toward animal death—the imagery and phrasing—thus risks becoming distancing.

CONCLUSION

The analysis shows that the three aspects of grief that Butler discusses are present in the cards, thus emphasizing the tragedy of a lost companion animal. However, each aspect is also played down, framing pet loss as manageable to some extent. The ways by which the grievability of pets are downgraded vary: companion animals are recurrently represented as replaceable, the loss is sometimes framed as predictable or in other ways manageable, and the sometimes objectifying depictions of nonhuman bodies in the cards suggest a somewhat distanced approach to animals' embodied experiences. Although pets are sometimes compared to humans in the cards, they are thus not framed as fully and normatively human.

The analysis has shown how the condolence cards on the one hand emphasize the tragedy of the loss of a companion animal, and make pet loss manageable in various ways on the other. The cards reflect a dilemma: they recognize the grievability of nonhuman life but are concurrently dependent on using the kind of familiar language and imagery that fuel the anthropological machine and thus also human exceptionalism. It may seem like the contradictory framing of nonhuman animals in the condolence cards takes the edge off a potential challenge against the pet grief taboo. However, the cards' paradoxical language and imagery may in fact alter humans' approach to animal death as the cards point to a crucial but productive maladjustment in the constellation of mirrors making human exceptionalism possible. As the condolence cards highlight pets' complex position both as loved friends and family members, and as members of the vague category of ungrievable "animals," they consequently make visible the differential allocation of grievability. By offering a set of shared knowledge alternative to the ordinary anthropocentric language of human loss and grief the cards confuse grievable political life and ungrievable bare life. By using a medium traditionally reserved for human beings—the condolence card—and tweaking its aesthetics, the anthropological machine is hence turned against itself and creates a space for grieving nonhuman animals within a human society founded on the exclusion of "the animal." Furthermore, the cards not only defy the pet grief taboo, but they also resist the taboo on death in Western society as they create a space for acknowledging and discussing difficult issues such as euthanasia and the fact that most pets have a comparatively short life span.

The condolence cards analyzed in this article may be read as a sort of posthuman postmortem postcard that provides sender and receiver both with a language to speak of nonhuman loss and grief, and a tool that can be used to make visible the anthropocentric frames for the allocation of grievability. In short, condolence cards for bereaved pet keepers bring to light pets' role as "werewolves" in Western society. According to Agamben, the werewolf, this "monstrous hybrid of human and animal," was invented as a way to manage the often diffuse border between human and nonhuman life, or *bios* and *zoē*, and the fact that both humans and other animals may pass across and thus challenge that border.[21] Werewolf stories have scared people for hundreds of years because they point to the fundamental instability of the boundary between human and animal. The condolence cards accentuate pets' ambiguous werewolf status—they frame companion animals as grievable, but they also make the grief manageable in various ways—and accordingly they draw the problematic distinction between human and animal into the limelight. As Butler points out, violence against beings that are not grieved is accepted because the discourse existing concerning their deaths "is a silent and melancholic one in which there have been no lives, and no losses."[22] Condolence cards for humans who have lost companion animals break this silence because they underscore the ambiguous status of pets by expressing grief for werewolves.

NOTES

This chapter has benefited immensely from my friends' and colleagues' many insightful comments. I especially want to thank Clara Iversen, the participants of the Higher Seminar Series in Sociology and Social Psychology at Mälardalen University, and the members of the HumAnimal Group at the Centre for Gender Research, Uppsala University. The chapter was written with generous support from Örebro University.

1. See e.g. Christine Morley and Jan Fook, "The Importance of Pet Loss and Some Implications for Services," *Mortality* 10, no. 2 (2005): 127–43; Debra Lynn Stephens and Ronald Paul Hill, "The Loss of Animal Companions: A Humanistic and Consumption Perspective," *Society & Animals* 4, no. 2 (1996): 189–210; Tania Woods, "Mourning the Loss of a Companion Animal: An Evaluation of the First Six Years of a Pet Loss Support Service," *Bereavement Care* 19, no. 1 (2000): 8–10. For a theoretical discussion concerning the ban on treating humans and other animals equally, see Marc Shell, "The Family Pet," *Representations*, no. 15 (1986): 121–53. I am using the terms "pet" and "companion animal" interchangeably in this chapter. One may object that "companion animal" should be the preferred term as "pet" is objectifying and suggests that nonhuman animals mainly have a passive role in human–animal relationships. Nevertheless, I am using both terms consciously to emphasize the tension-filled status of pets. Furthermore, "pet" is commonly used in the cards analyzed in this chapter, and as search terms at websites selling condolence cards for pet keepers. For a further discussion concerning the term "pet," see David Redmalm, "An Animal Without an Animal Within: The Powers of Pet Keeping" (doctoral thesis, Örebro University, 2013), 17.
2. For a discussion on pets' liminal position, see Clinton R. Sanders, "Killing with Kindness: Veterinary Euthanasia and the Social Construction of Personhood," *Sociological Forum* 10, no. 2 (1995): 195–214.
3. Judith Butler, *Precarious Life: The Powers of Mourning and Violence* (London: Verso, 2004); Judith Butler, *Frames of War: When Is Life Grievable?* (London: Verso, 2009). While I draw on these two texts by Butler, loss and grief is a theme that recurs throughout her authorship.
4. Butler, *Precarious Life*, xiv–xv.
5. Butler, *Precarious Life*, 19–31; Butler, *Frames of War*, 26–32.
6. Pierpaolo Antonello and Roberto Farneti, "Antigone's Claim: A Conversation with Judith Butler," *Theory & Event* 12, no. 1 (2009).
7. Giorgio Agamben, *The Open: Man and Animal* (Stanford: Stanford University Press, 2004), 26–27.
8. Agamben, *The Open*, 26–27, 37. The argument concerning the evasive character of "the human" and "the animal" is also informed by Jacques Derrida's *The Animal that Therefore I Am* (New York: Fordham University Press, 2008), see especially 47–48.
9. Giorgio Agamben, *Homo Sacer: Sovereign Power and Bare Life* (Stanford: Stanford University Press, 1998), 18. See also Agamben, *The Open*, 37–38.
10. Agamben, *Homo Sacer*, 13; Agamben, *The Open*, 27. See also Butler, *Frames of War*, 16; James Stanescu, "Species Trouble: Judith Butler, Mourning, and the Precarious Lives of Animals," *Hypatia* 27, no. 3 (2012): 567–82.
11. Information about the cards (photographs of the cards together with any inside images and texts) was retrieved from theinkypaw.com and etsy.com.
12. Butler, *Precarious Life*, 20–21; Butler, *Frames of War*, 98.
13. Redmalm, "An Animal Without an Animal Within", 17.
14. Cheryce Kramer, "Digital Beasts as Visual Esperanto: Getty Images and the Colonization of Sight," in *Thinking with Animals: New Perspectives on Anthropomorphism*, ed. Lorraine Daston and Gregg Mitman (New York: Columbia University Press, 2005), 138–71.
15. Butler, *Precarious Life*, 46.
16. See Nickie Charles and Charlotte Aull Davies, "My Family and Other Animals: Pets as Kin," *Sociological Research Online* 13, no. 5 (2008).
17. Butler, *Frames of War*, 29–31.

18. Stanescu, "Species Trouble."
19. See David Redmalm, "Pet Grief: When Is Non-Human Life Grievable?," *Sociological Review* 63, no. 1 (2015): 19–35.
20. Redmalm, "Pet Grief."
21. Agamben, *Homo Sacer*, 63.
22. Butler, *Precarious Life*, 36.

Claire
Last Days

JULIA SCHLOSSER

Claire came to live with me in 2009. I made the decision to euthanize her on July 5, 2011, because she suffered from osteomyelitis, a painful bone infection. I've lived with animals since I was four. In my adult life, I have loved, nursed, and mourned the loss of beloved animal companions. But when I reflect on Claire's life, I am haunted by questions that I never had to ask when those other animals died. Would she have rather I left her where I met her, living in a cardboard box in a windowless bathroom? Or would she have made the choice to live out her short life in my house where she shared the space with seven cats and a dog? Was she lonely living with us? How did she get the bone infection? I've always felt that if I had known more about rabbits, I would have noticed that she was sick sooner and could have helped her. When it became clear that Claire wasn't going to get better, I made a series of scanned images of objects associated with her life. After she died, I scanned her body before she was cremated.

Julia Schlosser, *Claire: Last Kiss (after Beuys)*, 7/5/2011. (From the series "Claire: Last Days," 2011.)

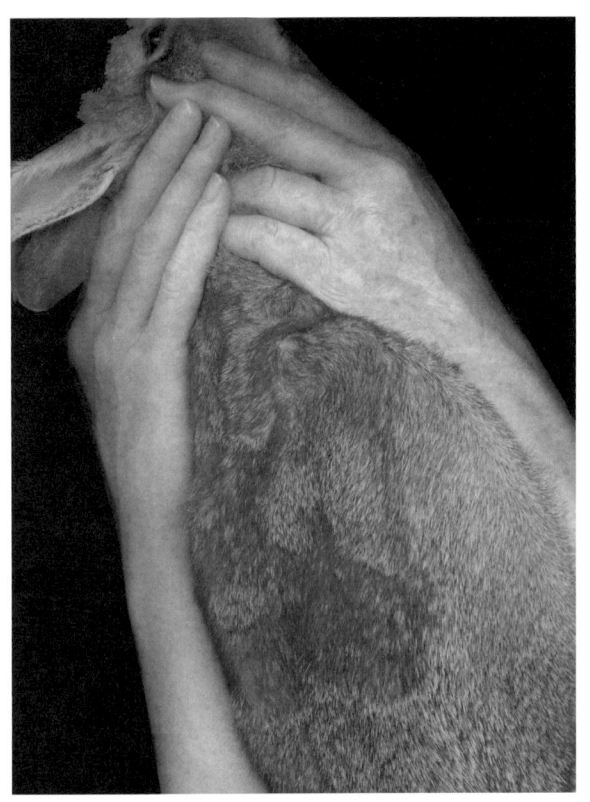

Julia Schlosser, *Claire's body, 7/5/2011, 1:58 p.m.* (From the series "Claire: Last Days," 2011.)

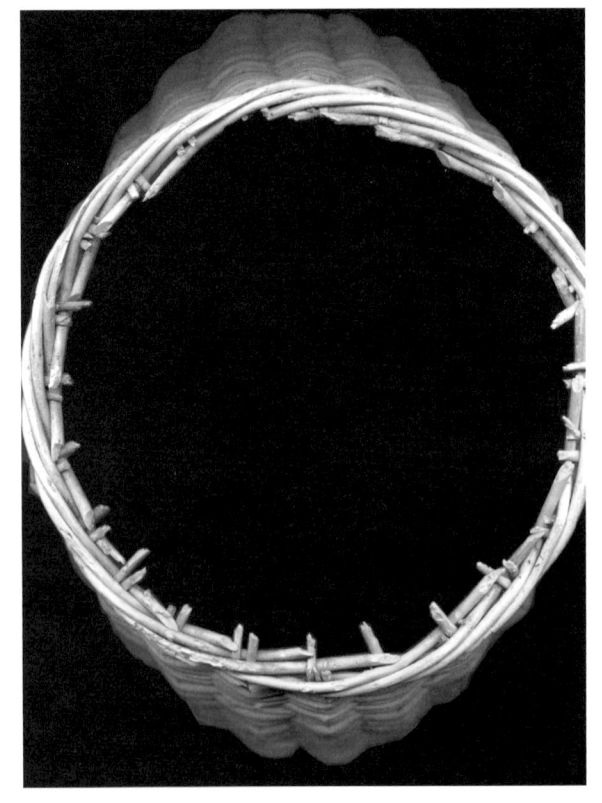

Julia Schlosser, *Basket (Claire chewed the bottom out of this basket)*. (From the series "Things Claire: Chewed," 2011.)

Julia Schlosser, *Alfalfa Hay (I bought this to stimulate Claire's appetite when she was sick)*. (From the series "Claire: Last Days," 2011.)

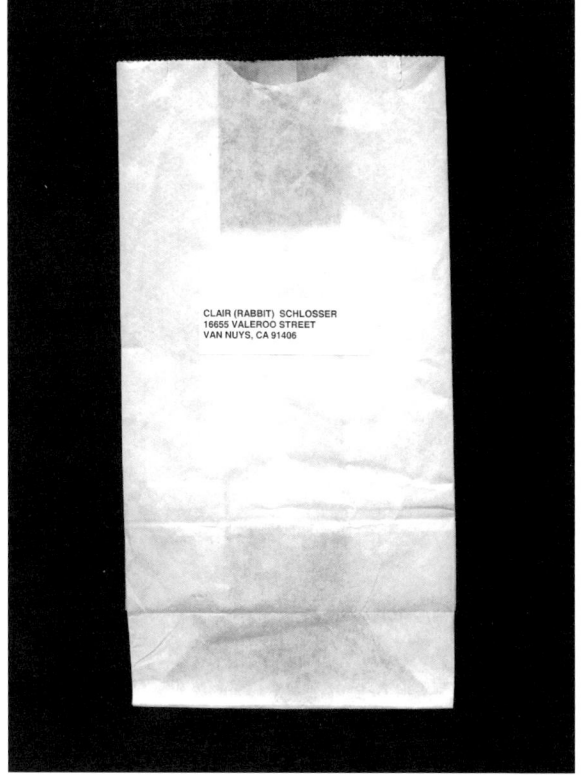

Julia Schlosser, *Pharmacy Bag (I got two of Claire's medications, enrofloxacin and cisapride, from a compounding pharmacy next door to my vet's office)*. (From the series "Claire: Last Days," 2011.)

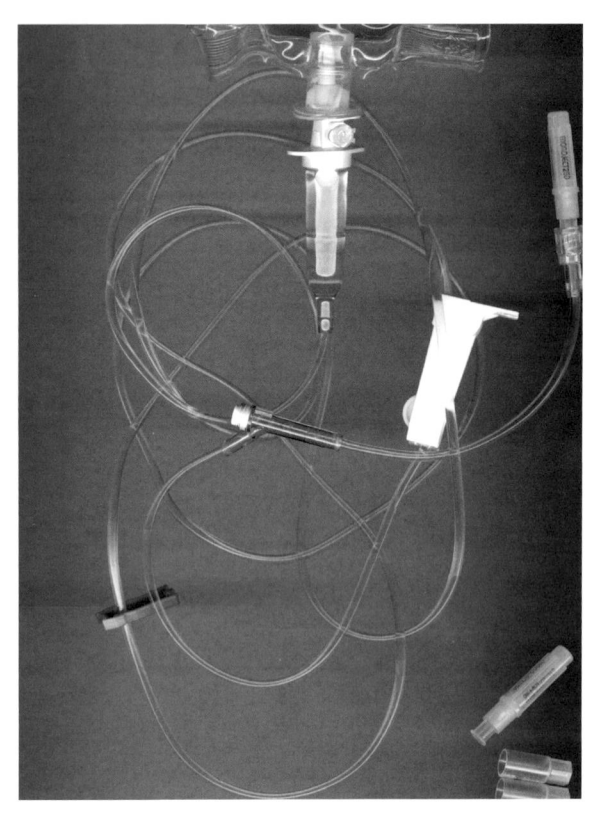

Julia Schlosser, *Lactated Ringer's solution (I had to give Claire subcutaneous fluids when she was sick)*. (From the series "Claire: Last Days," 2011.)

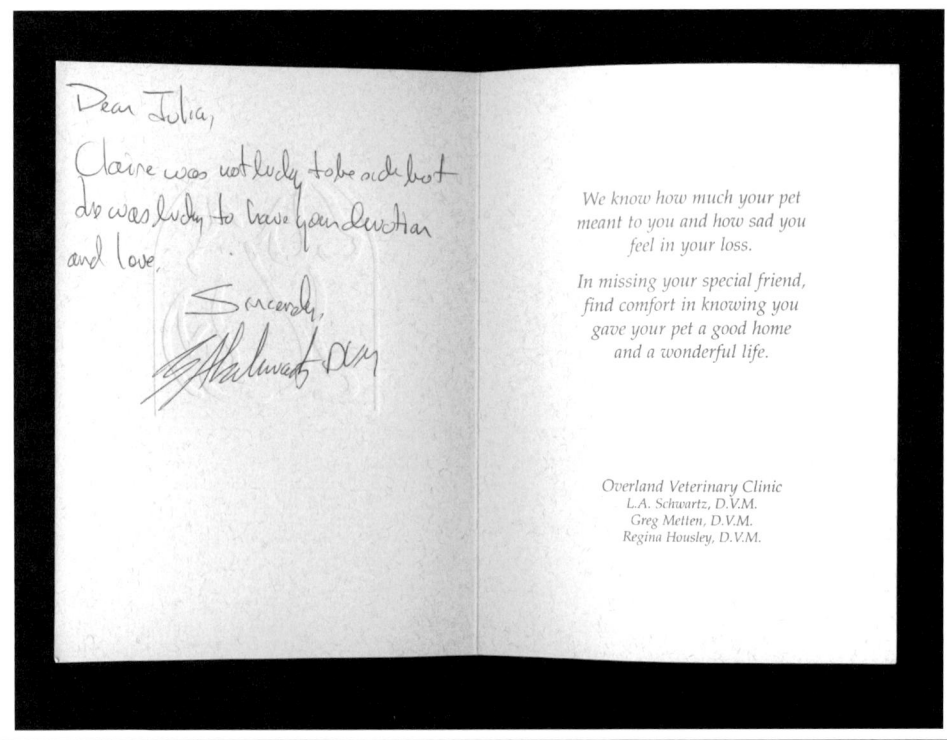

Julia Schlosser, *Sympathy Card (Dear Julia, Claire was not lucky to be sick but she was lucky to have your devotion and love. Sincerely, LA Schwartz DVM)*. (From the series "Claire: Last Days," 2011.)

PART 3

Memorials and the "Special" Treatment of the Dead

Britain at War
Remembering and Forgetting the Animal Dead of the Second World War

HILDA KEAN

In recent decades when contested invasions of Afghanistan and Iraq have resulted in human and nonhuman animal combatant and civilian war dead—and massive demonstrations against such adventures—the British remain obsessed with commemorating the Second World War. The 1939–45 war has remained as a "good" war in public memory. Despite—or perhaps because of—the passing of the years new memorials have been erected to discrete groups of humans previously not specifically commemorated. These include one to firefighters near St. Paul's Cathedral (which they helped to ensure was not destroyed by fire), one to women in the site of national war memory in Whitehall, near to Lutyens's Cenotaph that it imitates in form, and one to Bomber Command in the somewhat strange setting of Piccadilly.[1] In the Midlands—on land reclaimed from gravel workings that had no connection with war memory—a National Memorial Arboretum was first created in the late 1990s. By 2007 in the center there was a vast circular earthwork surmounted by stonework and bronze memorials listing all the names of British war dead since 1945. Blank walls have been kept free for the addition of future names.[2] However, in what has been called the "nation's principal alternative site to the Cenotaph,"[3] discrete groups and events from the Second World War still physically dominate the landscape.

The 1939–45 war is still remembered in public and popular memory as the "People's War" in which Britain "stood alone" and the nation came together united in a common cause and transcending class differences—despite debunking from various historians.[4] Yet this memorialized "good" war has no monument to commemorate the thousands of companion animals who died not through enemy aerial bombardment, but through the decisions taken by their human owners to kill them in the first days of the war in September 1939. This was not a state directive: official bodies, veterinary organizations, and animal welfare charities all advised people that the safest place for their animals was with their human companion. Such advice was ignored, and some four hundred thousand cats and dogs in London alone in the first week of the war were needlessly killed.[5] This was months before any bombing. Although this event is largely unknown today it was never covered up. It was widely reported in national newspapers and the BBC. Today, however, it is known within family stories and personal memories, but there is no public memorial to what animal campaigners at the time called a "massacre" or "holocaust."[6]

Moreover, as noted by scientist Julian Huxley, far fewer animals were killed through actual bombardment than had been anticipated. The animals' ability to go to ground often ensured their survival.[7] They were often found in bombed houses by special animal wardens and reunited with human members of their families. They would also direct air raid wardens to buried animals and people.[8]

MEMORIALIZATION OF INDIVIDUAL ANIMALS

Some individual animals have been embraced within the existing narratives of the Second World War, and these have been publicly commemorated. In Liverpool's Calderstones Park, for example, there is a plinth and plaque to Jet of Lada, a local German shepherd dog who was translocated to the capital to rescue people from bombed houses (figure 1).[9]

Another example is Faith the cat who guarded her newly born kitten in the church of St. Augustine and St. Faith in the City of London near St. Paul's Cathedral despite heavy bombardment in the first days of the Blitz in September 1940.[10] Her actions of standing firm were represented as being at one with the narrative of Britain (and particularly with mythologized London) standing alone against the odds. It is significant that the church was near St. Paul's: images of the cathedral surrounded by firestorms and clouds but still standing would become a key icon of the time (and decades after).[11]

EARLIER MEMORIALS TO ANIMALS IN WAR

However, there exist no memorials to nonhuman animals in general during this time. In some ways this is surprising since the role of animals in previous British military activities has not been ignored. The deaths of horses and mules in the South African Wars of the late nineteenth and early twentieth centuries were commemorated in various locations by animal campaigners seeking to bring to public attention the massive

Figure 1. Jet of Lada memorial, Liverpool. (Photo courtesy of Hilda Kean.)

Figure 2. The Tunnellers' Friends, Edinburgh. (Photo courtesy of Hilda Kean.)

loss of life caused by poor veterinary attention.[12] In Port Elizabeth in South Africa—as well as in various sites in England—drinking troughs, a long-standing feature of the public landscape, were constructed both to provide water for horses and cattle but also to commemorate the loss of animal life.[13]

The actions of animals working with the armed forces during the First World War—alongside details of the numbers killed and injured—were also memorialized, for example, at the local Kilburn dispensary of the RSPCA in London in a bronze frieze by F. Brook Hitch in the 1930s. Here a plaque enumerated the 484,143 horses, mules, camels, and bullocks and hundreds of dogs, carrier pigeons, and other creatures who died during the war and the role of the RSPCA in tending to 725,216 sick and wounded animals. The wording on the plaque described animal "love, faith and loyalty" and argued that, in return, humans should reciprocate by "showing kindness and consideration to living animals."[14]

In Scotland's National War Memorial in Edinburgh Castle in a bronze commemorative relief by Morris Meredith-Williams draught horses and messenger dogs have their place. Even rats and mice who accompanied tunnellers in the trenches of France were depicted in friezes carved by Phyllis Bone in 1927 (figure 2) in an adjacent chapel that also sported roundels of a camel, mule, horse, and reindeer with the inscription "Remember also the humble beasts that served and died." All such public memorials focus on the deaths—or "sacrifice"—of animals in warfare in another country. Difficulties, hardship, and death faced by animals on the home front in either the First or Second World War are ignored.[15]

ABSENCES IN THE PDSA CEMETERY

A specific example worth exploring in some detail is the People's Dispensary for Sick Animals (PDSA) animal cemetery on the outskirts of East London in Ilford. The PDSA was founded by Maria Dickin in 1917 to give veterinary services initially free (or subsequently cheaply) to those whose owners could not afford them. By 1928 an animals' sanatorium, the first of its kind in Europe, was opened in Ilford.[16] In 1943 with the support of the War Office it instituted a "Dickin Medal" described as the animals' Victoria Cross awarded "on an exceptional basis to animals displaying conspicuous gallantry or devotion to duty in saving human life during military conflict."[17] In 2006 Heritage Lottery Funding of £50,000 was obtained to restore memorials in the cemetery to individual animals, mainly dogs (figure 3). These animals were those who were awarded a Dickin Medal.[18]

However, although the animal welfare charity highlights the restored individual memorials in its exhibition at the cemetery and gives potted accounts of the animals' achievements, it fails to even mention that in the same site are buried thousands and thousands of animal corpses deposited there in September 1939. As it recorded in its *Annual Report of 1945*, as other animal societies and veterinary surgeons were "unable to cope with the burial of these poor Animals [the PDSA offered] the use of a meadow in the grounds of our sanatorium. Then, our real difficulties began, for, as far as can be estimated, we buried half a million Animals."[19]

However, this aspect of the allies' treatment of animals in the war is not wanted to be remembered. So although the PDSA grounds might well be defined as a "site of memory," only certain, individual, animals—whose exploits are put in a narrative to fit within the notion of a "good" war—are actually remembered. The hundreds of thousands of companion animals who died before any bombing (by the "enemy") are not remembered in this cemetery, a place of memory. It is not that the PDSA is unaware of these events, but they do not fit easily within the organization's own constructed history of benign concern and charitable endeavors. All major animal charities killed animals at the start of the war, but others did not have large burial sites, and although there is also evidence that employees attempted to dissuade people from killing their animals, nevertheless these deaths did happen.[20]

Figure 3. Rex's grave, PDSA cemetery, London. (Photo courtesy of Hilda Kean.)

REMEMBERING AND FORGETTING DOGS AT DUNKIRK

If the mass killing at the start of the war is an event that people want to forget since it shows them in a bad light, the evacuation at Dunkirk of the British Expeditionary Force (BEF) is even more problematic. In summary, with France subject to Nazi invasion in May 1940 the British troops were pushed to the coast in Dunkirk. By May 26 some twenty-eight thousand nonfighting British personnel had been evacuated to Dover; more than three hundred thousand were left in Dunkirk.[21] However, despite the odds, and aerial bombardment from the Nazis, hundreds of thousands of troops were evacuated in both very difficult and mythologized circumstances. This military defeat was refigured, partly through the journalist skills of "Cato," as a victory for the "common man" against an alien force. In particular, in terms of propaganda, much attention was paid to the "little ships," rather than naval vessels, that went across from England to France. The situation in reality was rather more complicated. Suffice it to say that the story of "getting on with it" and "muddling through" was reconfigured as a typical and laudable British trait.[22] However, although animals, specifically dogs, gathering together with the defeated men on the French beaches figured prominently in these actual events, they too have also been written out of modern accounts and public memory, for the human treatment of the dogs was not a simple, positive, story. Certainly many soldiers were keen to repatriate dogs who had followed them through France (including dogs who had often deserted from the Nazi side). Thus Frances Partridge recorded the story of Colonel Dick Rendel who had been on the English south coast beaches receiving evacuated men and needing to make provision to sort out the dead from the living humans:

> In the midst of all of this horror . . . Dick saw men making a cage on the beach. "What's that for?" he asked. "The dogs."
> "What dogs?"
> "Why the ones from France, the strays the soldiers are bringing back."
> "What will happen to them?"
> "They'll be sent to quarantine, after being carefully marked with that rescuer's name and number."[23]

A similar story of apparent compassion amid horror was also recounted by the RSPCA. The organization saw the canine attachment to the retreating troops as "testimony to the humanity of our men that in such circumstances dogs should seek refuge from them."[24] But human relationships with companion animals even in crises are never homogeneous or straightforward.[25] Thus the little dog Blackie yapping to alert his human companion to another's presence was shot—by a comrade: "The bloody stupid thing! The enemy's here, and he's giving the game away!" The soldier who accompanied Blackie later explained: "It broke my heart because I'd become very familiar with Blackie."[26] Certainly some stories of rescued dogs endorse the compassionate story the RSPCA and Dick Rendel conveyed. Thus a terrier-type mongrel who only understood French was being "taken on the staff of the parish" where a sublieutenant's father was vicar.[27] But other stories give a very different impression of the canine–human relationship in Dunkirk. A sailor in the Royal Navy remembered the stance of military police:

> When the troops arrived alongside us it was very sad—a lot of them had got dogs with them that they'd picked up. But as the men arrived with their dogs, the military police were shooting them

and throwing them in the harbour. Every time they did this, there was a great "Boo!" from the sailors on the ships loading up the men. We couldn't see any reason why these dogs shouldn't be taken back to Britain.[28]

These stories of different human relationships with dogs in extreme circumstances, which do not form part of the usual narrative of Dunkirk, do not just indicate that the presence of animals should be included to provide a bigger and more inclusive picture. Rather, by embracing animals in this mythologized event one is also opening up, and perhaps questioning, the public memory of this occasion.

In recent years accounts of the roles played by companion animals have been remembered in family stories and collected oral histories of the war. Individuals have remembered the way in which cats and dogs alerted humans to imminent bombing—before the air raid warnings—so that together animals and humans would shelter from bombardment. Many have reflected on the emotional support provided by animals in these stressful times, a feature also acknowledged later in the war by the state. Cats continued to play a utilitarian role killing rats and mice, but also many achieved the status of companion, a status that had been less common prior to the war.[29]

However, even this aspect of the wartime animal–human relationship is missing from public memorials. On the massive "Animals in War" memorial in London's Park Lane (figure 4) there is no reference to those who died on the Home Front: war is seen to be an event that happens in other countries (and this is reinforced by the iconography and type of animals including elephants and camels). The statement on the memorial, "They had no choice," could, of course, apply to the animal deaths in London in 1939 and those on the beaches of Dunkirk perpetrated by "friendly" military police. However, alongside such sentiments on the memorial are the words explaining that animals died for human freedom—exclusively *on* the allies side rather than *by* the allies.[30]

Considering such omissions may help us explore the complex relationship between companion animals and humans, showing, as Erica Fudge has noted, the disposability of

Figure 4. Close up of Animals in War memorial, London. (Photo courtesy of Hilda Kean.)

animals, even those deemed worthy of human affection.[31] While not necessarily suggesting that we need another public memorial about the Second World War, nevertheless drawing public attention to these forgotten events may remind us again that the construct we call British society is one in which both humans and animals live and die. It also reminds us that companion animal deaths inevitably occur within the framework of an animal–human relationship.

NOTES

1. Philip Ward-Jackson, *Public Sculpture of the City of London* (Liverpool: Liverpool University Press, 2003), 392–94; Philip Ward-Jackson, *Public Sculpture of Historic Westminster*, vol. 1 (Liverpool: Liverpool University Press, 2011), 428–32; and Alex Kleiderman, "Bomber Command Memorial Moves Veterans," *BBC News*, June 28, 2012.
2. See Paul Gough, "'Garden of Gratitude': The National Memorial Arboretum and Strategic Remembering," in *Public History and Heritage Today: People and Their Pasts*, ed. Paul Ashton and Hilda Kean (Basingstoke: Palgrave Macmillan 2012), 95–112.
3. Gough, "'Garden of Gratitude,'" 95.
4. Most importantly Angus Calder in *The People's War: Britain, 1939–1945* (London: Jonathan Cape, 1969); Angus Calder, *The Myth of the Blitz* (London: Pimlico, 1992).
5. Initially Sir Robert Gower, president of the Royal Society for the Prevention of Cruelty to Animals (RSPCA), gave a figure of 750,000 ("RSPCA," *Veterinary Record*, June 22, 1940, 475). The RSPCA's own commemorative postwar book *Animals Were There*, gave the figure of 400,000 pet animals killed in Greater London. Elizabeth Kirby and Arthur Moss, *Animals Were There: A Record of the Work of the RSPCA during the War of 1939–1945* (London: Hutchinson, 1947), 18–19. This figure was corroborated by John Clabby, *A History of the Royal Army Veterinary Corps, 1919–61* (London: J. A. Allen, 1963), 41. For further discussion see Hilda Kean, "The Dog and Cat Massacre of September 1939 and the People's War," *European Review of History: Revue europeenne d'histoire* 22, no. 5 (2015): 741–56.
6. Louise Lind-af-Hageby, *Bombed Animals—Rescued Animals—Animals Saved from Destruction* (London: Animal Defence and Anti-Vivisection Society, 1941), 19; National Canine Defence League, "September Holocaust," *Dogs' Bulletin* 114 (December 1939); Philip Ziegler, *London at War, 1939–45* (London: Sinclair-Stevenson, 1995), 74; Calder, *The People's War*, 34.
7. Julian Huxley, "War-time Reactions of Cats," *The Cat* 11 (1941): 88–89.
8. Cyril Demarne, *The London Blitz, a Fireman's Tale* (London: Parents' Centre Publications, 1980), 65; Frank R. Lewey, *Cockney Campaign* (London: Stanley Paul, 1944), 92.
9. For example, press cuttings from December 17, 1944, HO 186/2671, The National Archives, Kew.
10. Hilda Kean, *Animal Rights: Political and Social Change in Britain since 1800* (London: Reaktion, 2000), 194–96.
11. Paul Addison, "National Identity and the Battle of Britain," in *War and the Cultural Construction of Identities in Britain*, ed. Barbara Korte and Ralf Schneider (Amsterdam: Rodopi, 2002), 236.
12. Hilda Kean, "Animals and War Memorials: Different Approaches to Commemorating the Human–Animal Relationship," in *Animals and War: Studies of Europe and North America*, ed. Ryan Hediger (Leiden: Brill, 2012), 245–46.

13. Sandra Swart, "Horses in the South African War, c.1899–1902," *Society & Animals* 18, no. 4 (2010): 348–66.
14. Kean, "Animals and War Memorials," 248–49.
15. For an excellent account of the plight of dogs on the home front, see Philip Howell, "The Dog Fancy at War: Breeds, Breeding, and Britishness, 1914–1918," *Society & Animals* 21, no. 6 (2013): 546–67.
16. PDSA, *A Commemorative Brochure Documenting 80 Years of the People's Dispensary for Sick Animals* (Telford: PDSA, 1997).
17. PDSA, *PDSA Dickin Medal* (Telford: PDSA, 2014).
18. Gail Parker, "The Dickin Medal and the PDSA Animal Cemetery," *After the Battle*, no. 140 (2008): 46–55; Laura Clout, "A Better Resting Place for the Animal VCs," *Daily Telegraph*, December 14, 2007, 12.
19. PDSA, *Annual Report 1945*, (London: PDSA 1946), 4–5.
20. There was concern that if charities did not kill animals humanely then animals would be abandoned and, inter alia, be prey to vivisectors or, in the case of cats in particular, rogue furriers.
21. John Lukacs, *Five Days in London, May 1940* (New Haven: Yale Nota Bene, 2001), 130. Calder, *The Myth of the Blitz*, 90–101.
22. Michael Foot, Frank Owen, and Peter Howard, who called themselves "Cato" created this image in their hugely popular book, *Guilty Men* (London: Victor Gollancz, 1940). See Calder, *The Myth of the Blitz*, 90–101.
23. Frances Partridge, *A Pacifist's War: Diaries, 1939–1945*, vol. 1 (London: Phoenix, 1999), 152. This was the first occasion she had seen her brother-in-law since Dunkirk.
24. RSPCA 117th *Annual Report*, 1940, (London: RSPCA, 1940), 10. It also praised its own inspectors serving in the Dunkirk army who "did useful work in shooting animals which were hopelessly injured by bombing or shelling" (3).
25. See, for example, Erica Fudge, *Pets* (Stocksfield: Acumen, 2008).
26. Private Frank Curry in Joshua Levine, *Forgotten Voices of Dunkirk* (London: Ebury, 2010), 134.
27. Ordinary Seamen Stanley Allen in Levine, *Forgotten Voices of Dunkirk*, 240.
28. Able Seaman Ian Nethercott in Levine, *Forgotten Voices of Dunkirk*, 213.
29. Hilda Kean, "The Home Front as a 'Moment' for Animals and Humans: Exploring the Animal–Human Relationship in Contemporary Diaries and Letters," in *The Home Front: Images, Myths and Forgotten Experiences, 1914–2014*, ed. Maggie Andrews and Janis Lomas (Basingstoke: Palgrave Macmillan, 2014), 152–69.
30. See Kean, "Animals and War Memorials" for a fuller analysis.
31. Fudge, *Pets*.

Now on Exhibit
Our Affection for, Remembrance of, and Tributes to Nonhuman Animals in Museums

CAROLYN MERINO MULLIN

VIRTUALLY EVERY ASPECT OF SOCIETY—FROM SPAM TO BROKEN RELATIONSHIPS—HAS been curated in the museum field, and such is the case with mourning and death, albeit few and far between. Just a few thematic institutions exist, like the Museum of Mourning Art at the Arlington Cemetery (no reference to animals, as far as my research indicates) and the Museum of Death in Hollywood, California. The latter has a small gallery dedicated to taxidermy and jarred animal bodies, and the owners' own potbellied pig, now stuffed, greets visitors as they enter the theater.

MILITARY REMEMBRANCE: A MULTITUDE OF EXHIBIT MEDIUMS

In terms of mourning and commemoration, more common apparitions of animals in museums arrive with the themes of war and service. Domestically, Sergeant Stubby (catalog #58280M) and Cher Ami, the pigeon (#30714), relive their roles in World War I as part of the Smithsonian's exhibit *The Price of Freedom: Americans at War*, where their mounts are on view. Sergeant Stubby, a beloved mascot and the most decorated canine in WWI, saved his regiment from unexpected mustard gas attacks, found and comforted the injured, and even caught and restrained a German soldier by the seat of his pants.

Cher Ami, a carrier pigeon with the Seventy-Seventh Division, effectually rescued 194 survivors of a battalion through his delivery of a lifesaving message, a twenty-five-mile journey in which he faced the threat of shrapnel and poison gas and suffered from gunshot wounds, blindness, and the loss of a significant portion of one leg. A military hero, he succumbed to his battle wounds on June 13, 1919 and was mounted by the Smithsonian.

Legermuseum in the Netherlands opened *Brave Beasts* in 2008, described by the designer, Todd van Hulsen, as a "fun and compelling family exhibit about animals and war," which forged "a risky and stimulating marriage between Army and Carnival." Sergeant Stubby and Cher Ami made an appearance, as did Tacoma the dolphin (mine detection in the Gulf War, 2003), Chetak the horse (Battle of Haldighati, 1576), and Surus the elephant (Hannibal's Second Punic War, 218 BC). The museum contracted the design services of Studio Louter, which envisioned sculpted black shadow animals "carrying the collection on rotating carrousels and multimedia ensconced in carnivalesque army tents." The subtext of the exhibit: "War is not a Circus."[1]

Belgium's Remember Museum houses the second animals in war memorial in Europe, a relief that recognizes the contributions of animals in wartime and depicts a horse and a dog bearing the weight of the world, while a carrier pigeon is perched atop an orb, ready to deliver a message of peace. Other museums such as the Australian War Museum (*A Is for Animals: An A to Z of Animals in War*) or the National WWII Museum in New Orleans (*Loyal Forces: The Animals of WWII*) have also approached this subject matter through temporary or permanent exhibits.

The war on terror is observed through New York City's National September 11 Memorial & Museum. Dogs were active in the rescue and recovery efforts, but one canine did not live out the day, a yellow lab named Sirius. Port Authority Police Lt. David Lim, a survivor of the North Tower collapse, lost Sirius, his companion and coworker, when the South Tower collapsed. Lim donated Sirius's leash and badge, which are on display at the museum. In the gift shop, one can purchase Sirius key chains, buttons, mugs, and other items artistically rendered by Rob Burns.

Uniquely, this museum also operates an online Artists Registry, a database/ gallery of artistic work created in response to 9/11. Seasoned and novice artists are represented, and one can find stunning pieces about the rescue dogs, such as Patricia Davis's sculpted "Semper Fi":

> It is intended to be a tribute; the dog having an expression of a "find" on his face. The title "Semper Fi" seemed fitting in light of the overtones of war. I know of no soul more faithful than that of a dog.
>
> The structure that the Shepherd is balanced on began as the girders of a collapsed entryway. As I was working one evening, I noticed the cast shadows from the sculpture across the wall. It was three crosses. The "coincidence" of this and the implied symbolism of the crosses became the emotional center of this piece. The girders in the sculpture represent this ancient practice of crucifixion (far preceding Christianity) which reflects the darker side of mankind, in contrast to the faithful and pure nature of the animals we employ.[2]

These military tributes prove great examples for the diversity of mediums museums employ to communicate and nurture a legacy: from the more traditional taxidermy mount to a statue to a community-driven, twenty-first-century online art database down to the offerings in a gift shop.

ZOOLOGICAL MOURNING: THE NATURE OF OBJECTS IN A COLLECTION

Zoos and aquariums are museums with living collections, and when some of their more famous residents pass on, the public seeks a way to mourn and remains curious to know what will transpire with their bodies. Germany's Knut the polar bear, who died (2011) young at the Berlin Zoo, is a wonderful case in point. A poster bear for global warming in life and death, Knut was mounted for display at the local natural history museum (NHM), but not before the public enshrined the entrance to the zoo and the area adjacent to Knut's enclosure with flowers, candles, pictures, notes, stuffed animals, and drawings. The chairman of the

Friends of the Berlin Zoo remarked, "Knut will live on in the hearts of many visitors, but it's important to create a memorial for coming generations to preserve the memory of this unique animal personality."[3] The statue *Knut—The Dreamer*, by Ukrainian artist Josef Tabachnyk, was funded by donations from fans.

To much ethical controversy, Knut's mount has been exhibited at Berlin's NHM as well as the Netherlands' Naturalis Biodiversity Center. Currently, he is on view as part of a special exhibition, *Highlights of Taxidermy*, and will later be featured in an exhibit on climate change and environmental protection.

The ability to be exhibited and interpreted under a number of different themes comes with the territory of being in a collection. If shown in a context other than biographical, does this impact the public's view and understanding of an animal's legacy? And what influence does time have in how Knut and his mount are appreciated? How will museum visitors see Knut if and when polar bears go extinct or if other polar bear mounts are brought into the collection?

HACHIKŌ: THE IMPORTANCE OF INTERPRETATION

Japan's Hachikō (d. 1935) remains one of the most famous canines of the twentieth century. Known and adored for his devotion to Professor Ueno, his human whom he greeted at the Shibuya train station daily for years, Hachikō continued the regular practice of visiting the station even after Ueno passed away. He impressed upon the Japanese public the importance of familial loyalty, renewed an interest in and preservation effort of the Akita dog breed, and inspired educators to convey important values through his story. While statues commemorate his legacy at both the Shibuya and Odate stations and a Hachikō monument was erected next to Ueno's grave in Tokyo, his body was mounted and continues to be on display at the National Museum of Nature and Science in Tokyo, alongside other canines of importance.

For a number of months in 2012, the Shibuya Folk and Literary Shirane Memorial Museum held an exhibition, *Shin Shuzo Shiryoten*, of new acquisitions to their collection, including rare photos from Hachikō's life. Evoking widespread empathy and serving as a testament to the human–animal bond across regions and cultures, one of the photos went viral and has been shared with countless networks on social media. The image shows his death on March 8, 1935. Hachikō had been found lifeless near the Shibuya station; his body was carried to the station's baggage room, reportedly one of his favorite places. It was here that the famous photo was taken, showing Yaeko (Ueno's wife) and station staff members lamenting over Hachikō; this scene is forever preserved within the museum. One of the station employees, Yoshizo Osawa, had given this photograph—one of the only primary artifacts depicting Hachikō's existence to survive—to his daughter, Nobue Yamaguchi; she in turn donated this prized piece of visual history to the museum, commenting "My father loved dogs. . . . He told me, 'Hachi came to our station every day and we shared our box lunches with him.'"[4]

While museums are critically important for preserving these public histories, they also serve as venues for interpretation. The curator of the museum, Keita Matsui, remarked, "People in the photo are praying for the repose of Hachi's soul. . . . [From the photo,] we can see how beloved he was in those days."[5]

While there can be little doubt as to how much Hachikō was and still is revered, having inspired several books and films, Matsui and his colleagues have called into question

Hachikō's motives for visiting the station. According to an article in the *Asahi Shimbun*, these museologists interviewed around one hundred individuals, including members of the Ueno family, and deduced that

> Ueno commuted from his home in Shibuya Ward to his school campus in the Komaba district on foot, not by train. Hachi used to see him off to work and meet him back along the way with Ueno's two other dogs, and went only occasionally to Shibuya Station.
>
> Why then, one might ask, did Hachi alone continue to wait at the station for his owner to return, even after he had died.
>
> Matsui thinks he has stumbled onto a likely reason.
>
> Ueno once departed from Shibuya Station to go on a long business trip without telling anyone of his planned return date. When the professor arrived back in Tokyo, he found Hachi alone waiting for him at the ticket gate. The excited professor gave him a piece of grilled chicken, the dog's favorite food.
>
> "That happy event probably went down into Hachi's memory," Matsui said. "He may have continued to wait for the return of his owner at Shibuya Station in the belief he would reappear there if he was absent for many days on end."[6]

Matsui has some supporting evidence of Hachikō's preferential palate to chicken. The taxidermist in charge of preserving Hachikō back in 1935 discovered bamboo skewers in his belly. But chalking up Hachikō's patronage of the Shibuya station to chicken leaves much to be desired by any animal lover or advocate and is a dramatic leap from the "man's best friend" legacy we've all come to know and love through Hachi's story.

Renowned animal ethologist, scientist, and bestselling author Dr. Jonathan Balcombe of the Humane Society of the United States shared his thoughts on this interpretative debacle with me.

> Matsui's theory is interesting in light of the apparent fact that Ueno typically didn't take the train to work. Nevertheless, I'm puzzled by this rather cynical attempt to refute a beloved and credible story so long after it occurred. To suggest that Hachi was only self-interested fits poorly with the highly social canines, who read our emotions in our faces, and who recent fMRI brain imaging studies show respond with rewarding feelings when they see their guardian.
>
> I find it curious that the report fails even to ascribe individuality to the dog, calling him "it" throughout the rest of the piece. I imagine that once he had become famous, Hachi received handouts from many people and not just at the train station, yet he continued to go to the station where he had met Ueno.
>
> Whether or not Matsui's theory is correct, there are other cases of dogs showing site-loyalty to lost owners, most notably Greyfriars Bobby, who returned each night to his late master's gravesite in Edinburgh for over a decade.[7]

A poll sponsored by the American Association of Museums in 2011 found that 87 percent of those surveyed (adult Americans) viewed museums as one of the most trustworthy sources of objective information. But can any museum curator, taxidermist, or educator operate without some personal interest and subjectivity? Will animal lovers resist the objective findings of curators like Matsui if they tarnish the legacy of a beloved animal?

MARTHA: A TOKEN SYMBOL REINVISIONS THE FUTURE

On September 1, 1914, at the Cincinnati Zoo, Martha the passenger pigeon passed away and was the last of her kind. As I write this, museums across the country have recently opened commemorative centennial exhibits in honor of Martha and her species.

While Martha's body was acquired and mounted by the Smithsonian and continues to be one of their most iconic taxidermy specimens, the Cincinnati Zoo staff transformed a national historic landmark into the Passenger Pigeon Memorial. This Japanese-pagoda-style building, the last of its kind in the United States, which served as an aviary in the late 1800s, became a site to pay tribute to Martha. The exhibit's message then is that humans have the ability to do untold amounts of damage, including hunting a species—one of the most numerous on earth—to extinction. A century later, the zoo has renovated and transformed this exhibit "from a single-species memorial to an educational exhibit with a positive and hopeful conservation message that segues from the story of the passenger pigeon to modern wildlife conservation efforts."[8] Visitors learn the story of the species and its decline, discover how this occurrence prompted the conservation movement in America, understand how close we've come to losing other species, and, finally, see how the zoo is involved in global conservation efforts.

Martha, like Hachikō, is a fascinating example of how interpretation is integral to museum operations and speaks to our society's affection for, remembrance of, and tributes to nonhumans. In speaking with several NHM professionals, it was made clear that museological approaches to environmental stewardship have shifted to more hopeful tonalities, the idea being that we can and must turn the tide for animals and planet alike.

Helen James, curator of the Smithsonian's bird division, ensured that Martha made her way back into the public eye in 2014, after a fifteen-year hiatus in locked storage, for the exhibit *Once There Were Billions: Vanished Birds of North America*. In London, the zoo halted time on its Victorian birdhouse at noon on September 1 of that year to mark Martha's passing. Both the Museum of Natural History (*A Shadow Over the Earth: The Life and Death of the Passenger Pigeon*) and the EnviroArt Gallery (*Moving Targets: Passenger Pigeon Portrait Gallery*) at the University of Michigan–Ann Arbor have erected exhibits and a stellar lineup of programming to spotlight Martha, her species, and our communal need to act.

In a conversation on October 7, 2014, with Kira Berman (museum) and Sara Adlerstein-Gonzalez (gallery), I was able to get a better sense if there is indeed a component of mourning in these exhibits, which they both had a role in bringing to fruition. Sara a university scientist and an artist in the gallery show, acknowledged that "we have to really cry. This was an ecocide. . . . This shouldn't have happened. We first have to mourn . . . and then come of out it." Kira, the program coordinator, echoed her sentiments, "We do need to remember and mourn, but we also need to do something." And for this reason, both exhibits have calls to action, simple things visitors can do to stimulate biodiversity: garden, conserve water, lower energy consumption, slow our population growth, and more.[9]

These environmental educators brought to light an important psychological observation: the public is hammered with terrible news on a frequent basis and easily becomes immobilized. In such states of melancholy they are unable to effect change. Just as these exhibits connect people on an emotional level to the plight of animals, they must also provide hope. Their joint programming has done just this through origami bird making, which symbolically builds up the flock, chalk drawings, poetry readings, dancing, lectures, film screenings, and off-site programs at public schools that augment the exhibits' message and reach.

We've seen with the passenger pigeon exhibits a cautionary tale regarding species extinction, but what of species revival? Some museums are continuing the legacy of a certain animal or species through research departments.

Unbeknownst to many members of the public, most NHMs have scientists working behind the scenes or even off-site in remote parts of the world to protect biodiversity. NHMs are also treasure troves of specimens that scientists like Ben Novak (University of California–Santa Cruz) can use for their novel projects, in Ben's case to revive the extinct passenger pigeon. Once it succeeds, the techniques will be applicable to hundreds of other extinct species, adding further complexity to this discussion on animals, museums, and mourning.

HAM: RECOGNIZING AND TREATING ANIMALS AS "ALMOST HUMAN"

It's not entirely unheard of in the museum world for a grave to exist within a museum compound. Buffalo Bill and Robert Louis Stevenson, for example, have their own gravesites at their respective museums. But when it comes to animal graves within the museum setting, there are few to speak of, but one certainly proves a worthwhile detour.

Ham the chimp, who was famously shot up into space, passed away in 1983 at the National Zoo. His body was transferred to the Armed Forces Institute of Pathology for necropsy, with the understanding that his skin would be mounted for display at the Smithsonian. (The Soviets had done the same for space dogs Belka and Strelka.) Public fury erupted upon learning these intentions. One commentary from a newspaper read,

> Talk about death without dignity. Talk about dreadful precedents—it should be enough to make any space veteran more than a little nervous about how he is going to be treated in the posthumous by and by.
>
> Rest assured that we're not looking for full honors at Arlington here. We know that Ham was a chimp. We certainly don't want to offend our Creationist readers—at least, not any more than we always do. But stuffing and display? The only national heroes we can think of who are stuffed and on permanent display are V.I. Lenin and Mao Tse-tung. Does this nation really want to emulate the Soviet and Chinese models? There is not one shred of evidence that Ham was a Communist. . . .
>
> How about treating America's First Ape with a little respect? Bury Ham.

A response from a New York high school student, which is archived at the Smithsonian, noted

> By treating his body like that of a stupid beast, people will continue thinking of apes as stupid beasts, and not the intelligent, almost human animals they really are. In my opinion, a gravestone would honor Ham's life much better than would having his body filled with sawdust and stuck under a glass case for countless years to gather dust.[10]

Ham's cremated remains, sans skeleton (which is in the collection at the National Museum of Health and Medicine), were buried at the International Space Hall of Fame in Alamogordo, New Mexico. Colonel John Stapp, "the fastest man on Earth," gave the eulogy at the memorial service. To this day, museumgoers can visit Ham's grave. Many leave tokens such as flowers, rocks, and bananas.

What does it signify when Ham will have fruit left at this gravesite while mounts such as Cher Ami's or Hachikō's never or very rarely receive a memento at their exhibits? How many of these museum displays—mounts, statues, art, exhibits, or graves—can truly be considered tributes as opposed to memorials? Do some, in their very nature, elicit more emotion or certain types of emotion, like a grave? Offering Ham more human condolences leads me to believe that perhaps this might be the case, but more on-site research would say conclusively.

CONCLUSION

Museums play an important role in preserving, interpreting, and sharing the collective memory of society. Many of these institutions have reflected upon our communal traditions, momentous events, and changing trends as they relate to death, mourning, and remembrance. As shown here, animals too are woven into this cultural and institutional tapestry, and museums bring nuanced attention to our society's understanding, treatment, and views of nonhuman animals, even in death.

NOTES

1. Todd van Hulzen, "'Brave Beasts' at the Royal Dutch Army Museum," December 28, 2008, http://vanhulzen.com/?p=2020.
2. Patricia Davis, "Artist's Statement," National September 11 Memorial & Museum, Artists Registry, https://www.911memorial.org.
3. "Preliminary Autopsy Results: Knut May Have Died of Brain Disease," *Spiegel Online*, March 22, 2011.
4. Kazuya Ohmuro, "Shibuya Museum Showcases Last Photo of Loyal Pooch Hachiko," *Asahi Shimbum*, June 16, 2012, http://ajw.asahi.com/article/behind_news/social_affairs/AJ201206160043.
5. Ohmuro, "Shibuya Museum."
6. Yuri Imamura, "New Theory Questions Hachiko's Loyalty, Says Chicken Tidbits the Answer," *Asahi Shimbum*, January 16, 2014.
7. Dr. Jonathan Balcombe, e-mail correspondence to author, September 29, 2014.
8. "Passenger Pigeon Memorial," Cincinnati Zoo and Botanical Garden website.
9. Sara Adlerstein-Gonzalez and Kira Berman, conference call with author, October 7, 2014.
10. Henry Nicholls, "Ham the Astrochimp: Hero or Victim?," *The Guardian*, December 16, 2013.

Another Death

EMMA KISIEL

THE QUESTION OF WHETHER OR NOT HUMANS MOURN ANIMALS IS PRESENT IN ALL OF my photographic work. This theme emerged in my art when I began looking closely at dead animals and making images of roadkill animals, photographing flower and stone memorials I built around their bodies. My recent project, "Another Death," portrays museum taxidermic animals that have suffered another kind of death after their initial demise. Frozen in time, they are presented either in the throes of death at another creature's hand or in a limp resting pose, having just passed. Moments like these appear frequently in natural history museum dioramas, just as dead animals are a common sight along roadsides. This often-grotesque visual rarely elicits more than a visceral pang of discomfort. Are we generally comfortable with the sight because we see not a human, but an animal; not a "real" animal, but a taxidermic one? There are many levels of separation between humans and animals, in life and in death. My photographs explore the tension between how we experience animals in life, how we recognize—or do not recognize—animals in death, and whether we realize that we, too, will meet the same inevitable end.

Emma Kisiel, *White-tailed Jackrabbit*. From the series "Another Death," 2013. (Photos courtesy of Emma Kisiel [emmakisiel.com].)

Emma Kisiel, *Ribbon Seal*.

Emma Kisiel, *Mule Deer 1*.

Emma Kisiel, *Mule Deer 2*.

Emma Kisiel, *Mouse*.

Emma Kisiel, *Elk*.

PART 4

Animals We Do Not Mourn

In the Heart of Every Horse

Combating a History of Equine Exploitation and Slaughter through the Commemoration of an "Average" Thoroughbred Racehorse

TAMAR V. S. MCKEE

IN MID-SEPTEMBER 2011, ON A BREEZY DAY EDGED WITH A HINT OF AUTUMN CHILL, I took a seat amid a modest collection of bright white folding chairs lined up outside the Hall of Champions complex at the Kentucky Horse Park. People were milling about, enjoying refreshments and chatting to each other before the memorial service began for a Thoroughbred racehorse by the name of Invisible Ink. On display in front of the chairs was a richly colored photograph of the horse, who was bay with a white, heart-shaped "star" on his forehead. Groomed to shine, he wore a fine leather halter and gracefully curved his neck so as to look over his front right shoulder. The photo was positioned before the gathering of chairs so that Invisible Ink, ears brightly perked forward, appeared as though he was looking over the gravesite that had been prepared for him: red chrysanthemums and white pansies planted in the shape of a horseshoe. On the other side of the grave, a podium had been set up where remarks for the memorial service would be delivered, and a stunning wreath made of carrots, radishes, cabbage, and white roses, topped by a peach-colored satin bow, had been placed before it.

As I waited for the service to begin, I studied the program for the event. Against a purple banner, the header announced in yellow font that this was a "Memorial Service for Invisible Ink." This yellow and purple color combination was in homage to the "silks" that the horse had raced under for Peachtree Racing Stable. Below the horse's name came the listing of his parentage that was so customary to the identity of Thoroughbred racehorses worldwide. Invisible Ink's father, or sire, was listed first as Thunder Gulch, while his mother, or dam, was Conquistress, whose own father was Conquistador Cielo, making him the "dam sire" of Invisible Ink. It is also custom in the racing world to name foals after some combination of the sire's and dam's names, so I mused over how the horse's owners, John and Elizabeth Fort, came up with "Invisible Ink." As I came to learn, the quixotic name afforded a very clever move on the part of John Fort. Inspired by the turf writer Steve Haskin's suggestion, when it came time to craft the brass nameplate that affixed onto the leather halter as standard issue for all Thoroughbred racehorses, Fort left the plate blank. From then on, whenever he was asked what the horse's name was, Fort would joke that "the name is on there; it's written in invisible ink."[1]

Compared to other horses enshrined at the Hall of Champions, Invisible Ink's interment there was highly unusual because while "Inky," as his close connections and dearest fans called him, had raced in most of the prestigious "stakes" races a horse could as a three-year-old,[2] including the 2001 Kentucky Derby where he came in second to Monarchos (who set the record for the second fastest time at the Derby, behind Secretariat's legendary campaign in 1973), he was not considered an evident "champion." As I learned from comments left on an online forum upon the horse's passing, even though Invisible Ink's racing career and bloodlines had been valuable enough to retire him as a breeding stallion, by the time he died in July 2011 at the age of thirteen from a neurological disorder, the amount of money paid to breed a mare to him was negligible in a horse industry where stud fees could be in the tens of thousands of dollars.[3] Therefore, while Inky did not fit the typical profile of what I have elsewhere called the "ideal type Thoroughbred,"[4] I came to realize that the reason why he came to be buried and commemorated amid his more elite brethren is because of what he represented at a critical time in U.S. horse-racing history and concerns over how (in)humanely horses were being treated.

The memorial service began with then executive director of the Horse Park, John Nicolson, delivering the welcoming remarks, which I recorded as part of my fieldwork research. He first reminded people that just as the park was conceived "a few decades ago" (in the 1970s, in fact) to "be a place that celebrates the love that exists between mankind and the horse," the site in the park that celebrates that relationship most "poignantly" was at the Hall of Champions where we were all gathered today. Established in 1984, the Hall of Champions is one of the many attractions available at the Kentucky Horse Park, a self-proclaimed "educational equine theme park," where visitors can interface with horses "up close and personal"—a rare opportunity even for some locals despite the fact that Lexington, Kentucky, and the surrounding Inner Bluegrass region is considered the "horse capital of the world." Especially for Thoroughbred racehorses, access to them is limited (or impossible) for people not considered part of a horse's "connections." This is not only because of the thousands (if not millions) of dollars of insurance and liability attached to these horses, but also because the prestige of being associated with these horses (even if just standing next to them) is maintained as a precious resource of status and power among the highly competitive "horse people" of the Bluegrass and Thoroughbred racing industry at large.[5]

In this light, the horse park had been created to democratize access to and appreciation of horses at a time when the industry of breeding, racing, and selling horses was becoming a multimillion-dollar affair and, in particular, Thoroughbred horse farms in the Bluegrass were reversing their once open-gate policies where visitors could visit without scheduled, guided tours.[6] Thus the Kentucky Horse Park and, moreover, the Hall of Champions were founded to make horses "easily accessible to fans who can watch them resting in their stalls, grazing in their paddocks or being paraded during daily demonstrations . . . in the small pavilion adjacent to the barn."[7] Or, as I witnessed on that mid-September day in 2011, to find their final resting places, as Invisible Ink did amid the graves of other celebrated horses, such as John Henry (1975–2007) and Cigar (1990–2014).

After Nicolson's preamble, the tone of the ceremony shifted to acknowledge the anomalous event of burying Invisible Ink at the park. "The racing statistics of Invisible Ink wouldn't necessarily lend himself to being here at the Hall of Champions, I think we all agree on that," Nicolson noted. "But his remarkable story lends himself to being a champion everywhere." Nicolson then explained, with effusive praise to John Fort as a "man of honor in the industry" with a "creative way of thinking," how he and Fort decided that "Invisible Ink will stand forever here as an example that all horses in some form or fashion are champions, and that he had the heart of a champion." Furthermore, Nicolson also announced that Fort had established a fund "that will serve all the horses at the Kentucky Horse Park" to "improve the lives of the horses that are here in several of our barns, and to increase the safety and accessibility of those horses to the people who want to get to know them." He then concluded: "Invisible Ink's work is still going forward."

What was it that made Invisible Ink, modest racehorse that he was, so worthy of mourning and memorialization upon his death? And why was his commemoration being used to make a larger statement (and fund) about the welfare and familiarization of horses? The answer lies in understanding his "story," as it was often referenced to throughout his memorial service, as well as taking stock of the issues the Thoroughbred racing industry was facing between 2000 and 2011, particularly as it relates to equine exploitation and slaughter.

The horse who came to be registered with the Jockey Club of North America under the racing name Invisible Ink was born on one of the many famous Bluegrass horse farms in 1998. John Fort, who was then struggling to get into the racing industry, bought him in 1999 as a "beautifully bred" yearling for $105,000 and brought him to his farm in South Carolina.[8] Then, when the horse was training as a two-year-old in Ocala, Florida, in 2000, he sustained a cut on his left hind ankle. As infection set in, he was treated with a combination of antibiotics and Butazolidan so intensely that, according to Dr. Robert Copelan, the veterinarian credited with saving Invisible Ink's life and who also delivered remarks at the horse's memorial service, "it had killed off most of the bacteria in his gut." As a result, gastric ulcers formed in the horse's stomach and he developed colitis and intractable diarrhea. In press interviews, Fort described how the horse's throat looked as though "battery acid" had been poured down it and his insides were like "raw meat."[9] In addition to his swollen esophagus and the endless saliva dripping from his mouth, the horse also suffered from ringworm lesions and a stomach and testicles that had swelled up to "the size of a beach ball."[10] So ravaged, the horse's weight had dangerously plummeted, from nine hundred pounds to five hundred, and he was "basically on life support" with $1,000 worth of plasma being given to him daily as he could barely lift his head up, much less eat or drink.[11] The veterinarian-approved suggestion was on the table that the horse be euthanized.

Furthermore, it was repeatedly mentioned in many of the articles that I came across—especially those detailing Invisible Ink's struggle in light of his 2001 Kentucky Derby campaign—that the horse had been insured for $200,000 and that the insurance company had informed Fort that he could collect the entire amount upon the horse's death. But, as it was also repeated in those articles and at Invisible Ink's memorial service, Fort had refused to let the horse die, much less collect the insurance money that would have basically given him a return (if not slight profit) on the horse.

This care, concern, and refusal to put Invisible Ink down and collect on the insurance money was considered so notable both in 2001 and again ten years later at his memorial service, I would argue, because it ran in contradistinction to the circumstances other, less fortunate racehorses often face during their careers and after. This is the so-called dark side of racing: the mass breeding of horses just to sell for incredible amounts of money and never to race; the harsh methods of training and ensuring race-day competitiveness, such as injections of pain-numbing drugs to performance-enhancing ones; and the selling of washed-out, often lame and otherwise injured horses to slaughter either via kill buyers who frequented the backstretch or by a slower, perhaps more cruel method of allowing the horse to go through a series of failed, abusive, or neglectful trades before winding up at auctions infamous for channeling horses to purchase for slaughter. What is more, at the time of Invisible Ink's struggle in 2000–2001, news had broken about the slaughter of Exceller in Sweden in 1998, and the process by which once-celebrated racehorses could succumb to the violence and taboo of horse slaughter (much less the violence and exploitation of racing) was beginning to be laid bare as never before. As the racing industry troubled over the growing visibility of human mistreatment of horses in 2001 even as it remained a multimillion-dollar sports and gambling industry, Invisible Ink's story was strategically interpreted as the antithesis of such problems. And it began with emphasizing Fort's extraordinary, priceless devotion to the horse.

What was it that so motivated Fort to save Invisible Ink? According to Steve Haskin, Fort made the connection between his service in the Vietnam War and his ability to know when someone, human or animal, is beyond hope. What is more, having thus been in "life and death situations," Fort "had a feeling this was a horse whose spirit was still alive" even as his physical condition threatened demise.[12]

With such moral compulsion and conviction in his ability to see that there was life left worth saving for the horse, Fort called up Dr. Copelan and, to the veterinarian's recollection, told him, "in his usual aphoristic manner" that "you're not going to let him die." While the attending veterinarian, Dr. Carole Clark, had "done a remarkable job," according to Copelan, he had one unusual, last-resort remedy that would fall more into the category of folk medicine than a bottle with a prescription formally printed on it. As Copelan explained at the memorial service: "I told Dr. Clark that I would like to give a gallon of buttermilk to the horse." He went on to explain:

> The way I've always done it, is on my way to the racetrack in the morning, which is very early,[13] I would pick up a gallon of buttermilk at the 7–11 and put it on the passenger's side floor in my car, leave the windows rolled up, and at 11 o'clock—four or five hours later—the buttermilk had an opportunity to replicate a number of bacteria that were present in that gallon of buttermilk and give a real dose of that [healthy bacteria].

After administering the buttermilk and "if the horse was still alive in the morning," as Copelan put it, Invisible Ink was to be given another half gallon of the fermented milk. At that point, the stool would hopefully begin to form again and the horse would begin to recover "if there was any chance at all."

Copelan continued. A year later, "I was at Barn 6 at Keeneland," the premier racecourse in Lexington, Kentucky, "and I ducked out of one of the stalls and there was John who said, 'do you know who that horse was that you just treated? His name's Invisible Ink. He's the one you gave the buttermilk to.'" At that point in the memorial service, people let out soft, delighted gasps with accompanying smiles at the touching serendipity of the encounter. Copelan then concluded his time at the podium reading the poem "The Racer" by British poet John Masefield, noting that in this 1923 poem Masefield had "elegant words" that summed up Invisible Ink's career and the "assembly here today." A particularly telling excerpt from the poem reads thus:

> Would that the passionate moods on which we ride
> Might kindle thus to oneness with the will;
> Would we might see the end to which we stride,
> And feel, not strain, in struggle, only thrill.

With that, John Fort stepped up to the podium to deliver the eulogy. He began by informing us in the audience that he was not here to retell the story of Invisible Ink, but rather to emphasize "how important having a friend and a companion" was for him in his relationship with Invisible Ink. In this way, he seemed to speak to Masefield's poem on feeling "oneness with the will" of the horse, as well as seeing Inky's death as not a "strain" in its struggle as it seemed in 2000, but rather as a "thrill"—especially when the horse came back from the brink of death to almost win the Kentucky Derby just one year later. Fort then considered how mutual the relationship between Invisible Ink and him was. "I know about my care and resolve," Fort said, "and I am sure he knew it too." Fort repeatedly told us how they formed "a team" during Inky's illness and recovery and that the "value of a team is how you can help each other." In Fort's eye, he helped the horse fight off the threat of death and premature demise, and the horse reciprocated by helping him "rub shoulders with greatness" by catapulting Fort from struggling horseman to Derby limelight. Fort then went on to make the point that no one should be above a partnership with their horses. "Inspire each other," he charged, "work hard, together."

Fort's emphasis on the mutuality of the bond he shared with Invisible Ink, and the moral advice and ethical action derived from it, seemed all the more poignant in 2011. At this point, the dark side of racing had grown even more since Inky first fought off death in 2000. Ferdinand had been found slaughtered in Japan in 2002,[14] and Barbaro and Eight Belles had had very public breakdowns (and even deaths) at prestigious, heavily televised races resulting from catastrophic leg injuries in 2006 and 2008, respectively. Then, the "unwanted horse" issue threatened the multimillion-dollar Thoroughbred racing industry.[15] Brought on by the closure of U.S.-based equine slaughter plants in 2007 followed by a worldwide economic recession in 2008–9 that drove yearling sales even below prices impacted by September 11, 2001, people were eager (if not desperate) to off-load unprofitable horses. Otherwise healthy, sound horses were sold to kill buyers who would in turn transport them sometimes for thousands of miles with minimal to no food or water to slaughter plants in Canada or Mexico. If not sent to slaughter, the other option was still an event of needless suffering, as horses were left to starve and fester in pastures until the intervention of animal patrol and rescue operations took place—and even then, finding a suitable niche for a rescued, unwanted horse was not guaranteed.[16]

Such was the zeitgeist in which Invisible Ink's life and death were made all the more meaningful at his memorial service at the Kentucky Horse Park in September 2011. Instead of consigning a horse to slaughter, Fort had confronted the "raw meat" appearance of a horse ravaged by colitis (among other ailments) and committed to healing him. Instead of "humanely" and chemically euthanizing Invisible Ink and collecting the insurance money, Fort had initially poured thousands of dollars' worth of plasma into him, and then rancid buttermilk as a last resort. And instead of simply having the horse's body rendered upon his death, Fort and Nicolson conspired to bury him at the Hall of Champions as, according to the program for Invisible Ink's memorial service, "a reminder to all who visit his gravesite that the heart of a champion beats in every horse."

Fort concluded his remarks in a sob-choked voice: "this is the end of the journey for Invisible Ink." He noted how "this past spring" he had "stood in the winner's circle" at the 2011 Kentucky Oaks because "we had got to this point together."[17] "He's in the Hall of Champions," Fort said about Invisible Ink, "and I was in the winner's circle at Churchill Downs." Then, as if overcome by this comparison, Fort tried to go on, but emotion fragmented his words: "I don't think you can do that just . . . That's really Invisible Ink's. . . ." Fort quickly moved to conclude at this point before weeping overtook him, thanking everyone for "sharing this with me" and that it was a "real honor, thank you." He then stepped away to take hold of the marvelous wreath and place it in front of the horse's gravesite as the audience applauded. Then, a lone bugler attired in a red coat trimmed with green, gold top hat, and spotless white jodhpurs raised a long, thin bugle and played "Call to Post," a song traditionally heard ten minutes before every horse race. On this day, however, it served the purpose "Taps" does at the close of a military funeral for a human being. After the last, brassy note cut the chilly autumn air, all of us in the audience were taken into a stark, sudden, and strong invisible grip of silence, broken only by the heartbeat sound of hooves from the park grounds beyond.

NOTES

1. Steve Haskin, "The Loss of a Thoroughbred," *Hangin' with Haskin*, Blood-Horse blogs, July 7, 2011.
2. A horse's third year is a crucial campaigning year used to establish a horse's racing career.
3. Merlinsky, "RIP 'Inky': Invisible Ink Dies from a Neurological Disorder," Derby Trails Forum, July 7, 2011, http://www.derbytrail.com/forums/archive/index.php?t-42982.html.
4. Tamar V. S. McKee, "Ghost Herds: Rescuing Horses and Horse People in Bluegrass Kentucky," (PhD diss., University of British Columbia, 2014), 96.
5. See Rebecca Cassidy, *Sport of Kings: Kinship, Class, and Thoroughbred Breeding in Newmarket* (Cambridge: Cambridge University Press, 2002); Rebecca Cassidy, *Horse People: Thoroughbred Culture in Lexington and Newmarket* (Baltimore: Johns Hopkins University Press, 2007); and McKee, "Ghost Herds."
6. Bill Cook, director of the International Museum of the Horse, personal communication with author, May 2011.
7. Dale Leatherman, "Star Quality," *Discover Horses: The Kentucky Horse Park Magazine*, 2011–12, 54.
8. Judy Clabes, "Invisible Ink Left Indelible Mark on Hearts, Minds of His Loving Owners and His Fans," Kentucky Horse Park (website), September 15, 2011. All horses turn a year older on January 1 no matter their original birthdates.
9. Haskin, "The Loss of a Thoroughbred"; Dave Joseph, "Back from the Dead," *Sun Sentinel*, June 7, 2001.
10. Haskin, "The Loss of a Thoroughbred."
11. Clabes, "Invisible Ink Left Indelible Mark on Hearts."
12. Steve Haskin, quoted in Joseph, "Back from the Dead."
13. To put this in perspective, horses are usually out exercising on the track before the sun comes up during any time of the year.
14. Barbara Bayer, "Roses to Ruin," *The Blood-Horse*, no. 30 (July 26, 2003): 3918–23.
15. "Unwanted Horses: How the Industry Is Dealing with Life after Racing," *The Blood-Horse*, no. 40 (October 2, 2010).
16. McKee, "Ghost Herds."
17. The Kentucky Oaks is a prestigious race run by fillies (female horses) only on the day before the Kentucky Derby. That year, Plum Pretty had run and won the Oaks for Peachtree Stables.

Creating Carnivores and Cannibals
Animal Feed and the Regulation of Grief

KERIDIANA CHEZ

In the nineteenth century, the dog and the horse were man's best friends. Sagacious, affectionate, and loyal, dog and horse were represented as faithful and helpful creatures that had played key roles in the development of civilization. Frameworks like the animal protection movement enabled, and encouraged, the development and intensification of these affectionate ties. Yet in spite of these ties, the horse was systematically served up to the dog for dinner.

To be deemed killable, as Judith Butler says, entails being deemed not grievable. An unmournable life "is not quite a life; it does not qualify as a life and is not worth a note," and its passing is not deemed a loss.[1] Discursive frames can disenable the recognition of bodies that share the vulnerability of interdependence, and the mournable subject—whose intelligibility relies on the unintelligibility of these unmournable others—is invested in these ongoing erasures.[2] If we are to apply the idea of precariousness to nonhuman animals we must stretch it beyond Butler's original delineation, as Chlöe Taylor, James Stanescu, and Rebekah Sinclair have done in arguing for an alternative ethics that would allow for the mourning of animals we eat.[3] I join them in asking how we could extend Butler's ideas to challenge a status quo of unfathomable antianimal violence. In pursuing these arguments, we share Butler's belief that ungrievability degrades lives. As Taylor puts it, "as long as we do not grieve nonhuman animals, the instrumentalisation of their lives, and not only of their corpses, will continue."[4] For those of us whose engagement with animal studies is inseparable from our interest in the lives and deaths of real animals, how might grievability enable new avenues of inquiry and advocacy? And what are its limits?

The discourse of edibility has not merely replicated the human/animal boundary, designating the human as inedible and the animal as edible. Rather, the edible is a construct produced through the management of edibility across all species, designating which animals are fed to which others. The discourse of carnivorousness that enables the edibility of some animals, like horses, as well as the taboo against cannibalism that protects humans (and by extension, their dogs) from edibility, intersected to produce the frames that informed the recognizability of lives. Frames were drawn across all species, constructing what we call "food chains": detailed hierarchies affirming that dogs should eat horses, regardless of affective ties. As I will show, animal diets fell under willful human control, producing an interspecies power pyramid with the whole of natural creation.

I begin with the horse and dog because of the sheer irony of feeding one best friend to the other after a lifetime of companionship. In life, the horse was "the best friend of man" and his "faithful companion," but after death, he was dog food.[5] As pet dogs became ubiquitous members of nineteenth-century middle-class families, the carcasses of horses, whether cab or farm or pedigreed racer, were hacked up and boiled into three hundred pounds of "dog's meat" each. Unlike pet dogs, whose corpses were thought to merit some dignity,[6] beloved equine companions could be mourned and yet be denied the dignity of bodily integrity. In spite of their mournability, all horses were edible and wholly consumable. A horse's "posthumous utility"[7] was so great that it precipitated a unique disconnect between the living horse and its carcass, as evidenced here in this account:

> When he had finished loading the pistols, he went and stood in front of the mare. Polly, said he, I have rode thee these sixteen years over road and river, through town and country, by night and by day, through storm and sunshine, and thou never made a bolt or a boggle with me till now. Thou hast carried me over and five thousand dead bodies before breakfast, and twice saved my life. . . . We must both die soon, and should I go first, . . . it will be a bad day's work for thee. Thou wouldst not wish to be starved, and mauled, and worked to death, and thy carcase given over to the knackers, wouldst thou? Polly put down her head, and rubbed it against him, and while she was doing so, he tied a handkerchief over her eyes, and kissing her first on one side of the face, and then on the other, he said: Polly, God bless thee! and instantly fired one of his pistols right into her ear. She fell down, gave one kick, and never moved nor moaned afterwards; but I remember the tears gushed out of my eyes as if a Christian had been shot, and even Sam looked ready to cry as he stood over her, and said, poor Polly! We buried her in the hole. . . . No one could tell why he buried her in the yard, when the Squire's gamekeeper would have given a fair price for the carcase to feed the hounds. But old Harrison was an odd one.[8]

To his observers, Harrison's effusive mourning seems appropriate—the narrator himself weeps "as if a Christian had been shot"—but his insistence on burying the horse rather than profiting from her carcass appears "odd." Harrison defies convention by deeming this one particular horse inedible based on his affective ties to that horse. Mournability frames allowed for mourning the nonhuman,[9] but demanded that attachments be severed from its edible body. In spite of the evident love and respect a horse might have earned in life—here, even a war hero—it was presumed dog chow. Horses may thus be described as having had some measure of "mourning rights,"[10] but this did not spare the horse's body from edibility. It ought not have been buried—it was "unburiable," in Butler's terms.[11] To Butler, "open grieving is bound up with outrage, and outrage at the face of injustice or indeed of unbearable loss has enormous potential,"[12] but edibility abridges mourning, even mourning that is presumably sincere.

Edibility thus complicates the question of how much difference the mourning of animals would make for animal lives. Unlike the humans that are the subject of Butler's discussion, the bodies of select nonhuman animals are deemed "unburiable" because they are food. In the case of edibility, a death sustains another's life. Butler's original, anthropocentric discussion critiques the suppression of mourning for Palestinians in Gaza, in contrast to the imperative that we mourn Americans who died in the 9/11 attacks.[13] Many do regard Palestinian deaths as ungrievable, but those who position themselves as the "enemies" of Palestinians likely do more than not grieve: they celebrate fewer "terrorists" and more safety. A similar framework marks the deaths of certain species: from the point of view of its eaters, the death of an animal is a cause for celebration. Any mourning can be palliated by the legitimating, reassuring thought of essential vitamins and nutrients.

To be not only ungrievable but also edible is more than an ontological obliteration. Edibility transforms a death into a gain, for only the end of that life could create wonderful, glorious "food." As Noëlie Vialles has pointed out, the French word for edible meats, *viande*, is derived from the Latin *vivenda*, referring to "exalted" foods thought to particularly "sustai[n] life."[14] Both literally and figuratively, the edible constitutes the inedible. Ironically, in the name of "nutrition," the fundamental element of interdependence that for Butler might elicit ethical politics becomes instead an inexorable call for animal death. When a small but vocal minority tried to encourage Londoners to eat horseflesh, a merchant who sold the meat for pet food dramatically asked, "What is to become of . . . dogs if you take the food out of their mouths?" Dogs were, he argued, "entitled to be fed," suggesting that dogs would be fed horse or nothing.[15]

In the nineteenth century, animal death also created carnivores. While the dog had long been associated with maleness, his transition into a pet—an animal that provides emotional, rather than physical, services—represented the tragic taming of masculine force by the feminizing forces of domesticity. Although in 1827 meat was considered "more natural" and thought to "increas[e] their strength considerably," dog diets actually involved a lot of porridge.[16] As dogs became a ubiquitous part of American and British middle-class families, the human diet became a standard reference point for determining the dog's, so their diets also became increasingly meat-based.[17] In her seminal work, *The Sexual Politics of Meat: A Feminist-Vegetarian Critical Theory* (1990), Carol J. Adams explored the links between meat-eating and gender, and what she found regarding humans was also the case for dogs.[18] Eating meat was thought to be "stimulating," as opposed to vegetables, which would have a "cooling effect."[19] Particularly if the horsemeat was raw, it would have "a tendency to foster ferocity of disposition."[20] In affirming and reaffirming that, "the dog [was] unquestionably carnivorous,"[21] the dog's masculinity was cemented by the naturalization of meat in his diet. The horse's posthumous utility thus included the valuable work of making canine masculinity, which in turn enhanced human masculinity.

While the dog's body was protected from being eaten, he remained, for the most part, unburiable. We romanticize the nineteenth century if we focus on the elaborate rituals of a select few. Privileged canine hippophagists or not, only pet dogs were likely to be buried, and then only with constrained mourning and in cemeteries carefully segregated from human remains. An 1888 burial of a dog in a human cemetery Woodlawn, New York, for example, was denounced as "an insult to the dead and an outrage on the living,"[22] and a Kentucky court of appeals upheld an injunction against a similar burial on the grounds that, just as the whites-only cemetery would suffer a loss in value if one of "the negro race" were to be buried there, so would a dog's burial break the "dignity of our dead."[23] The more typical fate of dog bodies was likely joining horses at the rendering factory or some other ignominious end.[24] By such practices, the dog was carefully slotted above the horse and still firmly below man in the food chain.

Beyond food, the death of an animal also offered an opportunity for man's ingenuity. Taylor has explored how the discourse of "waste" has been used to rationalize the consumption of nonhuman bodies.[25] "Waste" operates posthumously, neatly sidestepping questions about the quality of an animal's life and death by shifting the focus on a predetermined question: Would it not be wrong to waste valuable food? But the focus on waste as an excuse can obscure the sense of victory involved in vanquishing waste. Horses were useful in life—the main motive power for industrializing societies—and assumed a whole other form of utility after death. "Posthumous utility" was about capital and man's ability to leverage scientific and technological acumen for remuneration: "In all civilised and densely populated countries, of the animals . . . it may be said that nothing is wasted, every part that is not eaten being turned to some useful purpose." Thanks to (civilized) man's ingenuity, the "disintegrated form of our once living friend re-enters the 'social swim'" of capital production.[26] Ultimately, even some who claimed deep sympathy for the fallen horse immediately dissociated the horse from its body. For example, one 1891 writer declared great pity for the horse, "whose life has been one of helpless, yet uncomplaining service to the will of man," but then methodologically detailed the lucrative deconstruction of the horse—skin stripped off and salted for leather, tendons pickled for glue, horseshoes sold for old iron, shin bones rendered into candles and buttons, hooves ground up into fertilizer, entrails processed into cheap soap, and so on.[27] Describing this dismantling as "life after death," the article neatly portions the pre- and postdeath horse in terms of ongoing friendship and service: "man's best and most faithful friend has . . . given his best services during life and its close has left us a rich legacy."[28]

The horse's "afterlife," however, impinged on its present life: from conception, horses were interpellated as future food and raw material. Posthumous utility cast a long shadow over equine life, but particularly toward its end. "No horse that enter[ed]" the knacker's yard "must come out again alive, or as a horse":[29] entering this predeath zone instantly stripped the horse of its mournable identity. As if being, in the words of one writer in London, "condemned meat"[30] after a lifetime of forced labor was insufficiently horrific, the suffering of many horses did not end upon delivery to the knackers' gates. Some horses, in fact, did "come out again alive": unscrupulous knackers resold them, and purchasers extracted the very last breath from the horse.[31] Others, in trying to manage the supply of their products against the demands of the market, did not kill the horses right away—but they refused to feed what they were going to eventually kill, so they left these "surplus" horses to slowly starve until it was lucrative to slaughter them.[32] Though there were complaints, particularly as the humane movement reeducated the middle classes into feeling sympathy for the suffering of nonhuman animals, these rising sentiments little improved conditions for the tens of thousands of horses "knackered" annually. I suspect that, as with the case of Polly's mercy-killing, these graphic depictions did more to inure the public from mourning the end of a life so horrible.

In the course of the century, animal farming also increasingly embraced systematized carnivorousness and even cannibalism. Horseflesh—the food of dogs (and cats and zoo animals)—had also been making its way into the troughs of poultry since at least the 1890s.[33] England claimed leadership in repurposing inedible animal offal and bones for feed.[34] In the United States, agriculture experiment stations and state colleges also revolutionized what farm animals would be fed, adding more and more animal matter to the diets of omnivores and herbivores.[35] This federally funded project was born out of anxiety over the unsustainability of feeding edible grains to an increasing number of farm animals. To reserve more of the edible for humans, scientists developed "tankage"—"the cooked meat, bone, and sinew remaining after the expression of fat" from all sorts of slaughtered animals[36]—for use in animal feed in place of edible grains. Described, by definition, as "always inedible,"[37] tankage was essentially the dregs of the animals that humans ate, which was then fed to other animals that humans would eat: the inedible maximizing the production of the edible. The president of the American Society of Animal Nutrition, founded in 1908, prophesied that "the feeder of the future" would "husband" by-product feeds "to an extent as yet unrealized," and he was quite right.[38] Yet this systematic creation of carnivores and cannibals would not be recognized as such.

According to the *Oxford English Dictionary*, the word "cannibal" originally referred to the Carib people of the West Indies, who were thought to eat human flesh. It was more than a hundred years later that the word "cannibal" took on the additional meaning of referring to any animal that eats its own species.[39] From its incipiency, the taboo protected only humanity, guarding against the danger of shifting the human to a lower position on the food chain, into the precarious position of edibility. The taboo against cannibalism, the "ultimate savage act,"[40] might be less about the unnaturalness of craving a bit of one's own and more about the horror of becoming edible to the world's greatest predator—the human.

Through the regulation of animal feed, the nineteenth century produced an interspecies power pyramid that organized animal life. The history of this traffic in animal meat sheds light on how and why over the last two hundred years we have become a society that feeds cows to cows, dogs to dogs—propagating the most unnatural food chain to date. This dog and horse story suggests that it is not necessarily grievability that would preserve or improve nonhuman lives. So long as a being's death has been preordained by the seemingly inexorable assignation of edibility or utility, it seems to make little difference whether that death is accompanied by mourning. To an extent, mourning nonhuman deaths can contest the larger speciesist framework, but the drive to capitalize on an animal's posthumous utility, including its edibility, and the ensuing impingement on the quality of its life would not likely be abated by mourning.

NOTES

1. Judith Butler, *Precarious Life: The Powers of Mourning and Violence* (London: Verso, 2004), 34.
2. Butler, *Precarious Life*, 5, 34.
3. Chloë Taylor, "The Precarious Lives of Animals: Butler, Coetzee, and Animal Ethics," *Philosophy Today* 52 (2008): 60–72; James Stanescu, "Species Trouble: Judith Butler, Mourning, and the Precarious Lives of Animals," *Hypatia* 27, no. 3 (2012): 567–82; Rebekah Sinclair, "Who's on Butler's Plate: Mourning, Vulnerability, and the Consumption of Others," (paper presented on the panel "Women, Animals and Religion: From Fleshy Objects to Embodied Subjects" at the American Academy of Religion National Conference, Atlanta, GA, October 30–November 1, 2010).
4. Chloë Taylor, "Respect for the (Animal) Dead," in *Animal Death*, ed. Jay Johnston and Fiona Probyn-Rapsey (Sydney: Sydney University Press, 2013), 85–101, 98.
5. Edward W. Gough, *"Centaur"; or the Turn Out: A Practical Treatise on the (Humane) Management of Horses* (London: Henry Thacker, 1885), 217. Adolf Cluss, "Modern Street-Pavements," *Popular Science Monthly* 7 (1875): 88.
6. Teresa Mangum, "Dog Years, Human Fears," in *Representing Animals*, ed. Nigel Rothfels (Bloomington: Indiana University Press, 2002), 35–47. See also Hilda Kean, "Human and Animal Space in Historic 'Pet' Cemeteries in London, New York and Paris," in *Animal Death*, ed. Jay Johnston and Fiona Probyn-Rapsey (Sydney: Sydney University Press, 2013), 21–42. I should note that cats also ate horsemeat, but as cats were not considered *man*'s best friend, I do not conflate discussion of the two species.
7. A. F. M. Willich, "Bones," in *The Domestic Encyclopedia* (Philadelphia: Abraham Small, 1821), 263.

8. Horace Smith, "The Old White Hat—and the Old Grey Mare," in *Gaieties and Gravities: A Series of Essays, Comic Tales, and Fugitive Vagaries* (London: Henry Colburn, 1825), 61–62.
9. Anna Sewell's 1877 *Black Beauty*, an international bestseller, stirred sympathy for the plight of workhorses.
10. I do not mean to invoke the idea of "rights" as inalienable just deserts, but rather as the product of the same kinds of frameworks shaping the intelligibility of grievableness and of valuable lives.
11. Butler, *Precarious Life*, 34.
12. Judith Butler, *Frames of War: When Is Life Grievable?* (New York: Verso, 2009), 39.
13. Butler, *Precarious Life*, 4–5.
14. Noëlie Vialles, *Animal to Edible* (Cambridge: Cambridge University Press, 1994), 4.
15. James Greenwood, "Mr. William Spavinger's Speech on Hippophagy," *London Society* 13 (1868): 467.
16. John Rydge, *The Veterinary Surgeon's Vade Mecum: A Complete Guide to the Cure of All Diseases Incident to Horses, Cattle, Sheep, and Dogs* (London: Clerc Smith, 1827), 242.
17. George B. Taylor, *Man's Friend, the Dog* (New York: Frederick A. Stokes, 1891), 40. For histories of meat-eating, see Maureen Ogle, *In Meat We Trust: An Unexpected History of Carnivore America* (Boston: Houghton Mifflin, 2013) and Roger Horowitz, *Putting Meat on the American Table: Taste, Technology, Transformation* (Baltimore: Johns Hopkins University Press, 2006).
18. Carol J. Adams, *The Sexual Politics of Meat: A Feminist-Vegetarian Critical Theory* (London: Continuum, 2010). See also Jean O'Malley Halley, *The Parallel Lives of Women and Cows: Meat Markets* (New York: Palgrave Macmillan, 2012).
19. Henry Clay Glover, *Diseases of the Dog and How to Feed* (New York: H. Clay Glover, 1897), 4.
20. William Chambers and Robert Chambers, eds., *Chambers's Information for the People* (London: W. & R. Chambers, 1874), 694.
21. Wesley Mills, *The Dog in Health and in Disease* (New York: D. Appleton, 1892), 103.
22. "Paragraphs of Natural and Unnatural History," *Current Literature* 1, no. 4 (1888): 350.
23. *Hertle v. Riddell*, 106 S.W. 282 (1907), Kentucky Court of Appeals, 800.
24. "Dogs and Cats into Soap," *American Soap Journal and Perfume Gazette* 5, no. 10 (1895): 335–36. Some suggested using impounded New York City dogs to feed poultry as well. P. L. Simmonds, *Waste Products and Undeveloped Substances: A Synopsis of Progress Made in Their Economic Utilisation during the Last Quarter of a Century at Home and Abroad* (London: Robert Hardwicke, 1873), 66.
25. Chloë Taylor, "Respect for the (Animal) Dead," in Johnston and Probyn-Rapsey, *Animal Death*, 86.
26. Simmonds, *Waste Products and Undeveloped Substances*, 40; A., "Gone to the Boneyard," *Wallace's Monthly* 18, no. 4 (1892): 261.
27. R. W. Snowden, "The Life after Death," *Street Railway Review* 1 (1891): 560.
28. Snowden, "Life after Death," 561.
29. W. J. Gordon, *The Horse-World of London* (London: Religious Tract Society, 1893), 184.
30. Jack Rag, ed., *Streetology of London* (London: James S. Jodson, 1837), 26.
31. John Styles, "The Knacker's Yard," in *The Animal Creation: Its Claims on Our Humanity* (London: Thomas Ward, 1839), 328.
32. Styles, "Knacker's Yard," 328.
33. A., "Gone to the Boneyard," 268.
34. Simmonds, *Waste Products and Undeveloped Substances*, 40.
35. E. W. Allen, *Experiment Station Record*, vol. 22 (Washington, DC: Government Printing Office, 1910).

Katherine C. Grier explores the history of by-products in pet food in "Provisioning Man's Best Friend: The Early Years of the American Pet Food Industry, 1870–1942," in *Food Chains: From Farmyard to Shopping Cart*, ed. Warren Belasco and Roger Horowitz (Philadelphia: University of Pennsylvania Press, 2009), 132–34. Grier notes that in the twentieth century, as humans used horses less, they turned more to the by-products of other farmed animals.

36. L. B. Zapoleon, *Inedible Animal Fats in the United States* (Stanford: Stanford University Press, 1929), 59.
37. Zapoleon, *Inedible Animal Fats*, 59.
38. H. P. Armsby, "The Food Supply of the Future: A Problem for Agricultural Institutions," *Scientific American Supplement* 69, no. 1792 (1910): 303; Grier, "Provisioning Man's Best Friend," 132.
39. *Oxford English Dictionary Online*, s.v. "cannibal," http://www.oed.com/view/Entry/27102?isAdvanced=false&result=1&rskey=VPL1YW&.
40. Adams, *Sexual Politics of Meat*, 55. See Analía Villagra, "Cannibalism, Consumption, and Kinship in Animal Studies," in *Making Animal Meaning*, ed. Linda Kalof and Georgina M. Montgomery (East Lansing: Michigan State University Press, 2011), 45–56, 49.

Mourning the Mundane
Memorializing Road-Killed Animals in North America

LINDA MONAHAN

I forced myself to look. Turned away from approaching traffic, but visible in profile as my car crawled to a stop was the bloodied face of a fawn. The young deer must have been killed a few days ago as skin was still largely intact, but exposed wounds were black with rot. In that time, tens of thousands of drivers and even more passengers would have passed his or her body. How many noticed? How many had time to take note of the species, possible age, and likely circumstances of the killing? And how many felt compelled to mourn the scene?

While most nonhuman animals remain outside the realm of acceptable human mourning, those that are able to transcend the species barrier typically do so through social ties to a human community. Companion animals, for example, are increasingly mourned in ways traditionally reserved for humans. Farmed animals, on the other hand, are sequestered from the daily lives of most people in North America, making their killings largely invisible and therefore largely unmournable. Animals that have been hit by cars, however, popularly known as "roadkill," seem to constitute a unique class of animal death. As wild species, road-killed animals lack the strong ties to a human community that companion animals—even those hit by cars—can claim.[1] The highly public nature of their killing, however, requires a human response in a way that the invisibility of farmed animal killing forecloses.

The question considered here is whether road-killed animals are permissible subjects of human mourning. Every day, roughly one million animals are killed by vehicles in the United States alone.[2] Bodies of large mammals like deer are usually moved from traffic lanes by state transportation authorities, but they remain visible on shoulders and ditches as they decompose. The majority of animals we routinely kill with our cars, however, are smaller mammals, birds, reptiles, and amphibians whose bodies stay on roadways to be driven over and over to disintegration. With nearly four hundred million animals killed by cars annually, roadkill is the second largest cause of animal death in the United States, behind animals killed for flesh.[3] Despite these figures, road-killed animals remain on the outskirts of acceptable human mourning.

BECOMING ROADKILL

The idea of roadkill is necessarily a twentieth-century invention. The phenomenon of animals being routinely struck and killed by humans in vehicles requires, of course, frequent automobile use and extensive road networks that only began to develop in the United States and Canada at the turn of the century. A historically contingent term, "roadkill" as shorthand for "animals killed by humans in vehicles" requires some unpacking.

In his Marxist examination of roadkill and commodity fetishism, labor studies scholar Dennis Soron explains, "As a human creation, 'road kill' is just as de-animalized as 'beef' and just as open to cultural meanings that are bracketed off from the embodied experience of the suffering animal."[4] For this reason, I use the term "road-killed animals" in place of "roadkill" to emphasize that the way in which these animals die does not exclusively define their relationship to the human community. As individual beings, road-killed animals have full and varied lives independent of the final violence inflicted upon them by humans.

By the late 1930s, this particular vehicular violence had become common enough to warrant a book-length study. James R. Simmons's *Feathers and Fur on the Turnpike* (1938) was the first to examine "automobile-killed animals," a precursor for "roadkill."[5] By rationalizing the presence of dead animal bodies on roadways and presenting knowledge obtained by focused analysis thereof, Simmons's study did more than simply enter road-killed animals into the realm of professional and lay scientific interest. His work translated a relatively recent, disconcerting phenomenon into an identifiable taxonomy of "roadside casualties" over which humans could exercise ontological control through data collection, scientific discourse, and, ultimately, cultural assertion of the inevitability of car-related animal killing.

The rapid expansion of car ownership, road construction, and urban and suburban sprawl that exploded in the postwar years necessarily correlated with an increased frequency of road-killed animals. This heightened visibility prompted the Humane Society of the United States (HSUS) to quantify the problem: in 1960, HSUS released statistics that placed the number of animals killed by cars each day in the United States at one million, a figure that has remained an accurate estimate over forty years later.[6] While the HSUS initiative to count suggests a growing concern for road-killed animals, contemporary cultural developments suggest otherwise.

The escalating rate of car-related animal death was reflected on screen in midcentury cartoons that featured animal characters as humorous victims of car violence. For example, the 1949 Warner Brothers debut of the Road Runner and Wile E. Coyote, *Fast and Furry-ous*, made becoming roadkill the ultimate punch line.[7] In the final scene of the six-minute cartoon, Wile E. Coyote suddenly becomes wide-eyed with fear: an oncoming bus heads directly for him. As the exhaust clears, Wile E.'s body lies completely flattened on the road, straddled by tire tracks. The coyote woozily rises, his face badly injured, and sees the Road Runner taunt him through the window of the bus. In a series driven by creative methods of capture and injury, making car violence the last word in the episode heightens its status as a supremely humorous way to kill animals.

Temporary flattening by automobile became a popular animated event that made the idea of roadkill laughable. Cartoons like this one made the reality of road-killed animals less threatening by denying the permanence of the violence. Unlike the real victims of collisions, Wile E. Coyote could peel himself off the pavement and walk away. Likewise, viewers could release any trace of guilt over the repercussions of American car culture as they fixated on the mutable moment of death and its undoing.

This cartoon-style mockery of road-killed animals resurfaced in popular culture in the mid-1980s. Warner Brothers' cartoon tropes of permasurprise and tire tracks found new expression in 1985, when the *Original Road Kill Cookbook* heralded the beginning of a "road-kill cuisine" and gag-gift enterprise headed by former *Playboy* food and wine columnist Buck Peterson. Peterson's cookbook combines exaggerated cartoon illustrations of road-killed animals with recipes for cooking commonly road-killed species, such as "Pavement Possum," "Windshield Wabbit," and "Hushed Puppies."[8]

While the illustrations work in the same dismissive way as Warner Brothers cartoons, the genre of "road-kill cuisine" employed a new strategy in keeping road-killed animals outside the realm of human concern. By reclaiming road-killed animals as food, Peterson and others insert otherwise superfluous animal killing into the established framework of killing animals for food. Reframing roadside bodies as usable to humans makes road-killed animals a happy consequence of car culture rather than a problem to be solved. Indeed, Peterson goes so far as to provide pointers for acquiring road-killed animals that include intentionally hitting animals. This reframing effectively neutralizes concern for road-killed animals since "meat" is a category of dead animal bodies that the majority of North Americans are not required or encouraged to mourn.

Late twentieth-century cartoons and cookbooks, then, are expressions of a larger speciesist discourse that maintains a hierarchical divide between human and nonhuman animals. Narratives of human dominion and progress, along with the desire to travel further, faster, and more frequently in North American car culture work together to create conditions inhospitable to compassion for road-killed animals.

THE PHENOMENOLOGY OF DRIVING AND THE PRACTICAL LIMITS OF INSTANT GRIEF

Cultural expressions of empathetic disregard for road-killed animals are not the only barrier to their consideration as grievable life.[9] The experience of driving has perhaps even greater influence on people's inability to mourn road-killed animals. Indeed, most people only encounter road-killed animals en route to somewhere else. Assuming that drivers even notice the bodies they routinely pass, time constraints and safety concerns about stopping suddenly alongside busy roadways make expressing feelings of grief simply impractical. The detached and fragmented nature of visually encountering road-killed animals while driving emphasizes the decontextualization of wild animal lives by forcing individuals outside their natural habitat into built environments where humans see them primarily as dead things rather than as living beings.

Road-killed animals, of course, do not spontaneously appear in travel lanes as disfigured corpses. There are identifiable and, often, preventable factors that put animals at risk of being killed on the road. Road ecologists have studied what brings certain animals to the roadside and have long been working toward preventative measures.[10] Wildlife crossings like vegetation-covered bridge overpasses and tunnel- and gully-like underpasses have been proven effective in rerouting the migration behavior of many commonly road-killed species.[11] These measures, however, are far from commonplace in the United States. Lack of political and financial support for mitigation efforts stems from the lack of concern for the fate of other animals in our shared road ecosystem. As this empathy deficit stalls mitigation efforts, failure to prevent animal highway mortality and its accompanying visual evidence hampers the building of empathy that would buoy mitigation efforts in a stagnant feedback loop of perpetual "roadkill."

In the case of road-killed animals, the frequency of drivers' encounters with such violent imagery fosters a culture that is desensitized to the sight. The mundane visibility of bloody, dismembered wildlife on the road naturalizes this automotive violence in the same way that constant imagery of meat products in food advertisements naturalizes the consumption of animal flesh. It is possible, however, for the constant visibility of road-killed animals to disrupt these animals' cultural status as outside the realm of human mourning.

Engaging in a politics of sight surrounding road-killed animals takes up their broken bodies as productive sites of contestation over the legitimacy of human supremacy. As political scientist Timothy Pachirat defines it in his study of industrialized slaughter, politics of sight are "organized, concerted attempts to make visible what is hidden and to breach, literally or figuratively, zones of confinement in order to bring about social and political transformation."[12]

Pachirat understands visuality as a powerful political tool, yet not one that is absolute in its outcomes. A successful politics of sight assumes that illuminating a given issue will result in feelings akin to pity. And yet, in reality, desensitization to violent images is a likely outcome of full transparency.[13] This desensitization is evident when it comes to road-killed animals: mutilated animal bodies have shock value often coded as humorous (as in midcentury cartoons) or daring (as in those brave enough to eat road-killed meat). As we have seen, it is the constant visibility of these dead animals that renders them largely unmournable. How would Pachirat's politics of sight work as an activist tool for an issue like roadkill?

The bodies of road-killed animals are easy to spot. But the value of the individual lives that once filled those bodies remains largely invisible. Road-killed animals require not greater visibility, but rather a new visuality in an activist politics of sight that brings to bear not just the ecological issue of roadkill, but the social issue of entangled animal lives, both human and nonhuman.

CATALYZING CONCERN THROUGH THE STRATEGIC AFFECT OF MOURNING

Recognizing the individual value of road-killed animals is a critical step toward human accountability for their lives and deaths. Mourning is a powerful affect that can translate into concern for road-killed animals in ways that are familiar to humans. Mourning, in contrast to grief, connotes an *expression* of feelings of deep sorrow.[14] By making feelings of sadness and regret visible, audible, or otherwise public, mourning animals who have been violently killed mirrors the highly visible, public nature of road-killed animals. In recent years, road-killed animals have begun to be integrated into larger narratives of subjectivity and interspecies community through activism and art that seek to fit road-killed animals into established human mourning practices.

One example of emergent collective mourning practices is the petitioning of state legislatures to erect highway memorials for mass road kills. People for the Ethical Treatment of Animals (PETA) has petitioned legislatures in nine states and two provinces to erect highway memorials for farmed animals killed in transport.[15] While none of the petitions so far have been approved, PETA's strategy centers on animal-vehicle collisions as an accessible site for activism.

The established mourning practice of erecting roadside memorials for human deaths lends a strong affective corollary for how passersby should react to the deaths of sixteen cows in an automotive accident. Furthermore, the visibility of animal transport crashes breaches the otherwise invisible nature of contemporary slaughter. PETA's memorials would capitalize on this visibility in the same way that the bodies of individual road-killed animals linger long after the initial death.

Despite making their petitions in earnest, PETA was routinely dismissed by citizens who viewed the memorials as pointless, ridiculous, and even offensive to humans.[16] The perceived impossibility and even frivolity of mourning road-killed animals attempts to bolster the same dismissive beliefs toward mourning food-killed animals. In both cases, commenters on news items about PETA's memorials expressed that these animals' deaths were inevitable and, therefore, outside the realm of human accountability. PETA's proposed memorials question this framework for road-killed animals by emphasizing the role of human drivers in animal safety on the road while doing the same for farmed animals by reminding humans that supporters of nonvegan lifestyles, in fact, make active choices to support animal killing for which they can easily be held accountable.

Dead animal bodies on the road serve as violent markers of territory—of who belongs, and who doesn't. The cultural concept of "roadkill" reinforces the notion that certain spaces are meant exclusively for humans by treating as inevitable the deaths of nonhumans in those spaces. Roads, however, are ubiquitous and largely indiscriminate. Their construction bisects nonhuman territory, threatens habitats, and makes migrations difficult and more dangerous. While humans seem to recognize that roads are part of a larger, interspecies environment, we remain unprepared to reckon with the consequences of insisting on our desires above all others'.

How does our conceptualization of "roadkill" further displace accountability for routine violence against road-killed animals? A promising corollary emerges from another space where wild animals enter human territory: zoos. Cultural geographers Chris Wilbert and Chris Philo describe the function of zoos as spaces that "translate wild animals *from* 'the wilderness' *to* the special, enclosed and policed enclaves nearer to our human homes in the city."[17] We might understand the cultural space filled by the concept of "roadkill" as serving the same transitive purpose as zoos. Dismissive, mocking, or grotesque visuality of road-killed animals translates wild fauna from an independent space of "wilderness" to a space marked by humans as "our territory": the road.

The bodies of road-killed animals are visual reminders of the effects of North American car culture. To acknowledge each death would be to take accountability for its cause, a responsibility few are willing to shoulder. Instead, an imaginative referent—"roadkill"—steps in to displace the individual animal in favor of an anonymous aggregate. In this way, the concept of "roadkill" polices the movement of wild animals to "keep out," or else. Those who trespass leave the category of "wild animal" and enter the realm of "roadkill." Witnessing road-killed animals, however, calls our linguistic bluff: the collective "roadkill" is a fantasy in the face of individual animal victims.

In his essay "Apologia," Barry Lopez describes his encounters with individual road-killed animals as moments to take accountability. For Lopez, accountability means pulling over to move the broken bodies from the road. When people ask him why he does this, he explains, "The ones you give some semblance of burial, to whom you offer an apology, may have been like seers in a parallel culture. It is an act of respect, a technique of awareness."[18] With each act of apology, Lopez chips away at the anonymous violence of "roadkill." Awareness of the individual compels him to act, to express his apology through the ritual of burial.

American photographer Emma Kisiel has a similar response to witnessing wildlife mortality on U.S. highways. In her series *At Rest* (2011), Kisiel constructs and photographs makeshift memorials for found road-killed fauna. Kisiel's new visuality of road-killed animals allows us to recognize them as individuals worthy of mourning. The majority of the animals memorialized in *At Rest* are roadkill, but Kisiel's photographs resist the ambivalence of this culturally constructed category of death.

Instead, the subjects of *At Rest* invite us to mourn them. The careful arrangement of objects around each individual animal compels the viewer to recognize the deceased as worthy of mourning. Kisiel's circular memorials of fresh plant matter, imitation flowers, and smooth stones are inescapably tender, foregrounding the suggestion that their construction brought the artist into an intimate relationship with these road-killed animals. This transgression of modern spatial partitioning among human and wild animal, living and dead, translates to recognition of the intimate entanglements of human and nonhuman beings.

Kisiel's impromptu memorials codify these roadside sites as scenes of death by drawing on Euro-American human mourning practices. The stone and flower arrangements, she says, "reference the 17th century Netherlandish and later Spanish tradition of creating flower garlands around sacred objects, like the sacrificial lamb."[19] Her larger body of work, including two other photographic series of deceased animals, draws heavily on the Victorian practice of memento mori that posed dead children and adults for photographic family shrines. By inserting road-killed animals into these established narratives of grief, memory, and sacred honor, Kisiel provides the visual cues for a strong affective connection to otherwise grisly and culturally ignored death scenes.

Kisiel explains the individual attention she gives to each animal that she memorializes: She "never moves or alters her animal subjects. 'They are happened upon, visited with, remembered, and left to return to nature.'"[20] Beyond recognizing a rather uncontroversial ecological connectedness across species, the explicit memorialization depicted in *At Rest* suggests that these wild animals were, in fact, members of society who left behind beings—human and otherwise—who would mourn them.

Rather than pointing to an aggregate class of death known as "roadkill," Kisiel's work challenges the viewer to contemplate each individual death from the affective position of human mourning. In the case of animals who were clearly hit by cars, evidenced by asphalt or telltale fatal injuries, *At Rest* forces us to further acknowledge *human* participation in the killing. Drawing on the affect of mourning and its associated expressions of respect and regret forms a clear path away from the twentieth-century mockery of the lives of road-killed animals.

Kisiel, Lopez, and PETA encourage us to take the time to recognize each road-killed animal we pass. The collective force of these millisecond mournings can have political power: once the affect of care shrouds these animals, we can press for preventative measures such as wildlife crossings and driver education campaigns that value animal life. Alongside creative works of remembrance, these measures will help "roadkill" continue its cultural transformation from laughably grotesque to grievable animal death.

NOTES

1. Companion animals that have been hit by cars are generally set apart from roadkill. The deaths of these animals are more frequently accounted for and mourned.
2. Marcel P. Huijser et al. "Cost-Benefit Analyses of Mitigation Measures Aimed at Reducing Collisions with Large Ungulates in the United States and Canada: A Decision Support Tool," *Ecology and Society* 14, no. 2 (2009): 15.
3. Andreas Seiler and J.-O. Helldin, "Mortality in Wildlife Due to Transportation," in *The Ecology of Transportation: Managing Mobility for the Environment*, ed. John Davenport and Julia L. Davenport (New York: Springer, 2006), 166–68.
4. Dennis Soron, "Road Kill: Commodity Fetishism and Structural Violence," in *Critical Theory and Animal Liberation*, ed. John Sanbonmatsu (New York: Rowman & Littlefield, 2011), 63.
5. James R. Simmons, *Feathers and Fur on the Turnpike* (Boston: Christopher Publishing House, 1938), 26–29.
6. Huijser et al., "Cost-Benefit Analyses," 15.
7. Chuck Jones, dir., *Fast and Furry-ous*, Warner Brothers Cartoons.
8. Buck Peterson, *Original Road Kill Cookbook* (Berkeley: Ten Speed Press, 1985). "Windshield Wabbit" may be an allusion to Elmer Fudd, extending the cultural relevancy of midcentury animated violence toward animals.
9. Judith Butler, *Precarious Life: The Powers of Mourning and Violence* (London: Verso, 2004), xiv–xv. I credit Butler's exploration of the concept of grievable life, but do not engage further due to the emphasis on one species and conflation of the categories of "human" and "subject." Still, the concept already extends to animals in practice: humans grant it to some individuals and species while denying it to many others.
10. Seiler and Helldin, "Mortality in Wildlife."
11. Diana Balmori and David K. Skelly, "Crossing to Sustainability: A Role for Design in Overcoming Road Effects," *Ecological Restoration* 30, no. 4 (2012): 363–67.
12. Timothy Pachirat. *Every Twelve Seconds: Industrialized Slaughter and the Politics of Sight* (New Haven: Yale University Press, 2013), 236.
13. Pachirat, *Every Twelve Seconds*, 255.
14. *Oxford English Dictionary* defines "grief" (n) as "mental pain, distress, or sorrow," whereas "mourning" (n) is "the action of feeling or expressing sorrow, grief, or regret; sorrowing, lamentation; an instance of this."
15. Mike Wiser, "PETA Wants Memorial to Turkeys Killed in Sioux City Crash," *Sioux City Journal*, April 23, 2014.
16. Julie Mann, "PETA Wants Roadside Memorial for Cows," *CBS Chicago Newsradio*, January 20, 2012.
17. Chris Philo and Chris Wilbert, eds., *Animal Spaces, Beastly Places: New Geographies of Human–Animal Relations* (London: Routledge, 2000), 13.
18. Barry Lopez, "Apologia," in *A Road Runs through It: Reviving Wild Places*, ed. Thomas Reed Petersen (Boulder, CO: Johnson Books, 2006), 39.
19. Emma Kisiel, interview, *BLINK* 17, October 2012.
20. Emma Kisiel, "At Rest," *iGNANT*, July 17, 2013.

The Unmourned

LINDA BRANT

What do we do with this problem of anonymity . . .
With the knowledge that like them, we too will one day belong to oblivion?
The animals that interest me are the ones that are the most useful
The most used and the least remembered
The most needed and the least cherished
Anonymous victims of humane and more often inhumane slaughter.
I gather their bones,
Remembering.
I clean their bones,
Absolving.
I sand and polish their bones,
Mourning.
I present their bones,
Honoring.
I am indebted to them
Our shared anonymity unites us.

Linda Brant, *Anonymity*. (Photos courtesy of Linda Brant.)

Linda Brant, *Unmourned*.

Linda Brant, *Cleaning*.

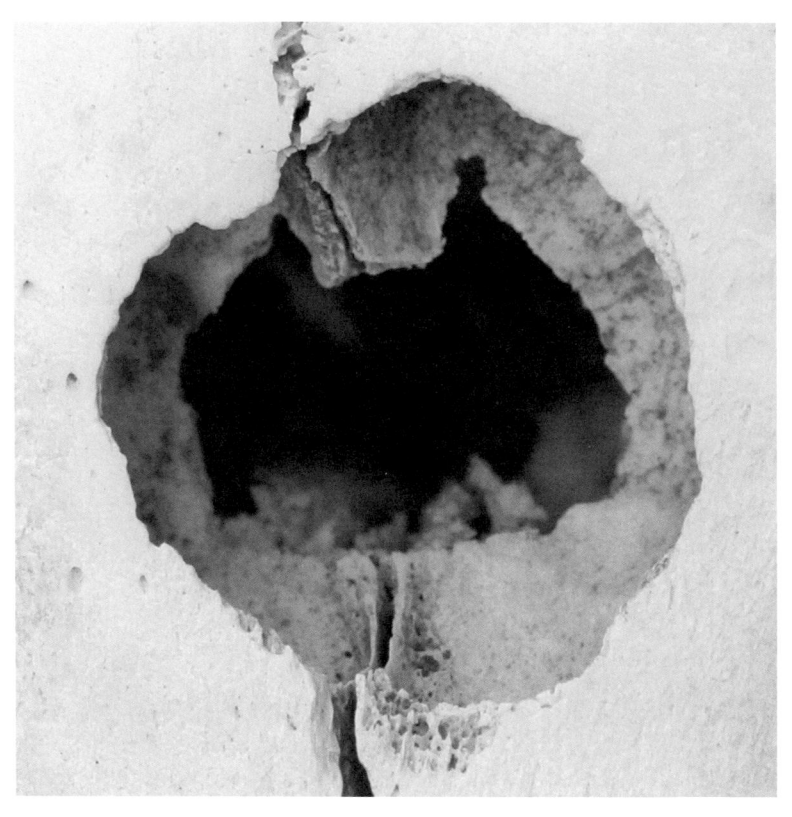

Linda Brant, *Remembering*.

Linda Brant, *Absolving*.

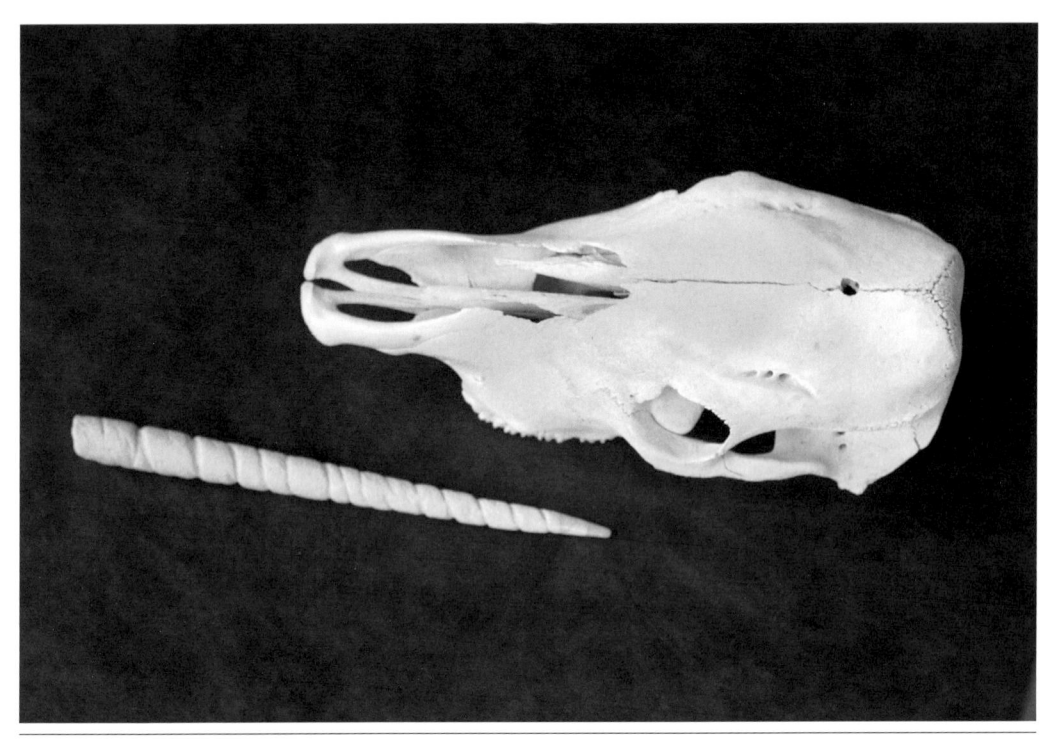

Linda Brant, *Third Eye* (detail).

PART 5

Problems with Coping and Human Responsibility

Beyond Coping
Active Mourning in the Animal Sheltering Community

JESSICA AUSTIN

ANIMAL SHELTER EMPLOYEES FACE EACH DAY WITH THE POSSIBILITY OF INHABITING antithetical roles: the caretaker, charged with ensuring the safety and well-being of the wards in their custody; and the executioner, overseer of these same animals' untimely deaths. With shelter euthanasia estimates reaching three million adoptable animals per year, shelter workers shoulder a considerable burden of grief, resulting in stress and manifesting in depression and even physical complaints, such as sleep disturbance and headaches.[1] While several authors describe coping mechanisms for those whose work involves death, both in general and specifically tailored toward shelter employees, little is written about how shelter workers mourn the animals they euthanize and how grieving for these beings shapes their sense of self. In this review, semistructured interviews with shelter staff explore the myriad emotions that inform shelter workers' outlook on their role in animal death and how personal mourning rituals and practices occur and empower them to continue in their bipolar role as both protector and life-taker.

Stress and its attendant negative effects—mental, emotional, and physical—are well documented among animal shelter workers, especially those who are involved in the euthanasia process. A seminal work in sheltering authored by Reeve, Rogelberg, Spitzmüller, and DiGiacomo describes the psychological strain induced by euthanasia-related duties in animal shelters.[2] The authors conclude that, compared to their counterparts whose job responsibilities do not include euthanasia, individuals involved in the euthanasia process experience substantially more work-related stress and lower job satisfaction. Perhaps more significantly, these individuals also report higher overall stress levels and job-related conflict within their families, reflecting a spillover into their private life and well-being. In the intervening years since Reeve and colleagues' study, this trend has continually been acknowledged, both formally and anecdotally. Shelter employees responsible for euthanasia have reported emotional responses, from unguarded rage to severe depression, and physical effects, such as insomnia and hypertension.[3] Reviews exploring stress in shelter employees do not explore the extent to which these outcomes pervade the general populace for purposes of comparison. However, Bernard Rollin, an internationally prominent veterinary ethicist, argues that individuals involved in euthanasia experience occupational stress differently, a phenomenon he terms moral stress: "It arises from a sense of discord and tension between what one is in fact doing and one's reason for choosing that field, between what one feels one ought to be and what one feels oneself to be, between ideal and reality."[4]

In the animal shelter employee, this stress often manifests in coping mechanisms that involve the technical aspects of euthanasia work or directing one's negative feelings to the belief that some animals are better off euthanized than experiencing any number of unpalatable alternatives, such as living as a stray in an unsafe location or staying with an abusive or negligent guardian.[5] A similar strategy involves redirecting anger at the general public regarding their lack of accountability in caring for pets and inaction to reduce the number of unwanted animals.[6] More extensive emotional strategies reported by many shelter workers include ensuring a healthy level of attachment and detachment, recognizing and venting feelings, and knowing one's limits with regard to the euthanasia process.

Mourning, as distinct from coping, generally occurs concomitant with punctuated instances of traumatic loss; it is therefore prudent to consider the *persistent* nature of occupational stress in the animal shelter employee. For these individuals, loss transpires regularly. While this loss is qualitatively different from the death of a close friend or family member, human or nonhuman, larger societal implications of euthanasia and understanding of one's role in the process may prove just as distressing, requiring examination of emotional processing beyond daily, on-the-job stress management. For purposes of this review, coping refers to "the mental and behavioral changes that people exert to manage specific stressful burdens or circumstances."[7] Likewise, mourning is defined as "responses to loss and grief involving efforts to cope with or manage those experiences and to learn to live with them by incorporating them into ongoing living."[8] Broadly, coping may be thought of as the short-term strategies employed to alleviate workplace stress on a daily basis, while mourning entails reflecting upon one's experiences and reconciling them with one's sense of self. In this view, coping may be perceived as a significant precursor to mourning. Contextually, separating coping from mourning entails examining both the proximate mechanisms that shelter personnel employ in order to continue to fulfill occupational obligations, as well as the ultimate emotional effects of ongoing loss and how they influence understanding of one's beliefs and values.

In considering Rollin's notion of moral stress, of particular interest is the process of meaning-making, the manner by which individuals assess the significance of traumatic scenarios and construct a sense of the implications within their own schemata and understanding of self. Rollin regards the genesis of moral stress residing in dissonance between how one conceives of oneself and one's actions. The ultimate outcome of meaning-making efforts is resolution of this conflict through adjustment of the frameworks through which one conceives the world and makes sense of one's purpose and ambitions.[9] In the context of mourning, emotional resolution of distressing events and their incorporation into the everyday necessarily involves transformation into higher meaning or purpose, or acceptance that, in the words of Janoff-Bulman, "we might not have the ability to prevent misfortune, but we have the freedom to create lives of value."[10]

For animal shelter employees, the source of conflict could originate from the violation of one's sense of purpose in working with homeless pets. Most animal shelter workers likely feel a strong love for nonhuman animals, desiring to care for them and ensure their welfare. These workers demonstrate a strong sense of empathy, constructing the animals in their care as beings worthy of safekeeping, attention, and a home that will provide not only the basic necessities of life, but healthy doses of affection and appreciation.[11] To pursue a career inspired by deep fondness for animals—both in the sense of individuals and collectively—only to participate in destroying them may create a perceived paradox in one's character, generating feelings of guilt and fractured self-worth. An additional chasm may form between the individual's views on society before and after entering shelter work. Employees may find themselves embattled with the public, constructing a wall between themselves and those whose actions, such as surrendering animals for dubious reasons or wishing to adopt an animal in less than ideal circumstances, they loathe. This resistance may, in some cases, create an "us versus them" mentality, forging the path for an effective coping mechanism to alleviate culpability and assign a scapegoat.[12]

Reconciling both internal and external sources of conflict in order to restore a sense of purpose to the world, decency to society, and fulfillment in one's life is the objective of meaning making. In order to describe how this process occurs in animal shelter employees, interviews with six individuals sought to describe the ways that individuals intimately involved with the euthanasia process cope with the routine realities of their occupation, as well as mourn the animals they must euthanize. Utilizing the definitions of coping and mourning outlined above, employees were asked to describe if and how they put each into practice, as well as their role in their organization's euthanasia process; how shelter work aligns with their initial expectations of the profession; the mental, physical, and emotional life changes that they ascribe to their involvement in euthanasia; and what self-transformations they have made or hope to make as a result of the mourning process. Interviewees comprised employees of municipal and non-profit shelters in the United States, in the West Coast, Southwest, Eastern Seaboard, and New England regions. All interviewees perform euthanasia at least occasionally, and all participate in euthanasia decisions or have the final say on each animal's fate. While a sample size of six individuals does not constitute generalizability, some noteworthy themes emerged and provide a starting point for further discussion of this topic.

Unsurprisingly, love for animals was universal among interviewees, with half mentioning animals as a significant childhood presence and influence on their career motivations. Most participants had worked with animals prior to their current position, either in a volunteer capacity or in other animal-related careers, such as veterinary technician and groomer. Despite the seemingly obvious presence of love for animals evident among those who choose this career path, interviewees frequently cited public criticism of shelter employees, operations, and euthanasia as sources of stress. One participant commented that the public could not ascertain "who's the enemy and who's not," and another described her feelings about the public: "[My] respect [for] and ability to trust people has dwindled since working in this field." Euthanasia in particular seems to foster consternation among the public, and even among other animal sheltering employees, both internal to the shelter and from other animal welfare groups. One interviewee, whose shelter provides overflow space for a no-kill rescue, related that she often hears the rescue employees joking about her in a passive-aggressive manner: "Oh, there goes [name redacted]; she likes to kill animals all day." Another interviewee described a memorial event for the shelter's euthanized animals, organized by the volunteer coordinator and open to both employees and volunteers. Staff members were reluctant to participate due to the friction between themselves and volunteers and the certainty of uncomfortable questions about euthanasia arising. Schisms between employees who perform euthanasia and those who do not prompt suggestions to promote consideration between the two groups.[13]

Emotional reactions to performing euthanasia varied among participants with some reporting the ability to compartmentalize the loss, taking a more pragmatic stance: "I've kind of grown a stone heart to it." Others experience a more externalized reaction on a regular basis, and some fall in the middle of the spectrum, with periods of punctuated emotion and detachment: "[I'm] able to convince myself to shield my heart a bit . . . [but] every few months, I sit in the shower and I cry over the injustice of it all." Several interviewees suffer physical effects that they attribute to participating in the euthanasia process, such as high blood pressure, excessive sleep, nightmares, and weight gain. Other effects reported include the inability to fully focus on family life, fixations on animals, and feeling a sense of guilt and regret over certain euthanasia cases.

Interviewees reported a vast range of mechanisms they employ in order to cope with the challenges that they encounter as a result of involvement with euthanasia. Many of these strategies occur at the workplace and involve not just the interviewee, but his or her coworkers. Most participants discussed the importance of having open dialogue with colleagues, accompanied by knowledge of each person's comfort level with the process. For example, one interviewee referred to her known discomfort with bagging animals after euthanasia, a procedure that other employees will complete in her stead. Several participants referred to institutional policies requiring employee rotation on euthanasia duty, the ability to remove an animal from the euthanasia list, and the capacity to switch out with other team members on cases involving, for example, an animal with whom the individual has forged a close relationship. Fellow euthanasia technicians are important players in other coping mechanisms, viewed as carrying the same burden as interviewees, and therefore able to understand their difficulties. Colleagues serve as sounding boards and sympathizers, as well as conversational partners about the mundane, such as movies or weekend plans, in order to maintain a sense of normalcy. Practices such as announcing adoptions over the public address system and matching found animals with advertisements on Internet bulletin boards help individuals maintain a focus on the positive aspects of the organization. Several interviewees reported finding solace in their own animals—either bringing them to the workplace to seek comfort while at work, or as a safe space at home, an animal for whom they are fully accountable and don't suffer anxiety about a bleak or unjust outcome.

When asked if they mourn, reactions among interviewees were mixed. Two individuals reported that they employ coping strategies, but that they do not extend to mourning. Two individuals replied that they do mourn the animals they euthanize, while two reported that they mourn only certain cases. The two individuals who feel they cope rather than mourn related that they are able to accept that euthanasia is part of their job and maintain a more matter-of-fact, detached view. These individuals both explained that they are able to take a more objective stance as they truly believe they are making the correct decisions, particularly in regard to public safety, in the case of animals with behavioral or aggression issues, and to suffering, for animals with terminal health conditions. Individuals who reported mourning for some animals spoke in terms of animals who particularly touched their hearts, either because they had worked with them extensively or because they regretted the euthanasia decision. For example, one respondent spoke of a decision she had made to euthanize a dog solely on the basis of the dog having entered the shelter pregnant. She later dreamed of the dog's predicament, with the dog speaking directly to her about the injustice of the verdict. Another reported mourning the dogs with whom he personally works, but not necessarily the animals with whom he is uninvolved.

Mourning for euthanized shelter animals takes many forms, most of which involve meaning making but some of which take ritual form. In keeping with the view of animals as individuals, one participant explained her routine of listening to each animal's heartbeat as the euthanasia drugs begin to take effect. The drugs produce a distinct response and pattern in each animal's heart rhythm, which she likens to music and the symbolic character of Native American drumming, diminishing the purely clinical atmosphere. In terms of meaning making, interviewees expressed a strong desire to direct their mourning to efforts at improving social conditions for animals and reducing the need for shelter euthanasia. One individual described her efforts both at her job and in her outside interactions to educate the public about conscientious animal care, a mission she has passed on to her children, expressing that she wants them to "put out into the world and community that responsibility with animals is important." Similarly, another participant explained her view of the process as fostering a sense of empathy and compassion, not just within herself, but as a lesson she can pay forward, such as when she teaches compassion fatigue workshops.[14] Some interviewees have recognized changes within themselves. One participant noted the significance of self-appraisal in one's outlook regarding the euthanasia process, a journey that led her to conclude, "While I still need to protect my heart, I don't need to stone it off so that nothing can get to it." After volunteering at a shelter with a very high euthanasia rate, one participant pursued a vegan lifestyle in order to promulgate her own sense of "most good, least harm." Another turns his mourning toward improving his professional skills, evaluating the cases of the animals that he mourns and applying lessons from each case to refine his approach to increasing adoptability.

In an occupation that one interviewee described as "a moderately terrible field to work in," it is hardly shocking that individuals who consider themselves mourners make meaning not just in ways that benefit their own views of self and society, but in ways that they hope will benefit animals. Bridging the perceived disparity between loving animals and taking part in euthanasia manifests in mourning practices that reach far beyond workplace coping mechanisms. Reconciled views of self and society are affected in long-term mourning strategies that typify the motivations and empathetic stances of shelter employees when choosing to enter the profession. Using the reinforced sense of purpose that mourning for homeless, ill, or unadoptable animals generates toward fostering compassion, these employees are able to partially neutralize some of the most emotionally demanding and unpleasant aspects of their occupation.

Though mourning is a highly personal process—typically explored on a solitary basis, as opposed to coping, which often involves coworkers and the work environment—pointing employees to resources to help them process grief may benefit the individual as they struggle to adjust to the reality of their occupation. While shelters sometimes have procedures in place to address compassion fatigue, the existence of these programs is hardly ubiquitous and sometimes amounts to little more than referral to a broker assigned to coordinate mental health benefits. While the interviewees in this study did not universally agree that they mourned for the animals they euthanized, most mourned at least some of the time. Ignoring the possibility of mourning does a disservice to these individuals and perhaps quashes some of the benefits to be realized both to employees and to the animals whom they may advocate for even more strongly through forging a new sense of purpose. The unique issues faced by animal caretakers—including active euthanasia of their charges, sometimes out of consideration of terminal health conditions, but often for less compassionate reasons—may benefit from specialized intervention by those trained in veterinary social work, a discipline created to address the emotional and psychosocial challenges of veterinary medicine, including compassion fatigue.[15] These individuals can point employees in the direction of not just coping mechanisms, but the process of meaning making and resolving the dissonance created by self-identification as both a friend to animals and their executioner, redefining their impressions of themselves, their future aspirations, and their life's purpose.

NOTES

1. "Pets by the Numbers," Humane Society of the United States, January 30, 2014.
2. Charlie L. Reeve et al., "The Caring-Killing Paradox: Euthanasia-Related Strain among Animal-Shelter Workers," *Journal of Applied Social Psychology* 35, no. 1 (2005): 119–43.
3. Debra J. White and Ruth Shawhan, "Emotional Responses of Animal Shelter Workers to Euthanasia," *Journal of the American Veterinary Medical Association* 208, no. 6 (1996): 846–49.
4. Bernard Rollin, "Euthanasia and Moral Stress," in *Suffering: Psychological and Social Aspects in Loss, Grief, and Care*, ed. Robert DeBellis et al. (London: Routledge, 2014), 119.
5. Benjamin E. Baran et al., "Euthanasia-Related Strain and Coping Strategies in Animal Shelter Employees," *Journal of the American Veterinary Medical Association* 235, no. 1 (2009): 83–88.
6. Reeve et al., "The Caring-Killing Paradox."
7. Baran et al., "Euthanasia-Related Strain and Coping Strategies," 84.
8. Charles A. Corr, Clyde M. Nabe, and Donna M. Corr, *Death and Dying, Life and Living*, 6th ed. (Belmont: Wadsworth, 2009), 249.
9. Crystal L. Park, "Making Sense of the Meaning Literature: An Integrative Review of Meaning Making and Its Effects on Adjustment to Stressful Life Events," *Psychological Bulletin* 136, no. 2 (2010): 257–301.
10. Ronnie Janoff-Bulman, "Posttraumatic Growth: Three Explanatory Models," *Psychological Inquiry* 15 (2004): 33.
11. See, for instance, Nik Taylor, "Animal Shelter Emotion Management: A Case of in situ Hegemonic Resistance?," *Sociology* 44, no. 1 (2010): 85–101.
12. Taylor, "Animal Shelter Emotion Management."
13. Steven G. Rogelberg et al., "What Shelters Can Do about Euthanasia-Related Stress: An Examination of Recommendations from Those on the Front Line," *Journal of Applied Animal Welfare Science* 10, no. 4 (2007): 331–47.
14. Compassion fatigue, or secondary traumatic stress, is a collection of psychological and physical symptoms experienced as a result of emotional identification with and empathy for one's charges or patients. See, for instance, Lila Miller and Stephen Zawistowski, *Shelter Medicine for Veterinarians and Staff*, 2nd ed. (Hoboken: Wiley-Blackwell, 2013), 470–71.
15. "Veterinary Social Work Certificate Program," University of Tennessee, Knoxville, http://www.csw.utk.edu/certificates/vsw.htm.

Mourning for Animals
A Companion Animal Veterinarian's Perspective

ANNE FAWCETT

I ALWAYS WANTED TO WORK WITH ANIMALS, BUT THE EUTHANASIA OF OUR FIFTEEN-year-old cat when I was fourteen catalyzed that ambition. My grief and sense of helplessness were overwhelming. I can still feel tears stinging my cheeks as I walked into school knowing that the cat I grew up with was being taken to the vet to be "put to sleep" and I could do nothing to save her.

Back then I questioned the judgment of my parents and our veterinarian in the end-of-life decision making. I believed I would have made different decisions.

Fast forward twenty years and I am a veterinarian, and I find myself—regularly—in the position of our family vet back then: counseling clients about euthanasia, explaining in some cases that every option has been explored and there is nothing we can do, comforting them about the loss of their pet.

The veterinary degree does not, as I believed in childhood, confer a God-like ability to save every animal. Veterinarians are inevitably witnesses to the grief and mourning of owners for their companion animals for many reasons—trauma, chronic illness, economic circumstances, and of course old age.[1]

The shorter life span of our patients and our ability to perform euthanasia means we're exposed to death more frequently than our medical counterparts. For example, where general medical practitioners have around twenty patients dying annually, companion animal first-opinion practitioners encounter at least ninety to one hundred patient deaths annually.[2] Yet only a sliver of time—around fifteen hours in the United States and twenty-one hours in the UK—in the veterinary curriculum is devoted to death, dying, and bereavement.[3]

That time is largely focused on learning the established phases of grief and what to do and say at the time of euthanasia. It gives the impression that grief is a finite, compartmentalized, linear progression of emotions that, if expressed in a healthy way, is followed by recovery to one's former self. If this happens, it is atypical. Grief is complicated, messy, and powerful enough to change lives. It may appear well before the loss of an animal (anticipatory grief) or months after. It might be behind the declaration that some make to "never get an animal again" or the decision to adopt a new puppy. It might influence someone's career choice.

As a veterinarian I have observed how grief and mourning around companion animal loss are different (and similar) to mourning for people, what we know about the extent of grief beyond the consulting room, and the impact of grief and mourning on the veterinary team.

IS MOURNING FOR COMPANION ANIMALS DIFFERENT FROM MOURNING FOR PEOPLE?

Our relationship with companion animals, at least in Western society, is widely understood through the lens of attachment theory—in short, our relationships with pets fulfill similar needs to some close human relationships.[4] In this sense, the grief may be similar.

In a survey of 242 heterosexual couples, men rated pet loss as about as stressful as losing a close friendship, while women rated it as about as stressful as losing touch with their married children.[5]

Many people describe the impact of losing a pet in terms of losing a family member.

"Seriously it was like losing a member of our family, which he was totally. I keep saying to my daughter and husband I think we need group counseling as I don't think we will ever get over the loss." —Michelle

"At the time, I was going through an IVF cycle. My IVF attempt was successful for only a few weeks. That was incredibly hard, but losing Heidi affected me tenfold." —Anonymous[6]

But grief for companion animals has been described as a type of disenfranchised grief—not unlike that experienced in cases of perinatal death or abortion—because the relationship with the companion animal is not sufficiently recognized by others.[7] Unlike people, pet loss is not commonly publicly mourned, depriving those grieving animal death of vital social support.

One study found that more than half of those who had recently lost a pet reported that they felt society did not view the loss of a pet as worthy of grief.[8] Numerous clients have confided similar concerns.

Owners of pocket or exotic pets may feel even more so as fewer vets treat these species and others may not appreciate the strength of the human–animal bond.

"A lot of people just don't understand and look at me as though I'm crazy because 'he was JUST a rabbit.' Well he was everything to me and I suffered so much through all of times of illness and the way he had to die. Nina lived inside with me for four years and we were very closely bonded. Not many people understood the bond—particularly, most of the vets I saw." —Taylor

There can be a tendency for veterinarians to construct the human–animal bond as an unhealthy substitute for social contact that may otherwise inoculate owners to pet loss.

"Many elderly people don't have a wide spectrum of interests, or circle of family and friends and tend to focus on their pets. It is far healthier to have a variety of life factors and if not then a loss of a loved pet is really devastating." —Anonymous (veterinarian)

However, vets can play an important role in normalizing and validating grief.

"I asked if my eldest son could come in to say goodbye, so I then drove home to collect him (nineteen-year-old) and he immediately came to the vet's to hug Maggie and say goodbye. We were not rushed, even though I was aware of other clients arriving with their pets. The vet was very empathetic, and commented how sad it was to lose Maggie. He had treated her all her life, and he knew she was loved by her family. This vet had lost a child when she was six, so has good insight into grief and its consequences." —Julia

Colleagues, friends, and family may do the same.

"I cried for a couple of days. . . . At first I tried to tough it out and go back to work, man-style, but a workmate spotted me looking a bit lost at my desk, and we had a talk. He'd lost dogs too; he understood. He talked to our boss for me, who was also very understanding and advised me to take a bit of time off." —Mark

In the case of animals that are euthanized, grief may be complicated by guilt. Of those clients who had chosen to euthanize their pet because it was the most humane option, approximately half questioned whether it was the right decision, and 16 percent stated that they felt "like a murderer."[9] The latter finding was a shock to me and highlights the need for more open, frank discussion prior to and post euthanasia.

"The vet can assist here by starting the conversation early to assist pet owners to prepare their minds. I understand that not all pet owners may be able to come to this realization and confirmation within themselves before euthanasia. Where it is possible, it will help the pet owners to avoid feelings of resentment afterwards. (Despite everything there is a small primitive cell in my mind that in some moments saw the vet in the way a child sees the old 'Dog Catcher'—mean, heartless, taking my dog away. I found this very strange to experience. I guess almost like reverting to childhood as a result of my grief.)" —Erin

The death of an animal can catalyze mourning for other loss.[10] Clients often discuss loss of family members at the time of euthanasia. A number have said that mourning for an animal is *easier* than mourning for a person.

In talking to clients about this, my impression is that while in general people have mixed feelings about people they have relationships with, their feelings about animals are very different. In many cases, the bond truly is unconditional.

"I think their loss is felt so keenly because with animals often there is a freedom to be who you are without any expectations or complications. I think the relationship is a lot less complex [than relationships with people], and that people often feel acceptance from animals that they don't get from their human relationships." —Adele (chaplain at the Lort Smith Animal Hospital)

In many ways, the bond between companion animal and owner is *closer* than the bond with other humans. For many, their pet is present more than a partner or family member— I've not met anyone who consistently walks with their partner twice a day or spends every single night sleeping beside them, but many do this with companion animals. Days may be bracketed by the animal's morning and evening routine—eating, toileting, getting ready for sleep. Companion animals are a constant in people's lives, often in the background but ever present.[11]

Of course, there are some clients who feel relief when a pet dies. Particularly in situations where an animal has been unwell for some time, there can be a sense of a burden lifted. It may be the first time for a while they feel that they can go away, or at least not return home to the dread that their pet may have passed away in their absence or that this may be the day to make that final decision.

As a veterinarian I have found it impossible to construct a blanket approach to grief, but I do see my role as one of normalization and validation.

GRIEF AND MOURNING BEYOND THE CONSULTATION ROOM

Mourning may begin in the veterinary clinic in some instances, but it doesn't end there. Clients face the difficult prospect of leaving the clinic, sometimes for the first time, without their pet. In a Canadian study involving 177 clients across fourteen practices, more than half said it was one of the most difficult things they had to do.[12]

That degree of grief experienced by owners remained reasonably consistent for around six weeks after the death of a pet. This trend is not unique. A study of 106 pet owners found that subclinical levels of grief and sadness lasted for six months or more in 30 percent of people following the loss of a pet, with 4.3 percent experiencing complicated grief.[13]

Owners may join grief support networks weeks, even months, after losing a pet.[14]

> "At the three-week post euthanasia mark, grief definitely felt different. In some ways it felt harder. Perhaps it is because the realization that the lost pet isn't coming back starts to hit home." —Erin

For some it is too much.

> "After losing Libby I would never get another dog. I am too old; it's too hard to cope with the loss; I could not bear it again." —Anonymous

Some owners grieve the loss of their relationship to the veterinary team, particularly those whose animal required frequent visits or hospitalization. Clients sometimes state that they will miss the vets and nurses almost as much as they will miss their pet.

Almost all owners surveyed believed that their veterinarian should provide emotional support before and after their pet's death, yet under 40 percent had the opportunity to communicate with their vet following the death of the animal.[15] That may be due to the busy nature of practice, or veterinarians feeling that their role is over once the animal dies. It could stem from a general discomfort around grief, which can challenge our self-image as "problem solvers."

> "Grief isn't fixable in the way a broken leg is. Grief is often very confronting, it can be very disturbing and you may not want to be there. The instinct can be to get out of the way, but if you can stay present it helps, because people need most to feel that their grief is allowed and accepted." —Adele

It is also a time when clients need us most, and small gestures can provide comfort. After having his German shepherd Pixie euthanized, Mark received a card from his vet.

> "In part he'd written 'Thank God for owners who love their pets as much as you.' I took that to mean that not only had I cared for Pixie and given her a good life, but it was right to end her pain

as peacefully as possible, and that the hurt I was feeling was part of that love, so in a strange sort of way it was a good thing. . . . I still have that card, nearly twenty years on."

Understanding the way people mourn their pets may aid our understanding of grief, afford us some closure, and provide insights that could assist other clients.

"It was not long after we brought the ashes home that my husband and I realized we did not want to part with the ashes or scatter them after all. They had become so precious to us now. All that we had left of her was in that box. It felt like she was still with us in a strange way. I was so shocked to be feeling all this." —Erin

"We brought a terracotta pot and a small plaque engraved for it and then put her ashes in the pot and planted a beautiful double yellow rose called 'Happy Child,' which she was. We are glad we did this, as we later moved. . . . Bronte's pot, ashes, and rose bush both traveled with us on all these moves and never stops flowering." —Joyce

THE IMPACT OF GRIEF AND MOURNING ON VETERINARIANS

"This must be the hardest part of your job" is a comment I frequently hear from clients during euthanasia. It can be.

In end-of-life decision making we are expected to offer a prognosis and provide an assessment of that animal's quality of life—one of the most difficult tasks in human medicine.[16] We may ourselves have formed an attachment to the patient and experience our own grief.

In the case of euthanasia, the veterinarian has the dual role of attending to both the suffering animal and the grieving client.[17] Where euthanasia is performed, the veterinarian may be distracted (rightly so) by technical considerations to ensure that a swift, humane, painless death is achieved.

"In many respects veterinarians and members of their team are actors whose job it is to stage a performance for their audience (the clients and sometimes their friends and family). As with any performance, the concern is likely to be with whether the show comes off or falls flat. Performances are considered successful when the audience perceives the death of the animal to be peaceful and painless and interprets the actions of the veterinarian to be competent, sincere, dignified and respectful."[18]

To some degree this is borne out by my experience, although I'm not sure the performance is so consciously contrived. But there is undoubtedly some comfort in being able to focus on the technical aspects—that in itself is a coping mechanism.

"I have found over the years that I have become in some ways insulated from the grief that I see, and I think this is a necessary reaction to avoid mirroring the very real emotional turmoil that our clients are experiencing and we are witnessing. Without distracting myself I would not be able to provide the professionalism and solemnity that the situation deserves." —Jenna

A veterinarian who describes herself as "a Jewish woman who doesn't believe in euthanasia" describes a "euthanasia process."

> "For me the grieving process starts when I acknowledge that the animal will not be able to pursue further treatment and the consequence of living is causing unnecessary suffering (this could be due to multiple factors—either animal, situational, or client related). I always acknowledge the life of the animal under its owner's care and refer to the lifespans of wild or homeless domestic animals and the reasons why they die, and this makes us all feel good that a life under our care is better than the alternative.
>
> "I always thank the animal for the companionship it has given the owner and for their life. And I always ask the owner if they are okay to drive, and I wish them a long life and good health (which is a Jewish tradition)."

During euthanasia, veterinarians, nurses, and technicians are expected to maintain a professional front. This is the "emotional labor"—documented in other professions from prostitutes to physicians—of suppressing our own anger, sadness, frustration, and so on to maintain the desired impression for clients.[19]

But time and again owners reported feeling great comfort when they caught a glimpse behind the facade.

> "We were totally devastated, our pets are our children and the grief was immense. We were crying, and the vet and her assistant were teary, too." —Joyce
>
> "I was crying uncontrollably, and the vet and her assistant started to cry uncontrollably also. It was the longest journey for all of us." —Taylor

In some ways I feel that veterinarians mourn vicariously through owners and benefit also from witnessing an outpouring of grief that we may internalize.

> "Certainly just listening to pet owners sharing their story of their pet's life assists the grieving process particularly for the owner but also for the vet." —Jan

However, more than one colleague has argued that dealing with grief and mourning on a regular basis does not necessarily equip veterinarians to deal with their own grief.

> "The decision to euthanize my unwell cat was easy; the grief and mourning process was not." —Anonymous

She was so distraught that she waited until others had left the clinic before sedating and euthanizing the cat and was unable to tell anyone else in the hospital for several days.

> "I think as professionals we do have a greater understanding of the mourning process and the different stages of grief associated with it, but that doesn't necessarily reduce how long we grieve or mourn for." —Anonymous

A study of medical oncologists found a lack of consistent strategies in coping with patient loss, with many feeling ill-equipped to manage their own grief.[20] The authors suggested that participating in bereavement rituals, making a phone call, or sending a condolence card may benefit not only the family of the patient but the oncologist. The same may apply for veterinarians.

CONCLUSION

Pet owners and indeed veterinarians may mourn for animals as they may for people—or they may not. Vets play a key role in normalizing and validating this grief and enabling clients to mourn. The extent to which clients grieve the loss of connection to the veterinary team requires further exploration. Veterinarians may only witness the tip of the iceberg when it comes to client grief, and an understanding of the potential extent of grief may enable veterinarians to counsel clients better. Developing protocols for coping with and mourning patient loss may improve bereavement care for pet owners as well as veterinarians.

NOTES

Thanks to Adele Mapperson, Jan Allen, Andrea Harvey, Felicity Spicer, Ilana Mendels, Jenna Moss-Davis, Di Johnstone, Erin Williams, Mark Goddard, Taylor Galbraith, Julia Mandziy, Joyce and Karl Webb, Michelle Ansen, Anne Douglass, Heather and Chrissie Apthorpe, Draga Dubaich, Susan Matthew, and those who requested not to be named.

1. For the purpose of this discussion, I take grief to refer to a subjective feeling of loss. Mourning, in contrast, is the behavioral, outward, or public expression of that grief. In this essay I will use the conventional term "owner," although other terms such as "guardian" may be substituted.
2. George E. Dickinson, Paul D. Roof, and Karin W. Roof, "A Survey of Veterinarians in the U.S.: Euthanasia and Other End-of-Life Issues," *Anthrozoös* 24, no. 2 (2011): 167–74; C. Hewson, "Grief for Pets Part 1: Overview and Update from the Literature," *Veterinary Ireland Journal* 4, no. 7 (2014): 380–85.
3. George E. Dickinson, Paul D. Roof, and Karin W. Roof, "End-of-Life Issues in United States Veterinary Medicine Schools," *Society & Animals* 18, no. 2 (2010): 152–62; G. E. Dickinson and E. S. Paul, "UK Veterinary Schools: Emphasis on End-of-Life Issues," *Veterinary Record* 174, no. 7 (2014). doi: 10.1136/vr.102152.
4. Hewson, "Grief for Pets Part 1."
5. M. Geraldine Gage and Ralph Holcomb, "Couples' Perception of Stressfulness of Death of the Family Pet," *Family Relations* 40, no. 1 (1991): 103–5.
6. Unless otherwise specified, the quotes come from a series of interviews conducted in 2014 by the author.
7. Kenneth J. Doka, *Disenfranchised Grief: Recognizing Hidden Sorrow* (Lexington, MA: Lexington Books, 1989).
8. Cindy L. Adams, Brenda N. Bonnett, and Alan H. Meek, "Predictors of Owner Response to Companion Animal Death in 177 Clients from 14 Practices in Ontario," *Journal of the American Veterinary Medical Association* 217, no. 9 (2000): 1303–9.

9. Adams, Bonnett, and Meek, "Predictors of Owner Response," 1305.
10. Hewson, "Grief for Pets Part 1."
11. In fact it would be very interesting to quantify the amount of time that people spend in the presence of a companion animal compared to that of their closest human companions. I suspect that an increasing number of owners would spend far more time in the presence of their animal than, for example, in the presence of their spouse over the course of a marriage in the same amount of years.
12. Adams, Bonnett, and Meek, "Predictors of Owner Response."
13. Julie A. Luiz Adrian, Aimee N. Deliramich, and B. Christopher Frueh, "Complicated Grief and Posttraumatic Stress Disorder in Humans' Response to the Death of Pets/Animals," *Bulletin of the Menninger Clinic* 73, no. 3 (2009): 176–87.
14. Adele Mapperson, personal communication with the author, 2014.
15. Adams, Bonnett, and Meek, "Predictors of Owner Response."
16. Bruce Fogle and David Abrahamson, "Pet Loss: A Survey of the Attitudes and Feelings of Practicing Veterinarians," *Anthrozoös* 3, no. 3 (1990): 143–50.
17. Dickinson, Roof, and Roof, "A Survey of Veterinarians in the U.S."
18. Patricia Morris, *Blue Juice: Euthanasia in Veterinary Medicine* (Philadelphia: Temple University Press, 2012), 51.
19. Morris, *Blue Juice*.
20. Leeat Granek et al., "Oncologists' Protocol and Coping Strategies in Dealing with Patient Loss," *Death Studies* 37, no. 10 (2013): 937–52.

You're My Sanctuary
Grief, Vulnerability, and Unexpected Secondary Losses for Animal Advocates Mourning a Companion Animal

NICOLE R. PALLOTTA

IT IS NOW WELL DOCUMENTED THAT THE LOSS OF A CHERISHED COMPANION ANIMAL can be as devastating, if not more so, than the loss of an important human relationship.[1] People can experience profound grief over the loss of a beloved animal.[2]

The societal acceptance of companion animals as legitimate objects of grief has become more widespread alongside other cultural trends that have elevated the status of dogs and cats in society, including the rising number of homes that include one or more companion animals and the shifting definition of those companion animals as family members. These trends have led to an increased awareness of companion animal welfare issues and enhanced legal protections for this relatively protected class of animals.[3] In addition, the social construction of animals as family members has led to greater acknowledgement of the strong bond that can be forged with an animal, and the resulting loss upon the animal's death.

This increased recognition of the potential importance of the relationship with a special pet is a relatively recent phenomenon, however, and pet loss can still lead to experiences of "disenfranchised grief," in which the emotions associated with the loss are not recognized by society as legitimate (embodied in the phrase "it's just an animal"). When a loss "is not or cannot be openly acknowledged, publicly mourned, or socially supported," there may be additional difficulties resolving grief.[4]

PRIMARY VERSUS SECONDARY LOSS

In addition to the primary loss, the bereaved may experience secondary losses that result from the death, such as loss of identity, social support, faith, confidence, or dreams for the future. Secondary losses can be as disorienting as the primary loss.[5]

The secondary losses experienced by an individual will be unique to their particular relationship with the loved one, personality and life situation, and other factors. But those who lose a cherished animal typically experience the loss of a dependable source of unconditional emotional support and more quotidian, yet still disruptive, changes, such as the loss of daily routine involved in caring for the animal.[6]

For the growing number of Americans whose pets are like family, the animal is woven into the fabric of daily life. Besides a constant presence and source of routine and stability, pets provide companionship, the perception of unconditional love, and emotional support to their human caregivers.

EMOTIONAL SUPPORT BENEFITS OF THE HUMAN–ANIMAL BOND

There is a growing body of research that demonstrates the mental, physical, and social benefits of living with a companion animal.[7] A bond with a special pet can provide emotional support, comfort, stability, and even therapy for individuals with a mental illness.

The potential psychological benefits of companion animals are now recognized in the mental health community and even legally protected in the case of "emotional support animals" (ESAs), who are prescribed by a physician to provide therapeutic benefit to an individual with a psychiatric disorder.[8] To receive protection under federal law a person must have a verifiable mental disability and a note from a medical professional, but notably, the animal needs no specific training to receive the designation of ESA, indicating that the mere presence of the animal can alleviate or mitigate certain psychological symptoms and mental distress.

Although the lack of a training requirement for ESAs has led to inconsistent court decisions with regard to legal protection and access issues for owners of ESA animals,[9] it is a rather remarkable testament to the therapeutic benefit animals can provide, just by "being there."

This effect is also seen in the arena of animal-assisted therapy, which uses the presence of animals as treatment in a variety of settings, including hospitals, nursing homes, mental institutions, and prisons. More recently, therapy or "facility" dogs are being used in courtrooms to comfort victims during their testimony, especially children in abuse cases.[10]

These therapeutic benefits are not limited to those with a mental illness; the presence of an animal companion can assuage feelings of anxiety and depression even among individuals who do not have a diagnosed psychiatric disability and can contribute to overall well-being generally, not just in therapeutic settings.

MOURNING THE UNMOURNABLE

For animal protection advocates, a strong bond with a companion animal may serve an additional, latent function: psychological buffer. For those who are heavily involved in animal advocacy work, companion animals can function as a psychological shield between themselves and the traumatic knowledge that constantly filters in on a daily basis about the multitude of other animals they cannot save.

Traumatic knowledge refers to learning the often gruesome facts about what routinely happens to animals used in society for food, research and product testing, clothing, and entertainment, as well as the perils faced by homeless pets and wild animals who are hunted and trapped. While abuse and neglect of pets in private homes is also an issue—and increasingly being recognized as a legitimate social problem, in part because of its link to violence against humans, including child abuse and intimate partner abuse[11]—animals defined as pets are at least nominally protected under criminal anticruelty laws.[12]

This is not the case for animals in institutional settings like research labs and farms.[13] For example, farmed animals and/or agricultural practices are specifically excluded from most state anticruelty laws, and there are no federal laws regulating their treatment on the farms where they spend the majority of their short lives. The two federal laws that apply to farmed animals only address transport (the Twenty-Eight Hour Law) and slaughter (the Humane Methods of Livestock Slaughter Act), and both exclude birds, who are 95 percent of the land animals killed for food in the United States.[14] The other main federal law that applies to animals, the Animal Welfare Act (AWA), regulates treatment of captive animals in certain facilities, such as research labs and zoos, but excludes farms. The AWA also specifically excludes birds, rats, and mice, who comprise 95 percent of the animals used in research. Therefore most animals used by humans are excluded from protection under the AWA.

Not only is there a dearth of laws that provide meaningful protections for animals, but in the cases where laws do exist, lack of enforcement provides another frustrating obstacle for advocates seeking justice for abused animals. Animals' strict definition as property under the law provides yet another barrier to advocating for them through the legal system.[15]

Awareness of not only the large-scale violence suffered by animals in these institutional settings, but also the lack of laws protecting them can induce a feeling of helplessness, even despair, with regard to being able to intervene to stop the abuse.[16] Further, witnessing and reporting violence against animals in a socially dismissive context where that violence is not acknowledged can result in the development of post-traumatic stress symptoms.[17]

While grief over the loss of a pet has undergone increasing social legitimization, farmed animals and other categories of animals who are socially constructed as commodities to be exploited, as opposed to "friends" or "family members," are culturally invisible as individuals (except in highly unique situations like sanctuaries), and to mourn them is to experience profound alienation from the mainstream culture and dominant social norms. The lack of a socially sanctioned outlet for mourning the billions of animals who remain hidden in the machinery of society, kept deliberately out of sight, can produce the kind of disenfranchised grief referenced above, which results from a loss that cannot be openly acknowledged.[18] Despite the invisibility of these hidden victims to the culture at large, animal advocates see them, and the suffering and abuse they have witnessed cannot easily be "unseen"; indeed, it may haunt them.[19]

A deep connection with an animal companion can serve as a psychological buffer against the despair that can be induced not only by the knowledge of how animals are hurt, exploited, and killed as part of the normal operations of society, but also by the absence of cultural support for these emotions, including a lack of social rituals validating feelings of grief for animals deemed "ungrievable." Although these feelings of grief are not connected to the loss of a specific animal with whom one shares a life, some qualities are similar, for example, feelings of helplessness and lack of control with regard to preventing the death.

Losing a cherished pet can induce not only feelings of depression over the loss of that animal and one's particular relationship with him or her, but also over the countless animals suffering and dying every minute of every day in slaughterhouses and other sites of animal exploitation. Animal advocates may have been aware of these other animal deaths, but losing a beloved pet can compromise their coping mechanisms in a way that complicates their grief experience.[20] With this one precious relationship gone—the individual animal whose happiness was in the bereaved person's hands, hence providing a modicum of control—it can become more difficult to shut out the horrors visited on the nameless others who are out of reach, and cannot be rescued no matter how hard they try.[21]

Losing the protective buffer this special relationship provided can exacerbate the experience of acute grief and contribute to heightened feelings of emotional vulnerability and social alienation. This complicating factor presents a unique and unexpected secondary loss for animal advocates.

ALEC

When my beloved rescued German shepherd Alec died, I was devastated and completely bereft. I have written a lot of words on my blog attempting to translate my experience loving him and, finally, losing him into language.[22] But words could never accurately capture the strength of our bond or the meaning of that relationship to me. For many reasons, he had become the most important thing in my life. Alec was my North Star. He was the love of my life.

All of this I knew when he was alive. What I didn't realize was that, in many ways, Alec protected me from unhappiness. I was not surprised by the depths of anguish, sadness, depression, and hopelessness that I experienced after he died. I had expected that, as much as I could have expected anything in the yawning abyss that awaited me after his death. I was overwhelmed not just with the lack of him—the sudden and nonsensical absence of his physical presence—but also flooded with sorrow over the circumstances of his death, which certainly complicated my grief. As I learned more about the experience of profound loss, I was somewhat comforted to learn that even when I felt I was losing my mind, my thoughts and feelings were all a relatively normal part of the grieving process.

What I didn't expect was the secondary (nonspecific to him) depression that began to close in—the crushing weight of the sadness of the world, specifically the images of farmed animals screaming in pain and fear that had so horrified and haunted me when I first learned of such things in my early days as an animal advocate. Back then, I didn't know how to live in a world where people were so cruel to helpless animals, and I thought there was something wrong with me that videos, photos, and descriptions of animal suffering didn't motivate me as an activist, but rather paralyzed me with despair.

Eventually I realized I just had a more sensitive temperament, and I was never going to develop the emotional "thick skin" that many activists do. I could still be involved in animal advocacy, but I had to find ways to keep the traumatic knowledge from flooding my psyche so I did not become overwhelmed with depression, which would be good neither for the animals nor for me. I developed ways to protect my emotional and mental health, which primarily involved assiduously avoiding graphic videos, pictures, and descriptions of animal cruelty (which abound once a person opens herself to the reality of animal exploitation in contemporary society).

But of course I can't "unknow" what I know, and occasionally, things really get under my skin and I begin to feel desperately sad and hopeless. But I try to minimize those experiences for my own sanity, employing many of the coping strategies used by other animal activists—seeking like-minded others, using humor, sanctuary visits and happy animal stories, and focusing on social change and positive gains. I didn't realize until he was gone that, alongside all the other positive benefits he brought to my life, Alec had a significant place in that constellation of coping mechanisms.

Although I had learned after those first growing pains as a sensitively tempered animal advocate that I could remain in the movement as long as I protected myself, I never thought of my companion animals as having anything to do with this protection. But when Alec died, I found myself living without a dog for the first time in my adult life. And suddenly, I could no longer shut out what I had been heretofore pretty successfully suppressing. This was very bewildering on top of the already shattering experience of losing Alec.

As I pondered why this was happening, the idea that my relationship with Alec had served as a psychological buffer occurred to me. I had poured into him all the love that I could not give to the others. I fiercely protected him and tried to keep him safe, and for a while, I was successful. Once his basic needs were taken care of (food, shelter, safety), I worked on the higher order ones—love, trust, physical exercise, mental stimulation, and species- and breed-specific needs. I would give him the best life possible, for him *and* for all the others I could never save. I never explicitly thought of it this way. But he provided an outlet for my desire to protect the helpless, and in turn he was my shield. With him gone, so went a coping mechanism I never even knew I had.

I have since written a bit on the subject and spoken with other animal advocates who immediately identified with what I was calling the "happiness buffer" effect. I began to realize—as with so many other bewildering emotions and thoughts I had in the acute stage of my grief—that my experience was not unique. Despite similarities and patterns that exist across grief experiences, individuals cognitively and emotionally process loss differently based on many factors, and I am not suggesting all animal advocates who lose an important companion animal will relate to this experience; I suspect (and my very limited experience suggests) that people who have a surfeit of empathy and emotional sensitivity will be more vulnerable to this secondary loss.

The psychological buffer effect is an outgrowth of the therapeutic benefits of companion animals discussed above, but specific to the experience of loss and unexpected complications that can arise for animal advocates who have formed an intense bond with their animal companion. The flip side of the beneficial therapeutic presence is that when the animal is gone, a crisis beyond normal grief can ensue and ignite symptoms of complicated grief that may not be fully understood.

SANCTUARY

When Alec died, I vowed I would never adopt another animal; I just didn't think I could survive a loss like that again. But that is one promise I am glad I did not keep. After the long period of mourning and depression I experienced upon losing Alec, the pivotal turning point, when the deep wounds of grief finally began to heal, was when I opened my heart again and adopted my sweet rescued dog Teagan. I began to be able to more successfully manage the despair over the others too. It is still there, but I can function.

This experience helped me to realize that, for me, one of the psychological antidotes to existential despair as it relates to massive animal exploitation is to love an animal, even if just one, with all my heart and to care for that animal as if he or she were the most special, cherished being on the planet—because to me, she is. The anthropocentric culture in which I live devalues animals,[23] but I do not. The disjuncture between my values and hegemonic social norms regarding animals can at times make me feel dizzy and alone, like a visitor from another planet. From the disorientation of alienation to the danger of developing post-traumatic stress symptoms,[24] animal advocacy work is emotionally difficult. But in a hostile political climate and culture that denigrates animal activists,[25] while sanctioning and even subsidizing the most ruthless exploitation of animals for the merest convenience,[26] love can provide safe harbor.

Love is a political act. As an ethical vegan, I resist systemic animal exploitation through my consumer choices. Through my relationships with my companion animals, I also resist the cultural idea, encoded in our laws, that animals are mere property, legal things who are interchangeable and, when it suits human interests, disposable. I may be unable to change the social structure or dominant ideology, or to stop the machinery of animal exploitation, but my ideals and values can be positively expressed through my relationships with the individual animals I love. Although they are statistically insignificant, proverbial drops in the bucket, they are the precious few whose lives I can directly affect. These relationships enhance feelings of self-efficacy, which can be eroded doing animal advocacy work due to the obstacles mentioned above.

Empathizing with animals, especially farmed animals, can lead to profound sorrow and feelings of powerlessness. But when I look into the eyes of my rescued dog, I know I am not completely helpless, although the scope of my agency is certainly limited. The ability to exercise direct positive influence on one or more animals' lives can help counteract the feelings of powerlessness every animal advocate faces. Love is affirmative resistance and can be a protective barrier against the potentially hazardous effects of traumatic knowledge and disenfranchised grief.

Nurturing relationships with companion animals are not the only protective barriers available for animal advocates. Volunteering at farmed animal sanctuaries and making connections with individual animals can be a healing experience. Rescued farmed animals, by the mere fact of their existence outside the means of production, are living signifiers of an alternate reality. Animal activists must continue to seek out, as well as create, safe spaces where their empathy, compassion, and grief can be validated and where an alternative vision of human–animal relations can be expressed. A mutually nurturing relationship with a special companion animal is one such safe space, and attention should be paid to the unique secondary losses that may occur in the wake of losing not only the animal but also the sanctuary they provided for the advocate's heart.

NOTES

1. Because both are used in legal and common parlance, I use the terms "companion animal" and "pet" interchangeably throughout this essay.
2. Tamina Toray, "The Human–Animal Bond and Loss: Providing Support for Grieving Clients," *Journal of Mental Health Counseling* 26 (2004): 244–59; Allison Werner-Lin and Teresa Moro, "Unacknowledged and Stigmatized Losses," in *Living beyond Loss: Death in the Family*, ed. Froma

Walsh and Monica McGoldrick, 2nd ed. (New York: W. W. Norton, 2004), 258–61; Betty J. Carmack, *Grieving the Death of a Pet* (Minneapolis: Augsburg Press, 2003); Kathleen V. Cowles, "The Death of a Pet: Human Responses to the Breaking of the Bond," *Marriage & Family Review* 8, nos. 3–4 (1985): 135–48; Thomas A. Wrobel and Amanda L. Dye, "Grieving Pet Death: Normative, Gender, and Attachment Issues," *Omega* 47 (2003): 385–93; Julie A. Luiz Adrian, Aimee N. Deliramich, and B. Christopher Frueh, "Complicated Grief and Posttraumatic Stress Disorder in Humans' Response to the Death of Pets/Animals," *Bulletin of the Menninger Clinic* 73, no. 3 (2009): 176–87.

3. David Grimm, *Citizen Canine: Our Evolving Relationship with Cats and Dogs* (New York: Public Affairs, 2014). Though still strictly defined as "property" under the law, pet dogs and cats are covered under criminal animal cruelty laws, and as of 2014 all fifty states now have a felony provision for animal cruelty and neglect ("SD Lawmakers Approve Making Animal Cruelty a Felony," *Rapid City Journal*, March 11, 2014). In sharp contrast, farmed animals are excluded from most anticruelty laws by specific or implied exemptions and receive virtually no legal protections. David J. Wolfson and Mariann Sullivan, "Foxes in the Hen House: Animals, Agribusiness, and the Law; a Modern American Fable," in *Animal Rights: Current Debates and New Directions*, ed. Cass R. Sunstein and Martha C. Nussbaum (Oxford: Oxford University Press, 2005), 205–33.

4. Kenneth J. Doka, ed., *Disenfranchised Grief: Recognizing Hidden Sorrow* (Lexington, MA: Lexington Books, 1989), 4.

5. Therese A. Rando, *How to Go on Living When Someone You Love Dies* (New York: Bantam Books, 1991), 15.

6. A unique hallmark of the human–companion animal relationship (for the human) is that the animal has often been present through many significant life changes, including changes in relationships, jobs, school, and sometimes geographic locations, representing an unchanging and constant stable presence during the vicissitudes of life.

7. See Andrea Brooks, ed., "The Health Benefits of Companion Animals," Pets Are Wonderful Support, 2007.

8. ESAs are protected under the Fair Housing Act but not the Americans with Disabilities Act (ADA), which only covers trained service animals. For more see Kate A. Brewer, "Emotional Support Animals Excepted from 'No Pets' Lease Provisions under Federal Law," Animal Legal & Historical Center, 2005, https://www.animallaw.info; Rebecca F. Wisch, "FAQs on Emotional Support Animals," Animal Legal & Historical Center, 2015, https://www.animallaw.info. ESAs are different from service animals, who do require special training to be recognized more broadly under the ADA.

9. See Rebecca J. Huss, "Why Context Matters: Defining Service Animals under Federal Law," *Pepperdine Law Review* 37, no. 4 (2010): 1163.

10. See Debra S. Hart-Cohen, "Canines in the Courtroom," *GPSolo* 26, no. 5 (2009): 54–57. Also "Legal Support for the Use of a Facility Dog to Assist Testifying Crime Victims and Witnesses: A Review of the Evidence Rule, Case Law, State Statutes, and Legislation," Courthouse Dogs Foundation, 2014.

11. Frank R. Ascione and Phil Arkow, eds., *Child Abuse, Domestic Violence and Animal Abuse: Linking the Circles of Compassion for Prevention and Intervention* (West Lafayette, IN: Purdue University Press, 1999).

12. Bruce A. Wagman, Sonia S. Waisman, and Pamela D. Frasch, *Animal Law: Cases and Materials*, 4th ed. (Durham, NC: Carolina Academic Press, 2010), 90–189.

13. "Animal Testing and the Law," Animal Legal Defense Fund, http://aldf.org.

14. "Farmed Animals and the Law," Animal Legal Defense Fund, http://aldf.org.
15. Carter Dillard et al., "Animal Advocacy and Causes of Action," *Animal Law* 13 (2006): 87–121.
16. Matthew Liebman, "Who the Judge Ate for Breakfast: On the Limits of Creativity in Animal Law and the Redeeming Power of Powerlessness," *Animal Law* 18 (2011): 133–50.
17. Taimie L. Bryant, "Trauma, Law, and Advocacy for Animals," *Journal of Animal Law and Ethics* 1 (2006): 63–138.
18. For more on how society is organized to conceal the massive, routine killing of farmed animals, see Timothy Pachirat, *Every Twelve Seconds: Industrialized Slaughter and the Politics of Sight* (New Haven: Yale University Press, 2013). Doka, *Disenfranchised Grief*, 4.
19. Nicole R. Pallotta, "Becoming an Animal Rights Activist: An Exploration of Culture, Socialization, and Identity Transformation" (PhD diss., University of Georgia, 2005); Kenneth Shapiro, "The Caring Sleuth: Portrait of an Animal Rights Activist," *Society & Animals* 2, no. 2 (1994): 145–65.
20. Animal advocates have other ways to cope with pent-up grief over the nameless others. Plugging into a like-minded community (vegan social groups or animal activist networks) and trips to farmed animal sanctuaries can also serve the function of a psychological buffer in an anthropocentric culture.
21. This secondary loss may be amplified in cases where the griever lived alone with the companion animal or, whether living with human others or not, the bereaved finds themselves in a pet-less household following the death; having a remaining animal or animals to care for can mitigate the disorienting aspects of loss of daily routine and other secondary losses resulting from the death of a special animal. Here I am referring specifically to adult loss of a companion animal, as the situation for a child losing an animal friend can present unique factors that would require a separate discussion.
22. Nicole R. Pallotta, *Alec's Story* (blog), http://www.alec-story.com.
23. Even dogs and cats, the most protected and elevated species of animals in human society, are put to death in animal shelter facilities every day in numbers that are staggering, simply because there are not enough homes for them all.
24. Bryant, "Trauma, Law, and Advocacy for Animals."
25. Will Potter, *Green Is the New Red: An Insider's Account of a Social Movement under Siege* (San Francisco: City Lights Publishers, 2011).
26. "Animal Testing and the Law," Animal Legal Defense Fund.

Keeping Ghosts Close
Care and Grief at Sanctuaries

PATTRICE JONES AND LORI GRUEN

When the gentle turkey called Dante began to flail and flap in the grip of a heart attack, VINE Sanctuary's recently hired bird caregiver Danielle Salino flung herself over him, using her own body to buffer him and others from the frantic spasms of his powerful wings. She whispered to him until the spasms subsided then remained draped over his body.

"I can't take it anymore! I can't take all this death!" she howled. Two other sanctuary workers, each with years of experience, made eye contact, wondering: How will this go? Danielle gulped, then switched gears and began reciting Dante's relationships and characteristics. "We'll miss you so much," she concluded as the other two allowed their own tears to flow, "we'll never forget you." She then gathered herself up along with Dante's body, bracing herself to assist with the necropsy. Now, split heart-shaped rocks hauled down from the mountain rest near the spot where Dante breathed his last breath, ensuring that Danielle's promise will be kept: He will not be forgotten.

Animals die at sanctuaries—often. This state of affairs poses a number of deep challenges for the sanctuaries and their supporters. It also opens up opportunities for more authentic engagement with animal death. Resisting the urge to retreat in the face of repeated grief takes work. Avoiding either going numb or being overcome by emotion also requires mindful effort. The ways that caregivers at sanctuaries strive to remain alive to and with other animals may provide models for activists at a time of mass slaughter and extinction.

ENTANGLEMENTS

We become ourselves in the context of relationships. It's not just that our social contexts help to shape our attitudes and behaviors, although that certainly is true, but we construct ourselves through interactions with others. The very elements of our "selves"—emotions, perception, the feeling of being a particular person—develop through our interactions with others. As inherently social animals we need to be with others or we go mad. Prisoners in solitary confinement report hallucinations, distorted perceptions, and an overall mental fuzziness that makes it difficult to form or hold onto thoughts.

For many people, the vital bonds that coconstitute the self include relationships with nonhuman family and community members. Many people live in family groupings that include companion animals. Some city residents interact with pigeons more often than they do with their human neighbors. Naturalists, both amateur and professional, attend carefully to nonhuman animals and often notice themselves changing as a result. And people at sanctuaries work and often live in communities in which animals are integral participants. In all of these instances, and many more, animals are among the others with whom we are entangled. With them we coconstruct our selves.

Since relationships make us, death undoes us. Others are, in various ways, parts of ourselves. When someone goes missing, we must find a way to keep their part of us alive if we are to try to remain whole. Death also changes our future relationships. If we retreat from communion, due to fear of further loss, our relationships (and, therefore, ourselves) become impoverished. This is a particular risk for those, like sanctuary workers, whose caregiving requires empathic engagement. If the ability to relate is damaged or distorted, caregiving that vitally depends on the ability to be emotionally attuned will suffer.

Death also changes the communities in which we are a part. The roles that the departed played in the group are suddenly vacant. The best friend of this one, the antagonist of that one, the jokester of the group—all gone. Meanwhile, those who remain grieve in their different ways. Captive chimpanzees will sometimes stay with the body of their companion, even refusing food. Others seem not to notice. In an account of the death of one of the very first captive chimpanzees in this country in the late 1800s, Arthur Brown recounts this poignant response of a male chimpanzee to the death of his partner:

> After the death of the female, which took place early in the morning, the remaining one made many attempts to rouse her, and when he found this to be impossible his rage and grief were painful to witness. Tearing the hair, or rather snatching at the short hair on his head, was always one of his common expressions of extreme anger, and was now largely indulged in, but the ordinary yell of rage which he set up at first, finally changed to a cry which the keeper of the animals assures me he had never heard before, and which would be most nearly represented by hah-ah-ah-ah-ah, uttered somewhat under the breath, and with a plaintive sound like a moan. With this he made repeated efforts to arouse her, lifting up her head and hands, pushing her violently and rolling her over. After her body was removed from the cage—a proceeding which he violently opposed—he became more quiet, and remained so as long as his keeper was with him, but catching sight of the body once when the door was opened and again when it was carried past the front of the cage, he became violent, and cried for the rest of the day. The day following, he sat still most of the time and moaned continuously.[1]

Reverberations of death can be lingering. The young chickens known as Violet and Chickweed were rescued together from the roadside after jumping or falling from a slaughterhouse-bound truck. Alone in the world together, they took refuge in each other, alternating in hiding beneath each other's wings as chicks do with their mothers. They grew up together at a sanctuary as Yin and Yang, with Violet's cautious thoughtfulness nicely balancing Chickweed's outgoing exuberance. They were what the poultry industry calls "broiler" chickens, bred to die young. Not long after they passed adolescence and entered young adulthood, Violet died suddenly as a consequence of what would have been, for any other kind of chicken, a minor injury. Chickweed watched her burial, then stood staring at the spot where she had disappeared into the ground. The next day, and for weeks thereafter, he stormed and stomped, wanting nothing to do with anyone. Over time, he became less angry and more sociable, but he never recovered his sunny personality.

Everyone is different. After a death, some tend toward sorrow while others tend toward rage. Some want comforting while others cannot be consoled. Some need company, others to be left alone. Some want and need to say their feelings loudly and immediately; others prefer nonverbal means of expressing feelings that take some time to become clear.

There is no right way to grieve. However, there may be methods of mourning that more (or less) effectively fulfill the functions of grief, which include not only self-repair but the reweaving of communities. We are interested in collective mourning practices by which sanctuary communities can or do continually reconstitute themselves after the deaths of residents.

This is a challenging task made all the more daunting by complicating factors such as the variability of mourning styles, the likelihood of grief overload, and the never-ending difficulty of making literally life-or-death decisions in the context of caregiving. What psychologists call complex bereavement can occur when emotions such as guilt or shame, or the emotional demands of a quick succession of deaths, make it difficult for a person to fully and wholly grieve the death of a beloved other. At sanctuaries, grieving also may be impeded by the need to immediately blunt one's feelings in order to move the body, arrange or even perform a necropsy, and continue to render care to surviving residents, some of whom themselves may be grieving.

MEMORIALS

Whether or not they do so intentionally, many people at sanctuaries engage in collective mourning practices with the aim of keeping the ghosts of former residents close by. The most common kind of memorial practice seems to be textual. In newsletters and on websites, blogs, and social media platforms, sanctuaries often post extended obituaries, with photos, of departed residents. Such stories also may be shared in the course of lectures or remarks at public events.[2]

When sanctuary workers write and tell the stories of the lives *and deaths* of sanctuary residents, they invite readers or listeners to share in both celebration and mourning. Even though perhaps only one person is writing, she may be doing so in collaboration with others or, as Danielle did with Dante, channeling the sentiments of the group. Sharing brings sanctuary supporters into the circle of mourners.

Many sanctuaries carry the spirits of departed residents forward by including their images and stories on banners, posters, picket signs, leaflets, or other materials intended to help other animals of their kind or in similar situations. This is a collective process in two ways. Many people from the sanctuary may carry the signs or distribute the leaflets, which then invites even more people to "meet" and remember the departed resident. At sanctuaries, the community member who died may be memorialized in some formal way, such as by naming a sanctuary structure or program after that animal. For example, the vegan education center at Eden Farm Sanctuary in Ireland is called "Matilda's Promise," after a beloved hen. Aptly, United Poultry Concerns set up a memorial fund named after the hen who inspired that sanctuary's creation. Those who donated to the sanctuary through its Fredda Flower Fund would have their own memories of beloved animals printed in the sanctuary's newsletter.

Informal or private memorials also are common at sanctuaries. Peace gardens planted over graves create places to which sanctuary staff may repair to remember those interred or to call on their spirits in some way. One might, for example, visit the resting place of a particularly persistent sheep when summoning up the fortitude for a protracted campaign.

Freed from the constraints of graveyards, sanctuaries may elect to site graves in central rather than inaccessible locations, so that the dead remain present. A horse might be buried in the center of a favorite pasture, a hen beneath a favored bush. Rock arrangements, wildflower plantings, or other markers over burial places offer reminders to sanctuary staff as they go about their days. In this way, former residents continue to "participate" in the life of the community.

Sometimes the memorials will be symbolic. Perhaps there might be a large vase tastefully displayed with an array of glass rocks around it, and sanctuary workers can be encouraged, when they are so moved, to think about someone who has died and add a rock to the vase. As with the Fredda Flower Fund, sometimes memorial sites can be for sanctuary residents and others. For example, supporters may plant a tree at the sanctuary in honor of someone they have loved and lost. At Chimpanzee Sanctuary Northwest, supporters are encouraged to "sponsor a day," and often those days are in memory of humans and other animals who have died, bringing the sanctuary into the collective process of a supporter's mourning.

Some caution is necessary. Sanctuaries deal with far more death than their supporters generally realize. Supporters tend to prefer upbeat stories of happy animals. In creating memorials that will be shared beyond the bounds of on-site staff and close supporters, sanctuaries may feel pressure to create overly sentimental or emotionally empty memorials that hide the often mixed and mixed-up feelings of mourning. While this may seem necessary, it might be even more useful for sanctuaries to help their supporters come into more authentic engagement with death and grief.

MAKING CHOICES, DIGGING GRAVES

Reflection in the process of repeated mourning leads many sanctuary people to embrace an ethos of connected care in the now. The accumulation of deaths leads to a deep-seated realization that *every* relationship will end, probably too soon. The demands of caregiving do not allow for self-protective retreat. Sanctuary workers are remarkably uniform in their solution to this dilemma: deliberately draw even closer to those who remain. Express care not only by adequately meeting needs but also by generous gestures, large or small, that increase the measure of happiness in any given day, knowing that each day might be somebody's last. These are practices that, if adopted more widely, might be broadly salutatory.

Sanctuaries must be always ready for death. For sanctuaries caring for large animals, this may mean predigging graves in the fall, before the ground freezes, given the likelihood that somebody will die over the winter. Who will fill that grave? Who will not live to see spring? Similarly unnerving questions arise when taking in large groups of physically compromised animals. Someone will die—too soon—but who? When? People at sanctuaries serving such vulnerable animals go about their days knowing that they might, at any moment, turn a corner and come upon a body.

Sanctuaries also must sometimes help others to brace themselves for death. Contributors who sign up to "sponsor" a particularly vulnerable sanctuary resident may need to be warned that the recipient of their largess is likely to die sooner rather than later. When an especially popular or otherwise notable sanctuary resident dies, not only sponsors or other contributors but also those who follow the sanctuary on social media must be notified. Answering expressions of grief can be soothing to sanctuary workers, who thereby feel less alone. But when death announcements are met with suspicion rather than sorrow, the ensuing drama may devastate already drooping morale. This is not to say that there are not irresponsible "sanctuaries" that ought to be scrutinized from the outside. But at reputable sanctuaries, every untimely death is already an occasion for anguished soul searching. Sanctuary people who provide exemplary care may struggle against feelings of shame, doubt, self-blame, and a nagging sense of having fallen short in response to even as clear-cut a case as an elderly resident dying of a heart attack. This problem is compounded by the fact that there will be deaths that are not so easily explained.

Sooner or later, every sanctuary worker has blood on her hands—literally and figuratively. In addition to coping with the inherently hard experience of witnessing death repeatedly, sanctuary workers also sometimes must grapple with their own culpability. This may range from the nagging awareness that different choices might have led to a different outcome to the horrifying realization that some misstep you made really did lead directly to somebody's death. Such reflections considerably complicate mourning.

A sanctuary staffer whose error caused or contributed to the death of an animal does not have the luxury of descending into guilt-ridden paralysis. Nor may she decline to confront her culpability. She and her organization must find a way to live with and work from within awareness of shortcomings and the injuries they have caused. Again, the responses to this are consistent across reputable sanctuaries and of potentially broader application. While sanctuaries generally dare not disclose their own errors to the general public, candor (both within and among sanctuaries) about errors and shortcomings is the norm, allowing everybody to learn from mistakes. Across the board, sanctuaries and their staffs tend to react to tragedies in a similar manner: double down on care-giving, doing what we can for who we can with the knowledge that we all are imperfect.

Sanctuary deaths occur in the broader context of a culture of killing. As one sanctuary mourns the death of a chicken, literally millions of other chickens are being killed. Sanctuaries mourn that one chicken with simultaneous awareness of the millions. In doing so, they gain determination to do all that they can to end the killing. When an elderly chimpanzee dies at sanctuary, there is all the more urgency to get more chimpanzees out of laboratories so that they don't die without experiencing relative freedom and being treated with respect. Mourning deaths can motivate action.

AWAKENING VIA MOURNING

Sandra Higgins of Eden Farm Animal Sanctuary says, "in my mind and in my heart, each and every resident who has lived at Eden is still alive, the memories of them acting as constant inspiration and source of hope to me."[3] People sometimes fear that grappling with death will deaden them, but when mourning practices keep the "ghosts" of sanctuary residents close, those spirits enliven the people and the place.

Thus sanctuaries ought, insofar as possible, to deliberately practice remembering, doing what they can to both care for mourners within the sanctuary community and extend the community of mourners. We like to imagine sanctuaries developing mourning practices that are even more creative and collective. What would the sanctuary equivalent of a jazz funeral be?

Supporters of sanctuaries can do the same in their own lives, but have an even more important role to play by being willing to join the virtual circle of mourners after a sanctuary death and by being mindful of the toll that constant grief takes on sanctuary workers. Be willing to hear the sad as well as the glad news, and encourage people at sanctuaries to speak of death as well as celebrations and to disclose mistakes or shortcomings without shame or fear of loss of support.

Death is an aspect of life. Loss is an aspect of love. To remain alive while confronting death, we need to embrace connection without flinching from culpability. By doing so, we resist paralysis and become better able to promote caring interspecies community.

NOTES

We would like to thank all of the people who work in sanctuary who have shared their stories with us. We have written about topics discussed in this chapter in pattrice jones, *Aftershock* (Lantern, 2007) and Lori Gruen, "Facing Death and Practicing Grief," in *Ecofeminism: Feminist Intersections with Other Animals and the Earth*, ed. C. J. Adams and L. Gruen (Bloomsbury, 2014) and *Entangled Empathy* (Lantern, 2015).

1. Arthur E. Brown, "Grief in the Chimpanzee," *American Naturalist* 13, no. 3 (March 1879): 173–75.
2. Most sanctuary websites include pages devoted to profiles of residents, including departed residents. Some sanctuaries have a special page just for memorials; others post memorials on blogs or social media soon after someone has died. Gruen has developed a memorial website for the first chimpanzees used in research at http://www.first100chimps.wesleyan.edu.
3. Sandra Higgin, personal communication to pattrice jones, November 23, 2014.

Grieving at a Distance

TEYA BROOKS PRIBAC

I hear their screams and witness their fear and suffering in hundreds of places including slaughterhouses, industrialized farms, darkened sheds, open paddocks, feedlots and inside transport trucks and ships on four continents.

—PATTY MARK

It is not often that, in the daily inundation of concise and carefully selected wordings accompanying images, jointly aiming at bringing the attention of the current-time ever-distracted and ever-rushing viewer to focus on some important plight or another, a verbal-image combination—an Internet meme—strikes me so powerfully as to remain with me for years, possibly forever. This was the case, however, with the photograph of a calf, removed from the mother far too young and placed in a barren crate with barely enough room to move. The calf is looking directly into the camera with pleadingly confused eyes. The crate is situated in rows of identical crates, designed to hold other infants, who were also taken away from their mothers at the delicate age when the mother's nurturance is of paramount importance, because, as the story goes, most humans supposedly cannot survive without cheese. The text to the left of this photograph of one of the many victims of the dairy industry reads: "We see you. We care. We are sorry. We are trying."

To *see* is to bear witness. Once you see, you cannot *un*see. Seeing brings about personal change. It may also bring about grief. The line is thin and souls are fragile. A failure to recognize and address the psychophysical pressure upon those who bear witness to nonhuman animals' torture and deaths en masse represents violence against the self and possibly violence against the very animals we seek to protect and whose plight we wish to bring to light.

Grief is a deeply intimate affair, affecting a range of psychobiological levels and exhibiting the potential for long-term compromising effects on the well-being of the affected organism, including threats to its mere existence. Simultaneously, in sociopolitical settings the outer expression of loss, or lack thereof, is almost by definition a political act, as it defies, or supports, the selective social normative with its tendency to dictate who is worthy of mourning and hence of life itself.[1] The latter is particularly reinforced in relation to the lives and deaths of nonhuman animals and is reflected in the widespread attitude toward human mourners of nonhuman animals, whose grief is usually not recognized, not admitted, and oftentimes even derided, hence falling under the category of disenfranchised grief.[2]

While human grief for nonhuman animal family members is rarely, if ever, considered to be on a par with the grief humans may experience at the loss of another human, the specter of speciesism and instrumentalization further dictates, in relation to nonhuman animals of various species, the dynamics of love and loss that a human is expected to adhere to in order to comply with social standards of "normality" and acceptable conduct. However, a growing number of humans have moved away from the culturally determined ethics based on species segregation and embraced and internalized the philosophy and praxis of interspecies equality. The empathic identification with other animals drives these people into animal rescue and direct care, advocacy aiming at educating about animal suffering and ways of preventing it, or a combination of both. As a consequence, these people are continuously exposing themselves as witnesses of direct or indirect violence, and as such become vulnerable to psychophysical stress and trauma with potentially detrimental outcomes. It is elemental to recognize that for many of these people this "lifestyle" is not a choice but an imperative defined by their inability to *un*see, which in turn defines who they are as individuals and informs an entire cognitive-emotional spectrum underpinning their existence. A pig, a cow, a goat, a sheep, a rabbit, and any other animal trapped in the system of exploitation and abuse, or victim of anthropogenic violence in the wild, is not simply a number, an object, somebody's property. Every single one of them is a living, feeling being who deserves a species-specific life, free of preventable suffering.

One does not need to know an animal personally, that is, develop a physically and emotionally proximal relationship with the animal, to identify with her/his misery and be deeply affected by her/his death. Grief "at a distance," which, for want of a better term, refers to the grief experienced by humans for animals whom they don't personally know and which includes but is not limited to vicarious grief, is a painful reality for many, and its dismissal will not eradicate it. Various theoretical frameworks supported by individuals' testimonies suggest that grief "at a distance" is *possible* and bears comparable emotional charge to the grief experienced in relation to the loss of proximal significant others; that such grief is *legitimate* based upon the violence that commodification imposes upon nonhuman animal subjects; and that the outer expression of such loss is *necessary* as it bears witness to both the reality of the human mourner's internal turmoil and the conceived reality of the mourned animals.

VICARIOUS GRIEF AND BEYOND

Professionals and volunteers working with victims of violence and ill-fated events and circumstances are vulnerable to vicarious trauma,[3] which describes traumatization induced by exposure to a primary victim's experience, manifesting symptoms mirroring those experienced by the primary victim. Like primary traumatization, vicarious traumatization may have long-term consequences for the vicarious sufferers' personal and professional lives and can negatively impact victims in their care. As such, the phenomenon of vicarious trauma has received increased attention in professional domains most at risk of the developing of such trauma within the human context, aiming at spreading awareness both of the risk and of diversified strategies promoting vicarious resilience and trauma stewardship, as helpfully summarized by Berthold.[4] People working with nonhuman animal victims, both in direct care and in advocacy, are equally vulnerable to vicarious trauma, potentially even more so since nonhuman animals' legal inequality—for example, animals being considered as property—may represent an additional impediment to helping the victim and preventing further abuse. However, their vulnerability—and the possible impact on the animals they seek to protect—is not always appreciated by the society at large and oftentimes even by the animal welfare groups themselves, though awareness among the latter is growing as symptoms become harder to neglect.[5]

The constellation of potential vicarious effects based on empathy toward and identification with other subjects includes vicarious loss. Termed "vicarious grief" by Kastenbaum and described as "the sorrow one feels for a loss suffered by another person,"[6] inducing affective states and responses comparable to those suffered by the individual experiencing direct personal loss, the concept of vicarious loss is later elaborated by Rando, who terms it "vicarious bereavement" and defines it as "the experience of loss and consequent grief and mourning that occurs following the deaths of others *not* personally known by the mourner."[7] Rando proposes the existence of two types of vicarious bereavement. Type-I involves losses that are solely vicarious; that is, upon empathic identification with the primary mourner, the vicarious sufferer feels what the grief must be like for the primary mourner. Type-II includes Type-I bereavement plus an added personal component, reflecting either or both an exacerbation of the vicarious mourner's reaction to direct personal losses and a perceived violation of one's assumptive world.

Vicarious grief, as the term implies, presupposes an intermediary subject—a primary mourner—who is directly affected by the loss and whose loss and its acuteness are then absorbed by another person, the secondary mourner. In many cases it may be this kind of vicariousness that induces humans' grief for unknown nonhuman animals. For instance, we may identify and suffer with the mothers and infants who are subjected to systematic separation and bond-breaking in various exploitative settings within the food production industry. We may feel the pain of the animals in the wild who have lost their children, companions, communities, and habitats—homes—due to hunting, misinformed conservation attempts based on killing, human material development, and other forms of anthropogenic violence. We may deeply grieve when species face extinction; besides the often-cited human voyeuristic interest in species preservation, the primary tragedy of extinction is the many individual animals' suffering before their own and their conspecifics' lives are permanently lost. Extinction doesn't affect exclusively the species in question, but also the entire multispecies ecology (also composed of individuals) that the vanishing species is embedded into, including participating human communities, as van Dooren elaborates.[8] Neither does extinction need to be imminently physical to be grievable. Bradshaw details the psychological extinction of animals in the wild,[9] which with its cross-generational transferability will change their inner landscape and outer relational patterns forever, much as in the case of animals exploited in agribusiness.

The nature of the pain some humans feel in the face of the above and similar violence cannot be reduced to mere sorrow as expressed by others who upon learning about such brutality may indicate their regret for the mass suffering and continue with their lives undisrupted. The pain of the human mourners for unknown animals can be deeply felt and comparable to the pain experienced after a direct proximal loss. Such feelings are possible as they originate in and rest upon the secondary mourner's empathic recognition of relatedness to both conspecifics and members of other species. We never in fact mourn the unknown; we always mourn the known.

The increasingly more open admission of human/nonhuman animal mental and emotional comparability,[10] including strong evidence predictive of nonhuman animals' capacity to experience grief,[11] substantiates the legitimacy of the empathic projection that gives rise to grief for unknown animals. While it would be naive, in fact potentially damaging, to promote sameness both in relation to nonhuman animals and to other humans, the relationality and relationability embodied in a transspecies space of being together and knowing, recognizing each other, confirms the existence of comparability beyond form. It is this subjective encounter with the other that informs our understanding of and attitude toward ourselves and the rest of the world. It also defines our spectrum of attention, as McGilchrist formulates in defiance of the myth of objectivity:

> The nature of attention one brings to bear on anything alters what one finds. . . . To attempt to detach oneself entirely is just to bring a special kind of attention to bear which will have important consequences for what we find.[12]

Let us take sheep, for example, a staple of many humans' diets and apparel, an objectified and instrumentalized lump of wool and tissue to be mutilated, traded, and eventually slaughtered for human interest. If one lives with sheep, as I do, in a transspecies intersubjective space aiming for equality rather than exploitation, the general instrumentalizing attitude is irreconcilable with what I see. My vision—like anybody else's vision—might be blurred, of course, by the nature of attention I apply. But should I seriously be worried about my intellectual integrity in my perception of the sheep when such is challenged by a visitor who cannot even distinguish among the highly distinctive faces of the sheep in question, which is usually the case? This phenomenon, which is known as "cross-race effect" within the human context—but is equally applicable to interspecies settings—and describes the elevated ease humans experience in recognizing faces of their own race compared to other races but which can be reversed by exposure to other races, does not reveal much about sheep's subjectivity. However, it does remind of the precariousness of detached agnosticism in regard to other animals' physical and mental experiences, when in practice such agnosticism hypocritically promotes objectification and further violence toward animals. While we live, we will inescapably continue to impact their lives, but will also to a great extent retain some choice concerning the nature of the impact.

The line between Rando's two types of vicarious bereavement is often diffused for the human mourner for unknown animals. In many cases, however, the grief goes beyond vicariousness. The terrified look of an individual in a transport truck destined for slaughter is coming from the eyes of a brother. I feel his fear; I feel his pain. I grieve his death and the death of each individual whose terrified gaze had been hidden from me but radiates from pieces of flesh on supermarket shelves, and other products of violence encountered daily. Grief may source from the unbearable lightness with which the ontological genocide of certain species is implemented—a genocide, based upon appropriation of a psycho-socio-biologically complex life and its conversion into a mere commodity, labelled as food, pest, workforce, or other, which has indelible repercussions for the individuals and the species at large. Grief may also arise from the savage disruption of these lives' imminent potentiality—of the kind Marder advocates for plants[13]—a gift and beauty that is not only grievable but worthy of fierce protection and defense that no sociopolitical imposition may be able to prevent. The scale of the horror of human violence against nonhuman animals may indeed represent the apical difference between the loss of a proximal significant other (human or nonhuman) and loss at a distance, and in the latter case the assumptive world is always therefore challenged.

The assumptive world, as the term suggests, is an individual's blueprint of assumptions and expectations consciously and unconsciously constructed from experience, which informs the way we perceive the world and ourselves in it, and against which we measure and evaluate the various events and situations in life.[14] When loss or other traumatic events occur—proximal or at some distance—one's assumptive world may be shattered. To promote personal healing and well-being a revision of the assumptive world and an adaptation to the new reality may be necessary. But unlike in the event of a loss of a proximal loved one where such revision is encouraged and may to various extents be possible, when it comes to grieving for unknown animal victims, the tension between the assumptive world and the reality of anthropogenic violence against nonhuman animals can never really be resolved. My assumptive world causes my grief, and the grief in turn sustains my assumptive world. If I adapt my assumptive world to the reality of violence I may be vulnerable to desensitizing. Desensitizing is not a healthy coping mechanism; it is a breakdown.

Hillman writes: "Of course I am in mourning for the land and water and my fellow beings. If this were not felt, I would be so defended and so in denial, so anaesthetized, I would be insane."[15] However, by and large, insanity—along with softness implying weakness—is usually not attributed to the "anaesthetized" human; instead it is attributed to those, including mourners of nonhuman animals, who are unable to make themselves perceive the rest of the world as an instrumentalized commodity. As Oliver points out referring mainly to human–nonhuman companion animal relationships: "To love animals is to be soft, childlike, or pathological. To admit dependence on animals—particularly emotional and psychological dependence, as pet owners often do—is seen as a type of neurosis."[16] The weakness that motivates people to conform to societal expectations, on the other hand, is perceived as sanity and strength. There is nothing insane, of course, about humans and other animals enjoying relationships with others and forming groups with social norms and expectations; it is a psychobiological need enhancing physical protection and emotional support. What *is* "insane," as far as the current Western-bound attitude is concerned, is to deny this innate vulnerability and attempt to disguise it even from ourselves by turning a simple and natural phenomenon like group formation with its capacities of empowerment into a system so oppressive to nonhuman animals and so fragile in itself that its very survival relies on most people's inability to look at what underlies it out of fear that, upon *seeing*, the self would spill like quicksilver. This is not strength.

Sullender notes: "Most of us, unless we are sociopaths, are touched by the tears and sufferings of other humans and even other living creatures. We are instinctually drawn to their aid."[17] If we agree with Sullender, by allowing the society, of which we are agent constituents, to attempt to "protect" our fragile selves by promoting safety based on disguise and denial of what a large majority may intrinsically perceive as ethically deeply compromised principles and practices (which is reflected, for example, in people's resistance to witness procedures in slaughterhouses, and, importantly, in increasing evidence of the impact of slaughterhouse work on the mental health of the workers themselves),[18] we are not growing safer and stronger, but more fragile and more vulnerable, both as individuals and as a society, heading toward sociopathy and a devastating internal split. Simultaneously, the human victim-turned-perpetrator of such denial is perhaps indirectly but nevertheless actively participating in the violence inflicted upon both nonhuman animals and fellow humans who have *seen* and can neither *un*see nor choose to look the other way.

SILENT NO MORE

To commemorate the deaths of innocent animal victims of anthropogenic violence, various animal rights and advocacy groups across the globe have begun to hold regular or occasional public vigils.[19] These vigils are not just another innovative method of bringing the plight of nonhuman animals to the attention of the broader public; their implications are far more profound.

Despite its potent emotional charge comparable to that experienced in relation to other humans, the grief for nonhuman animals, particularly those animals the purposive and systematic exploitation and murder of whom is socially acceptable and normalized, bears little social consent. Consequentially, many humans living with such grief do not only suffer the internal turmoil intrinsic to this feeling, but their grief, at the delicate time when a gentle, sympathetic hand may be most appreciated, is often met with indifference or even outright animosity.

Public vigils and other outer expressions of loss perform critical functions for the benefit of the mourner, the mourned, and each individual the mourned one may, in the eyes of the public, represent. Butler's notion of sociopolitically informed grievability as a determinant of a life's noteworthiness can be equally applied to transspecies contexts, as Stanescu suggests.[20] In this sense, the vigils and other forms of open mourning validate the lives of the mourned animals as well as the lives of their conspecifics who continue to suffer and die under the violent pretense of normality. Simultaneously, they validate the mourners themselves, who have found the strength to expose their vulnerability in a world where the latter is also regulated by socially determined modes and levels of affordability. Such mourning may also offer a much-needed support to the numerous humans who themselves bleed from the uncountable deaths of their perceived animal kin, but do so quietly, isolated, and perhaps isolating.

Grief, like love, remains a deeply intimate experience, and the modes of "dealing" with it are perhaps as varied as the number of sufferers. The recognition, admittance, and respect of an individual's grief and mourning represent a minimum of ethical decency. When such grief is directed at "unconventional" subjects, the opportunity arises to reconsider the tender foundations underlying conventions. However, as is the case with any socially unsolicited conduct, mourning for nonhuman animals may take some time and public exposure for most human animals to rid themselves of the burden of illusionary segregation.

NOTES

This chapter is dedicated to Gay Bradshaw and Lynda Stoner.

1. Judith Butler, *Precarious Life: The Powers of Mourning and Violence* (London: Verso, 2004). James Stanescu, "Species Trouble: Judith Butler, Mourning and the Precarious Lives of Animals," *Hypatia* 27, no. 3 (2012): 567–82.
2. Millie Cordaro, "Pet Loss and Disenfranchised Grief: Implication for Mental Health Counseling Practice," *Journal of Mental Health Counseling* 34 (2012): 283–94.
3. I. Lisa McCann and Laurie Anne Pearlman, "Vicarious Traumatization: A Framework for Understanding the Psychological Effects of Working with Victims," *Journal of Traumatic Stress* 3 (1990): 131–49.

4. S. Megan Berthold, *Vicarious Trauma and Resilience* (Sacramento, CA: CME Resource, 2011).
5. G. A. Bradshaw, Jeffrey G. Borchers, and Vera Muller-Paisner, *Caring for the Caregiver: Analysis and Assessment of Animal Care Professional and Organizational Wellbeing* (Jacksonville: Kerulos Center, 2012).
6. Robert Kastenbaum, "Vicarious Grief: An Intergenerational Phenomenon?" *Death Studies* 11, no. 6 (1987): 447.
7. Therese A. Rando, "Vicarious Bereavement," in *Death and the Quest for Meaning*, ed. Stephen Strack (Northvale: Jason Aronson, 1997), 259.
8. Thom van Dooren, "Pain of Extinction: The Death of a Vulture," *Cultural Studies Review* 16, no. 2 (2010): 271–89.
9. G. A. Bradshaw, "Elephants, Us, and Other Family: How Attachment Theory Has Started a Cultural Revolution" (paper presented at "Affect Dysregulation and the Healing of the Self," Annual Interpersonal Neurobiology Conference, UCLA, March 14–16, 2014).
10. For example, G. A. Bradshaw and Mary Watkins, "Trans-Species Psychology: Theory and Praxis," *Spring* 75 (2006): 69–94. *Cambridge Declaration on Consciousness* (proclaimed at the Francis Crick Memorial Conference, Cambridge, July 7, 2012).
11. For example, Teja Brooks Pribac, "Animal Grief," *Animal Studies Journal* 2, no. 2 (2013): 67–90.
12. Iain McGilchrist, *The Master and His Emissary: The Divided Brain and the Making of the Western World* (New Haven: Yale University Press, 2009), 29.
13. Michael Marder, "Is It Ethical to Eat Plants?," *Parallax* 19, no. 1 (2013): 29–37. Marder's plant rights advocacy aiming at deinstrumentalizing life generally is sometimes mistakenly perceived as undermining animal rights advocacy.
14. For example Joan Beder, "Loss of the Assumptive World: How We Deal with Death and Loss," *Omega* 50 (2005): 255–65.
15. James Hillman, "Aesthetics and Politics," *Tikkun* 11 (1996): 39.
16. Kelly Oliver, "Pet Lovers, Pathologized," *New York Times*, October 30, 2011.
17. R. Scott Sullender, "Vicarious Grieving and the Media," *Pastoral Psychology* 59 (2010): 193.
18. Jennifer Dillard, "A Slaughterhouse Nightmare: Psychological Harm Suffered by Slaughterhouse Employees and the Possibility of Redress through Legal Reform," *Georgetown Journal on Poverty Law and Policy* 15 (2008): 391–408.
19. One such group is the Toronto Pig Save. In October 2015 the group's co-founder, Canadian animal rights activist Anita Krajnc, was charged with criminal mischief for giving water to thirsty pigs on their way to slaughter during one such vigil. As this volume is going to print, Krajnc is facing ten years in jail.
20. Stanescu, "Species Trouble."

Who Is It Acceptable to Grieve?

JO-ANNE MCARTHUR

We grieve our companion animals when they die. Those with whom we share our homes, even our food and our beds. They are dogs, cats, sometimes rodents and winged creatures, sometimes horses or potbellied pigs.

Superficially, we grieve the charismatic megafauna whose numbers are in decline. The majestic, the exotic, and the beautiful, like the elephants in Africa and the polar bears in the north. We admire them from afar. We wring our hands and donate to organizations that support their conservation.

But there are other animals in our lives. The invisible, yet ever-present, who die unconsidered and unmourned. They number in the tens of billions. We euphemize them as spare ribs instead of pigs, leather instead of cows, test subjects instead of chimpanzees. They make up a great part of our lives as food, clothing, and entertainment and in products that are tested on animals, yet they remain within the shadows of our lives and outside of the sphere of our compassion.

These billions are as sentient as other animals, and all facets of the animal rights movement are engaged in making this fact known.

Sanctuaries take in, and give care and respite to, these animals. They give them a name instead of a number, and the animals become part of the sanctuary family. They are loved, respected, and mourned when they die. We're not accustomed to seeing a human grieve animals reserved solely for eating and exploitation, but it has happened time and again while I've been fortunate enough to be there to document the passing, the love, the rituals, and the mourning.

Jo-Anne McArthur, *Bronwyn*. After Bronwyn the sheep's rescue, he lived a happy life at Farm Sanctuary until he was humanely euthanized after a long illness. He was cradled in Susie Coston's arms as he passed, and his cow friend, Linda, watched on. The animals at Farm Sanctuary are cremated, and many are buried in their cemetery at the south end of the property. Photo taken at Farm Sanctuary Sheep Barn, New York, USA. 2007. (Photo courtesy of Jo-Anne McArthur/*We Animals*.)

Jo-Anne McArthur, *Shmuel and Patty*. Shmuel was a sickly piglet rescued by Animal Liberation Victoria. After Shmuel succumbed to his illness, Patty Mark and Felicity Andersen cradled him, shed tears, and mourned his loss. (Photo taken at Animal Liberation Victoria headquarters, Melbourne, Australia. 2013.)

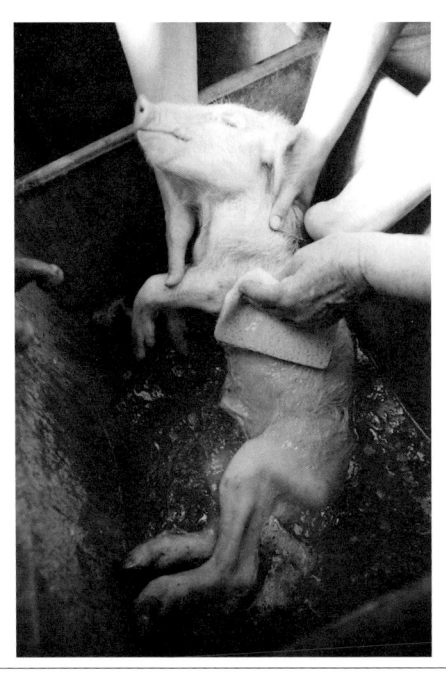

Jo-Anne McArthur, *Shmuel Being Bathed*. After Shmuel's death, the women honored his body by washing it, as humans do for their family members. (Photo taken at Animal Liberation Victoria headquarters, Melbourne, Australia. 2013.)

Jo-Anne McArthur, *Spock with Key*. When a chimpanzee dies at Save the Chimps, the deceased is given a key, symbolizing freedom. All of the chimps are cremated with a key. (Photo taken at Save the Chimps, Florida, USA. 2014.)

Jo-Anne McArthur, *Chimps Say Goodbye*. Spock was rescued from decades in the biomedical research industry by Save the Chimps. On the morning of his natural death at their sanctuary in Fort Pierce, Florida, his body was gently carried and shown to the other chimpanzees so that they would know that their friend had died. (Photo taken at Save the Chimps, Florida, USA. 2014.)

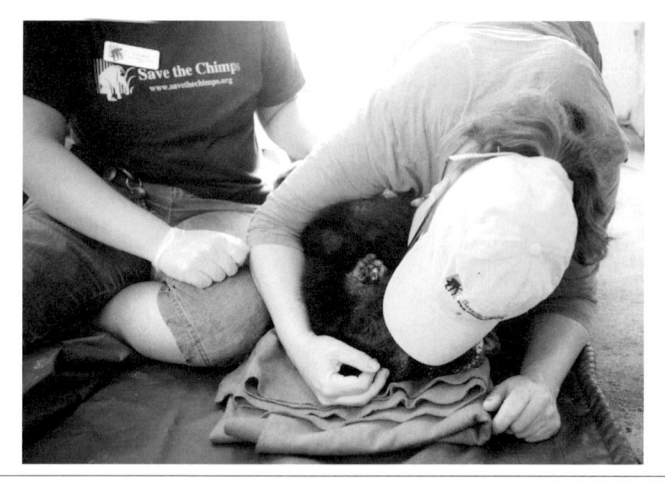

Jo-Anne McArthur, *Caressing Spock*. After Spock died, all Save the Chimps staff were alerted, so that they could see him one last time, if they so chose. One of the most bittersweet aspects of the death of their chimpanzee friends is that, for the first and last time, the human caregivers are able to touch the deceased. In life, there is a no-touch policy, to protect both the humans and the chimpanzees from injury. Only in death are the humans able to caress, cradle, and hold the hands of their chimpanzee friends. (Photo taken at Save the Chimps, Florida, USA. 2014.)

Bibliography

A. "Gone to the Boneyard." *Wallace's Monthly* 18, no. 4 (1892): 260–71.
Adams, Carol J. *Neither Man nor Beast: Feminism and the Defense of Animals*. New York: Continuum, 1995.
———. *The Sexual Politics of Meat: A Feminist-Vegetarian Critical Theory*. London: Continuum, 2010.
Adams, Cindy L., Brenda N. Bonnett, and Alan H. Meek. "Predictors of Owner Response to Companion Animal Death in 177 Clients from 14 Practices in Ontario." *Journal of the American Veterinary Medical Association* 217, no. 9 (2000): 1303–9.
Addison, Paul. "National Identity and the Battle of Britain." In *War and the Cultural Construction of Identities in Britain*, ed. Barbara Korte and Ralf Schneider, 225–40. Amsterdam: Rodopi, 2002.
Adrian, Julie A. Luiz, Aimee N. Deliramich, and B. Christopher Frueh. "Complicated Grief and Posttraumatic Stress Disorder in Humans' Response to the Death of Pets/Animals." *Bulletin of the Menninger Clinic* 73, no. 3 (2009): 176–87.
Agamben, Giorgio. *Homo Sacer: Sovereign Power and Bare Life*. Stanford: Stanford University Press, 1998.
———. *The Open: Man and Animal*. Stanford: Stanford University Press, 2004.
Alderton, David. *Animal Grief: How Animals Mourn*. Dorchester: Veloce Publishing, 2011.
Allen, E. W. *Experiment Station Record*, vol. 22. Washington, DC: Government Printing Office, 1910.
Ambros, Barbara. *Bones of Contention: Animals and Religion in Modern Japan*. Honolulu: University of Hawai'i Press, 2012.
———. "Vengeful Spirits or Loving Spiritual Companions? Changing Views of Animal Spirits in Contemporary Japan." *Asian Ethnology* 69 (2010): 35–67.
Animal Legal Defense Fund. "Animal Testing and the Law." Http://aldf.org.
———. "Farmed Animals and the Law." Http://aldf.org.
Antonello, Pierpaolo, and Roberto Farneti. "Antigone's Claim: A Conversation with Judith Butler." *Theory & Event* 12, no. 1 (2009).
Argent, Gala. "Toward a Privileging of the Nonverbal: Communication, Corporeal Synchrony and Transcendence in Humans and Horses." In *Experiencing Animal Minds: An Anthology of Animal–Human Encounters*, ed. Julie A. Smith and Robert W. Mitchell, 111–28. New York: Columbia University Press, 2012.
Armsby, H. P. "The Food Supply of the Future: A Problem for Agricultural Institutions." *Scientific American Supplement* 69, no. 1792 (1910): 302–4.
Ascione, Frank R., and Phil Arkow, eds. *Child Abuse, Domestic Violence and Animal Abuse: Linking the Circles of Compassion for Prevention and Intervention*. West Lafayette, IN: Purdue University Press, 1999.
Atter, Sheila. "Small Numbers, Big Responsibility." *Dog World*, February 15, 2013.
Bachelard, Gaston. *The Poetics of Reverie: Childhood, Language, and the Cosmos*. Boston: Beacon Press, 1969.

Back, Les. *The Art of Listening*. Oxford: Berg, 2007.

Baker, Steve. *The Postmodern Animal*. London: Reaktion, 2000.

Bakhtin, Mikhail. *Art and Answerability: Early Philosophical Essays*. Austin: University of Texas Press, 1990.

Balmori, Diana, and David K. Skelly. "Crossing to Sustainability: A Role for Design in Overcoming Road Effects." *Ecological Restoration* 30, no. 4 (2012): 363–67.

Baran, Benjamin E., Joseph A. Allen, Steven G. Rogelberg, Christiane Spitzmüller, Natalie A. DiGiacomo, Jennifer B. Webb, Nathan T. Carter, Olga L. Clark, Lisa A. Teeter, and Alan G. Walker. "Euthanasia-Related Strain and Coping Strategies in Animal Shelter Employees." *Journal of the American Veterinary Medical Association* 235, no. 1 (2009): 83–88.

Baxter, Ian L. "A Dwarf Hound Skeleton from a Romano-British Grave at York Road, Leicester, England, UK, with a Discussion of Other Roman Small Dog Types and Speculation Regarding Their Respective Aetiologies," in *Dogs and People in Social, Working, Economic or Symbolic Interaction: Proceedings of the 9th Conference of the International Council of Archaeozoology, Durham, August 2002*, ed. Lynn M. Snyder and Elizabeth A. Moore, 12–23. Oxford: Oxbow, 2006.

Bayer, Barbara. "Roses to Ruin." *The Blood-Horse*, no. 30 (July 26, 2003): 3918–23.

Becker, Gay. *The Elusive Embryo: How Women and Men Approach New Reproductive Technology*. Berkeley: University of California Press, 2000.

Beckes, Lane, and James A. Coan. "Social Baseline Theory: The Role of Social Proximity in Emotion and Economy of Action." *Social and Personality Psychology Compass* 5, no. 12 (2011): 976–88.

Beder, Joan. "Loss of the Assumptive World: How We Deal with Death and Loss," *Omega* 50 (2005): 255–65.

Behrens, Hermann. *Die Neolithisch-frühmetallzeitlichen Tierskelettfunde der alten Welt: Studien zu ihrer Wesensdeutung und historischen Problematik*. Berlin: Deutscher verlag der Wissenschaften, 1964.

Berthold, S. Megan. *Vicarious Trauma and Resilience*. Sacramento, CA: CME Resource, 2011.

Beyer, Gerry W. "Pet Animals: What Happens When Their Humans Die?" *Santa Clara Law Review* 40, no. 3 (2000): 617–76.

Bokovenko, Nikolai A. "The Origins of Horse Riding and the Development of Ancient Central Asian Nomadic Riding Harness." In *Kurgans, Ritual Sites, and Settlements: Eurasian Bronze and Iron Age*, ed. Jeannine Davis-Kimball, E. Murphy, L. Koryakova and L. T. Yablonsky, 304–10. Oxford: Archaeopress, 2000.

Bougeant, Guillaume Hyacinthe. *Amusement Philosophique sur les Langages des Bêtes*. Paris: Gissey, 1739.

Bouquet, Mary. *Reclaiming English Kinship: Portuguese Refractions of British Kinship Theory*. Manchester: Manchester University Press, 1993.

Bradley, Richard. "Darkness and Light in the Design of Megalithic Tombs." *Oxford Journal of Archaeology* 8 (1989): 251–59.

Bradshaw, G. A. "Elephants, Us, and Other Family: How Attachment Theory Has Started a Cultural Revolution." Paper presented at "Affect Dysregulation and the Healing of the Self," Annual Interpersonal Neurobiology Conference, UCLA, March 14–16, 2014.

Bradshaw, G. A., Jeffrey G. Borchers, and Vera Muller-Paisner. *Caring for the Caregiver: Analysis and Assessment of Animal Care Professional and Organizational Wellbeing*. Jacksonville: Kerulos Center, 2012.

Bradshaw, G. A., and Mary Watkins. "Trans-Species Psychology: Theory and Praxis." *Spring* 75 (2006): 69–94.

Brandes, Stanley. "The Meaning of American Pet Cemetery Gravestones." *Ethnology* 48, no. 2 (2009): 99–118.

Brewer, Kate A. "Emotional Support Animals Excepted from 'No Pets' Lease Provisions under Federal Law." Animal Legal & Historical Center, 2005. Https://www.animallaw.info.

Brooks, Andrea, ed. "The Health Benefits of Companion Animals." Pets Are Wonderful Support, 2007. Http://www.nps.gov/goga/parkmgmt/upload/Comment-4704-attachment_.pdf.

Brooks Pribac, Teja. "Animal Grief." *Animal Studies Journal* 2, no. 2 (2013): 67–90.

Brown, Arthur E. "Grief in the Chimpanzee." *American Naturalist* 13, no. 3 (March 1879): 173–75.

Brown, Jonathon. "Everybody Loved Vince: I Hope that When I Die, I'll Be as Fondly Remembered." *The Independent*, August 20, 2009.

Bryant, Taimie L. "Trauma, Law, and Advocacy for Animals." *Journal of Animal Law and Ethics* 1 (2006): 63–138.

Burman, Erica. *Deconstructing Developmental Psychology*. New York: Routledge, 1993.

Butler, Judith. *Frames of War: When Is Life Grievable?* London: Verso, 2009.

———. *Precarious Life: The Powers of Mourning and Violence*. London: Verso, 2004.

Byun Duk-kun. "Asia's Biggest Pet Store, Mega Pet, to Open in July." *Korea Times*, January 29, 2003.

Calder, Angus. *The Myth of the Blitz*. London: Pimlico, 1992.

———. *The People's War: Britain, 1939–1945*. London: Jonathan Cape, 1969.

Cambridge Declaration on Consciousness. Proclaimed at the Francis Crick Memorial Conference, Cambridge, July 7, 2012.

Carmack, Betty J. *Grieving the Death of a Pet*. Minneapolis: Augsburg Press, 2003.

Cassidy, Rebecca. *Horse People: Thoroughbred Culture in Lexington and Newmarket*. Baltimore: Johns Hopkins University Press, 2007.

———. *Sport of Kings: Kinship, Class, and Thoroughbred Breeding in Newmarket*. Cambridge: Cambridge University Press, 2002.

Chambers, William, and Robert Chambers, eds. *Chambers's Information for the People*. London: W. & R. Chambers, 1874.

Chang, Claudia, and Katharine Guroff, eds. *Of Gold and Grass: Nomads of Kazakhstan*. Bethesda: Foundation for International Arts and Education, 2007.

Charles, Nickie, and Charlotte Aull Davies. "My Family and Other Animals: Pets as Kin." *Sociological Research Online* 13, no. 5 (2008).

Clabby, John. *A History of the Royal Army Veterinary Corps, 1919–61*. London: J. A. Allen, 1963.

Clabes, Judy. "Invisible Ink Left Indelible Mark on Hearts, Minds of His Loving Owners and His Fans." Kentucky Horse Park (website), September 15, 2011.

Clandinin, D. Jean, and F. Michael Connelly. *Narrative Inquiry: Experience and Story in Qualitative Research*. San Francisco: Jossey-Bass, 2000.

Clout, Laura. "A Better Resting Place for the Animal VCs." *Daily Telegraph*, December 14, 2007, 12.

Cluss, Adolf. "Modern Street-Pavements." *Popular Science Monthly* 7 (1875): 80–89.

Coetzee, Jan K., and Asta Rau. "Narrating Trauma and Suffering: Towards Understanding Intersubjectively Constituted Memory." *Forum: Qualitative Social Research* 10, no. 2 (2009): art. 14.

Cordaro, Millie. "Pet Loss and Disenfranchised Grief: Implication for Mental Health Counseling Practice." *Journal of Mental Health Counseling* 34 (2012): 283–94.

Corr, Charles A., Clyde M. Nabe, and Donna M. Corr. *Death and Dying, Life and Living*. 6th ed. Belmont: Wadsworth, 2009.

Courthouse Dogs Foundation. "Legal Support for the Use of a Facility Dog to Assist Testifying Crime Victims and Witnesses: A Review of the Evidence Rule, Case Law, State Statutes, and Legislation." 2014. Http://www.courthousedogs.com.

Cowles, Kathleen V. "The Death of a Pet: Human Responses to the Breaking of the Bond." *Marriage & Family Review* 8, nos. 3–4 (1985): 135–48.

"Customer Letters." Anthony Eddy's Wildlife Studio. Http://www.pet-animalpreservation.com/.

Davis, Patricia. "Artist's Statement." National September 11 Memorial & Museum, Artists Registry. Https://www.911memorial.org.

Davis, Susan, and Margo DeMello. *Stories Rabbits Tell: A Natural and Cultural History of a Misunderstood Creature.* New York: Lantern, 2005.

de Waal, Frans. *The Age of Empathy: Nature's Lessons for a Kinder Society.* New York: Harmony Books, 2009.

Dean, Richard. *An Essay on the Future Life of Brutes, Introduced with Observations upon Evil, Its Nature, and Origin.* 2 vols. Manchester: J. Harrop, 1767.

Demarne, Cyril. *The London Blitz, A Fireman's Tale.* London: Parents' Centre Publications, 1980.

Derrida, Jacques. *The Animal that Therefore I Am.* New York: Fordham University Press, 2008.

Desmond, Jane. "Animal Deaths and the Written Record of History: The Politics of Pet Obituaries." In *Making Animal Meaning*, ed. Linda Kalof and Georgina M. Montgomery, 99–111. East Lansing: Michigan State University Press, 2011.

———. "Displaying Death, Animating Life: Changing Fictions of 'Liveness' from Taxidermy to Animatronics." In *Representing Animals*, ed. Nigel Rothfels, 159–79. Bloomington: Indiana University Press, 2002.

———. "Postmortem Exhibitions: Taxidermied Animals and Plastinated Corpses in the Theaters of the Dead." *Configurations* 16, no. 3 (2008): 347–78.

Despret, Vinciane. "The Becomings of Subjectivity in Animal Worlds." *Subjectivity* 23 (2008): 123–39.

Dickinson, G. E., and E. S. Paul. "UK Veterinary Schools: Emphasis on End-of-Life Issues." *Veterinary Record* 174, no. 7 (2014). doi: 10.1136/vr.102152.

Dickinson, George E., Paul D. Roof, and Karin W. Roof. "End-of-Life Issues in United States Veterinary Medicine Schools." *Society & Animals* 18, no. 2 (2010): 152–62.

———. "A Survey of Veterinarians in the U.S.: Euthanasia and Other End-of-Life Issues." *Anthrozoös* 24, no. 2 (2011): 167–74.

Dillard, Carter, David Favre, Eric Glitzenstein, Mariann Sullivan, and Sonia Waisman. "Animal Advocacy and Causes of Action." *Animal Law* 13 (2006): 87–121.

Dillard, Jennifer. "A Slaughterhouse Nightmare: Psychological Harm Suffered by Slaughterhouse Employees and the Possibility of Redress through Legal Reform." *Georgetown Journal on Poverty Law and Policy* 15 (2008): 391–408.

"Dogs and Cats into Soap." *American Soap Journal and Perfume Gazette* 5, no. 10 (1895): 335–36.

Doka, Kenneth J., ed. *Disenfranchised Grief: Recognizing Hidden Sorrow.* Lexington, MA: Lexington Books, 1989.

Donaldson, Sue, and Will Kymlicka. *Zoopolis: A Political Theory of Animal Rights.* Oxford: Oxford University Press, 2011.

Drummond, William H. *The Rights of Animals, and Man's Obligation to Treat Them with Humanity.* London: John Mardon, 1838.

Eco, Umberto. "Sull'anima delle bestie." In *Animalia*, ed. Ivano Dionigi, 67–86. Milano: Bur, 2012.

Engel, Susan. *The Stories Children Tell: Making Sense of the Narratives of Childhood.* New York: W. H. Freeman, 1995.

Fawcett, Leesa. "Kinship Imaginaries: Children's Stories of Wild Friendships, Fear, and Freedom." In *Routledge Handbook of Human–Animal Studies*, ed. Garry Marvin and Susan McHugh, 259–74. New York: Routledge, 2014.

Feh, Claudia. "Relationships and Communication in Socially Natural Horse Herds." In *The Domestic Horse: The Origins, Developments, and Management of Its Behaviour*, ed. D. S. Mills and S. M. McDonnell, 83–93. Cambridge: Cambridge University Press, 2005.

Fogle, Bruce, and David Abrahamson. "Pet Loss: A Survey of the Attitudes and Feelings of Practising Veterinarians." *Anthrozoös* 3, no. 3 (1990): 143–50.

Franklin, Adrian. *Animals and Modern Cultures: A Sociology of Human–Animal Relations in Modernity*. London: Sage, 1999.

Franklin, Sarah. *Embodied Progress: A Cultural Account of Assisted Conception*. London: Routledge, 1997.

Freud, Sigmund. *On Murder, Mourning, and Melancholia*. Trans. Shaun Whiteside. London: Penguin Classics, 2005.

Fudge, Erica. *Pets*. Stocksfield: Acumen, 2008.

Fulford, Michael. "Links with the Past: Pervasive 'Ritual' Behaviour in Roman Britain." *Britannia* 32 (2001): 199–218.

Fulford, Michael, Stephen Rippon, Steve Ford, Jane Timby, Brian Williams, Denise Allen, J. R. L. Allen, S. J. Allen, G. C. Boon, Tess Durden, Janet Firth, Sheila Hamilton-Dyer, M. Reid, D. Richards, and Elizabeth Somerville. "Silchester: Excavations at the North Gate, on the North Walls, and in the Northern Suburbs 1988 and 1991–3." *Britannia* 28 (1997): 87–168.

Gabałówna, L. "Pochówki Bydlęce Kultury Amfor Kulistych Ze Stanowiska 4 W Brześciu Kujawskim W Świetle Podobnych Znalezisk Kultur Środkowoeuropejskich." *Prace i Materiały Łódź* 3 (1958): 63–108.

Gage, M. Geraldine, and Ralph Holcomb. "Couples' Perception of Stressfulness of Death of the Family Pet." *Family Relations* 40, no. 1 (1991): 103–5.

Gaillemin, Bérénice. "Vivre et construire la mort des animaux: Le cimetière d'Asnières." *Ethnologie française* 39, no. 3 (2009): 495–507.

Gaita, Raimond. *The Philosopher's Dog*. London: Routledge, 2003.

Game, Ann. "Riding: Embodying the Centaur." *Body & Society* 7, no. 4 (2001): 1–12.

Garrett, Aaron V., ed. *Animal Rights and Souls in the Eighteenth Century*. 6 vols. Bristol: Thoemmes Press, 2000.

———. "Animals and Ethics in the History of Modern Philosophy." In *The Oxford Handbook of Animal Ethics*, ed. Thomas Beauchamp and Ray Frey, 61–87. New York: Oxford University Press, 2011.

Gilquin, Gaëtanelle, and George M. Jacobs. "Elephants Who Marry Mice Are Very Unusual: The Use of the Relative Pronoun *Who* with Nonhuman Animals." *Society & Animals* 14, no. 1 (2006): 79–105.

Glover, Henry Clay. *Diseases of the Dog and How to Feed*. New York: H. Clay Glover, 1897.

Gordon, W. J. *The Horse-World of London*. London: Religious Tract Society, 1893.

Gossip, James. *Excavations at York Road Leicester (NGR SK 585039)*. University of Leicester Archaeological Services, Report 99/111. Leicester: University of Leicester, 1999.

Gough, Edward W. *"Centaur"; or the Turn Out: A Practical Treatise on the (Humane) Management of Horses*. London: Henry Thacker, 1885.

Gough, Paul. "'Garden of Gratitude': The National Memorial Arboretum and Strategic Remembering." In *Public History and Heritage Today: People and Their Pasts*, ed. Paul Ashton and Hilda Kean, 95–112. London: Palgrave Macmillan, 2012.

Gower, Robert. "RSPCA." *Veterinary Record*, June 22, 1940, 475.

Granek, Leeat, Paolo Mazzotta, Richard Tozer, and Monika K. Krzyzanowska. "Oncologists' Protocol and Coping Strategies in Dealing with Patient Loss." *Death Studies* 37, no. 10 (2013): 937–52.

Grant, A. "Animals and Ritual in Early Britain: The Visible and the Invisible." In *Animal et pratiques religieuses: Les manifestations matérielles; Actes du colloque international de Compiègne, 11–13 novembre 1988*, ed. Patrice Méniel, 79–86. Paris: Association L'Homme et l'animal, 1989.

Grant, Annie. "Animal Husbandry." In *Danebury: An Iron Age Hillfort in Hampshire*, vol. 2, *The Excavations, 1969–1978: The Finds*, ed. Barry W. Cunliffe, 496–548. London: Council for British Archaeology, 1984.

Greenwood, James. "Mr. William Spavinger's Speech on Hippophagy," *London Society* 13 (1868): 467.

Grier, Katherine C. *Pets in America: A History*. Chapel Hill: University of North Carolina Press, 2006.

———. "Provisioning Man's Best Friend: The Early Years of the American Pet Food Industry, 1870–1942." In *Food Chains: From Farmyard to Shopping Cart*, ed. Warren Belasco and Roger Horowitz, 132–34. Philadelphia: University of Pennsylvania Press, 2009.

Grimm, David. *Citizen Canine: Our Evolving Relationship with Cats and Dogs*. New York: Public Affairs, 2014.

Grinsell, L. V. *Dorset Barrows*. Dorchester: Dorset Natural History and Archaeological Society, 1959.

Gryaznov, Mikail. *Pervyi Pazyrykskii Kurgan* [First Pazyryk Kurgan]. St. Petersburg: Hermitage, 1950.

Guido, Vecchi Gian. "Il Papa e gli animali 'Il Paradiso è aperto a tutte le creature.'" *Corriere della Sera*, November 27, 2014, 25.

Gupta, Anthea Fraser. "Foxes, Hounds, and Horses: Who or Which?" *Society & Animals* 14, no. 1 (2006): 107–28.

"Half Cat, Half Machine: Dutch Artist Turns Dead Cat Orville into the Orvillecopter." *The Telegraph*, June 4, 2012.

Hama, Haruyo, Masao Yogo, and Yoshinori Matsuyama. "Effects of Stroking Horses on Both Humans' and Horses' Heart Rate Responses." *Japanese Psychological Research* 38, no. 2 (1996): 66–73.

Hamerow, Helena. "'Special Deposits' in Anglo-Saxon Settlements." *Medieval Archaeology* 50 (2006): 1–30.

Hansen, Natalie. "Embodied Communication: The Poetics and Politics of Riding." In *Sport, Animals, and Society*, ed. James Gillett and Michelle Gilbert, 251–67. New York: Routledge, 2014.

Haraway, Donna. *The Companion Species Manifesto: Dogs, People and Significant Otherness*. Chicago: Prickly Paradigm Press, 2003.

———. *Primate Visions: Gender, Race, and Nature in the World of Modern Science*. New York: Routledge, 1989.

———. *When Species Meet*. Minneapolis: University of Minnesota Press, 2008.

Harcourt, R. A. "The Dog in Prehistoric and Early Historic Britain." *Journal of Archaeological Science* 1 (1974): 151–75.

Harris, Oliver. "Emotional and Mnemonic Geographies at Hambledon Hill: Texturing Neolithic Places with Bodies and Bones." *Cambridge Archaeological Journal* 20 (2010): 357–71.

Harris, Oliver, and Tim Flohr Sørensen. "Rethinking Emotion and Material Culture." *Archaeological Dialogues* 17 (2010): 145–63.

Hart-Cohen, Debra S. "Canines in the Courtroom." *GPSolo* 26, no. 5 (2009): 54–57.

Haskin, Steve. "The Loss of a Thoroughbred," *Hangin' with Haskin*, Blood-Horse blogs, July 7, 2011.

Hearne, Vicki. *Adam's Task: Calling Animals by Name*. New York: Skyhorse, 2007.

Hewson, C. "Grief for Pets Part 1: Overview and Update from the Literature." *Veterinary Ireland Journal* 4, no. 7 (2014): 380–85.

Hildrop, John. *Free Thoughts upon the Brute Creation; or, an Examination of Father Bougeant's Philosophical Amusement &c. in Two Letters to a Lady*. London: R. Minors Bookseller and Stationer, 1742.

Hill, J. D. *Ritual and Rubbish in the Iron Age of Wessex: A Study on the Formation of a Specific Archaeological Record*. Oxford: Tempus Reparatum, 1995.

Hillman, James. "Aesthetics and Politics." *Tikkun* 11 (1996): 38–40.

Homer. *The Iliad*, trans. Robert Fagles. New York: Penguin, 1986.

Horowitz, Roger. *Putting Meat on the American Table: Taste, Technology, Transformation*. Baltimore: Johns Hopkins University Press, 2006.

"How to Preserve Your Pet Forever." *American Stuffers*. Http://www.animalplanet.com/tv-shows/american-stuffers/videos/how-to-preserve-your-pet-forever/.

Howell, Philip. "The Dog Fancy at War: Breeds, Breeding, and Britishness, 1914–1918." *Society & Animals* 21, no. 6 (2013): 546–67.

———. "A Place for the Animal Dead: Pets, Pet Cemeteries and Animal Ethics in Late Victorian Britain." *Ethics, Place & Environment* 5, no. 1 (2002): 5–22.

Huijser, Marcel P., John W. Duffield, Anthony P. Clevenger, Robert J. Ament, and Pat T. McGown. "Cost-Benefit Analyses of Mitigation Measures Aimed at Reducing Collisions with Large Ungulates in the United States and Canada: A Decision Support Tool." *Ecology and Society* 14, no. 2 (2009): 15.

Humane Society of the United States. "Pets by the Numbers." January 30, 2014.

Huss, Rebecca J. "Why Context Matters: Defining Service Animals under Federal Law." *Pepperdine Law Review* 37, no. 4 (2010): 1163–1216.

Huxley, Julian. "War-time Reactions of Cats." In *The Cat*, 88–89. Cats Protection League, 1941.

Iliff, Susan A. "An Additional 'R': Remembering the Animals." *ILAR Journal* 43, no. 1 (2002): 38–47.

Imamura, Yuri. "New Theory Questions Hachiko's Loyalty, Says Chicken Tidbits the Answer." *Asahi Shimbum*, January 16, 2014.

Ipsos-Reid. "Paws and Claws: A Syndicated Study on Canadian Pet Ownership." June 2001. Http://ocpm.qc.ca/sites/import.ocpm.aegirvps.net/files/pdf/P56/7a1a.pdf.

Irvine, Leslie. *Filling the Ark: Animal Welfare in Disasters*. Philadelphia: Temple University Press, 2009.

———. *If You Tame Me: Understanding Our Connection with Animals*. Philadelphia: Temple University Press, 2004.

Jackson, Peter. "Bomber Command Fliers in Their Own Words." *BBC News*, June 27, 2012.

Jacobson, Esther. "The Issyk Headdress: Symbol and Meaning in the Iron Age Nomadic Culture." In *Of Gold and Grass: Nomads of Kazakhstan*, ed. Claudia Chang and Katharine S. Guroff, 65–70. Bethesda: Foundation for International Arts and Education, 2007.

Janoff-Bulman, Ronnie. "Posttraumatic Growth: Three Explanatory Models." *Psychological Inquiry* 15 (2004): 30–34.

Johnston, Jay, and Fiona Probyn-Rapsey, eds. *Animal Death*. Sydney: Sydney University Press, 2013.

Jones, Chuck, dir. *Fast and Furry-ous*. Warner Brothers Cartoons.

Joseph, Dave. "Back from the Dead," *Sun Sentinel*, June 7, 2001.

Kastenbaum, Robert. "Vicarious Grief: An Intergenerational Phenomenon?" *Death Studies* 11, no. 6 (1987): 447–53.

Kean, Hilda. *Animal Rights: Political and Social Change in Britain since 1800*. London: Reaktion, 2000.

———. "Animals and War Memorials: Different Approaches to Commemorating the Human–Animal Relationship." In *Animals and War: Studies of Europe and North America*, ed. Ryan Hediger, 237–62. Leiden: Brill, 2012.

———. "The Home Front as a 'Moment' for Animals and Humans: Exploring the Animal–Human Relationship in Contemporary Diaries and Letters." In *The Home Front in Britain: Images, Myths and Forgotten Experiences, 1914–2014*, ed. Maggie Andrews and Janis Lomas. London: Palgrave Macmillan, 2014.

———. "Human and Animal Space in Historic 'Pet' Cemeteries in London, New York and Paris." In *Animal Death*, ed. Jay Johnston and Fiona Probyn-Rapsey, 21–42. Sydney: Sydney University Press, 2013.

Kearney, Richard. *On Stories*. New York: Routledge, 2002.

Kelly, Lucretia. "Beyond Food: the Role of Animals in Ritual and Ideology." *Illinois Antiquity* (2010): 8–10.

Kenney, Elizabeth. "Pet Funerals and Animal Graves in Japan." *Mortality* 9, no. 1 (2004): 42–60.

King, Barbara J. *How Animals Grieve*. Chicago: University of Chicago Press, 2013.

Kirby, Elizabeth, and Arthur Moss. *Animals Were There: A Record of the Work of the RSPCA during the War of 1939–1945*. London: Hutchinson, 1947.

Kisiel, Emma. "At Rest." *iGNANT*, July 17, 2013.

Kleiderman, Alex. "Bomber Command Memorial Moves Veterans." *BBC News*, June 28, 2012.

Kramer, Cheryce. "Digital Beasts as Visual Esperanto: Getty Images and the Colonization of Sight." In *Thinking with Animals: New Perspectives on Anthropomorphism*, ed. Lorraine Daston and Gregg Mitman, 138–71. New York: Columbia University Press, 2005.

Lagerås, Per. "Burial Rituals Inferred from Palynological Evidence: Results from a Late Neolithic Stone Cist in Southern Sweden." *Vegetation History and Archaeobotany* 9 (2000): 169–73.

Laurier, Eric, Angus Whyte, and Kathy Buckner. "Neighbouring as an Occasioned Activity: 'Finding a Lost Cat.'" *Space and Culture* 5, no. 4 (2002): 346–67.

Lawrence, Elizabeth Atwood. "The Centaur: Its History and Meaning in Human Culture." *Journal of Popular Culture* 27, no. 4 (1994): 57–68.

Leatherman, Dale. "Star Quality." *Discover Horses: The Kentucky Horse Park Magazine*, 2011–12, 54.

Lestel, Dominique, Florence Brunois, and Florence Gaunet. "Etho-ethnology and Ethno-ethology." *Social Science Information* 45, no. 2 (2006): 155–77.

Levine, Joshua. *Forgotten Voices of Dunkirk*. London: Ebury, 2010.

Lévi-Strauss, Claude. *Le Totémisme aujourd'hui*. Paris: Presses Universitaires de France, 1962.

Lewey, Frank R. *Cockney Campaign*. London: Stanley Paul, 1944.

Liebman, Matthew. "Who the Judge Ate for Breakfast: On the Limits of Creativity in Animal Law and the Redeeming Power of Powerlessness." *Animal Law* 18 (2011): 133–50.

Lind-af-Hageby, Louise. *Bombed Animals—Rescued Animals—Animals Saved from Destruction*. London: Animal Defence and Anti-Vivisection Society, 1941.

Lopez, Barry Holstun, and Robin Eschner. *Apologia*. Athens: University of Georgia Press, 1998.

Lopez, Barry. "Apologia." In *A Road Runs through It: Reviving Wild Places*, ed. Thomas Reed Petersen, 39–43. Boulder, CO: Johnson Books, 2006.

Losey, Robert J., Sandra Garvie-Lok, Jennifer A. Leonard, M. Anne Katzenberg, Mietje Germonpré, Tatiana Nomokonova, Mikhail V. Sablin, Olga I. Goriunova, Natalia E. Berdnikova, and Nikolai A. Savel'ev. "Burying Dogs in Ancient Cis-Baikal, Siberia: Temporal Trends and Relationships with Human Diet and Subsistence Practices." *PLoS ONE* 8, no. 5 (2013): e63740, doi: 10.1371/journal.pone.0063740.

Luff, Rosemary M., and Marta Moreno García. "Killing Cats in the Medieval Period: An Unusual Episode in the History of Cambridge, England." *Archaeofauna* 4 (1995): 93–114.

Lukacs, John. *Five Days in London, May 1940*. New Haven: Yale Nota Bene, 2001.

Madden, Dave. *The Authentic Animal: Inside the Odd and Obsessive World of Taxidermy*. New York: St. Martin's Press, 2011.

Madgwick, Richard, Naomi Sykes, Holly Miller, Rob Symmons, James Morris, and Angela Lamb.

"Fallow Deer (*Dama dama dama*) Management in Roman South-East Britain." *Archaeological and Anthropological Sciences* 5 (2013): 111–22.

Maher, Lisa A., Jay T. Stock, Sarah Finney, James J. N. Heywood, Preston T. Miracle, and Edward B. Banning. "A Unique Human-Fox Burial from a Pre-Natufian Cemetery in the Levant (Jordan)." *PLoS ONE* 6, no. 1 (2011): e15815, doi:10.1371/journal.pone.0015815.

Maltby, M. "The Animal Bones." In *The Prehistoric Settlement at Winnall Down, Winchester: Excavations of MARC 3 Site R17 in 1976 and 1977*, ed. P. J. Fasham, 97–125. Winchester, UK: Hampshire Field Club, 1985.

Maltby, Mark. "The Animal Bone from a Romano-British Well at Oakridge II, Basingstoke, Hampshire." *Proceedings of the Hampshire Field Club and Archaeological Society* 49 (1994): 47–76.

———. *The Animal Bones from the Excavations at Owslebury, Hants., an Iron Age and Early Romano-British Settlement*. English Heritage, Ancient Monuments Laboratory Report 6/87. Southampton: University of Southampton, 1989.

———. "Sheep Foundation Burials in Roman Winchester." In *The Ritual Killing and Burial of Animals: European Perspectives*, ed. Aleksander Pluskowski, 152–63. Oxford: Oxbow, 2012.

Mangum, Teresa. "Dog Years, Human Fears." In *Representing Animals*, ed. Nigel Rothfels, 35–47. Bloomington: Indiana University Press, 2002.

Mann, Julie. "PETA Wants Roadside Memorial for Cows." *CBS Chicago Newsradio*, January 20, 2012.

Mapes, Diane. "When I Die, So Does My Dog: Some Pet Owners Take Animals to Their Graves." *MSNBC News*, November 30, 2010.

Marcella, Kenneth. "Managing Grief Responses: Bereavement Could Deteriorate the Health of Your Horses." *DVM 360 Magazine*, October 1, 2004.

Marciniak, Arkadiusz. *Placing Animals in the Neolithic: Social Zooarchaeology of Prehistoric Farming Communities*. London: UCL Press, 2005.

Marder, Michael. "Is It Ethical to Eat Plants?" *Parallax* 19, no. 1 (2013): 29–37.

Martin, Emily. "The Egg and the Sperm: How Science Has Constructed a Romance Based on Stereotypical Male–Female Roles." *Signs* 16, no. 3 (1991): 485–501.

Marvin, Garry. "Enlivened through Memory: Hunters and Hunting Trophies." In *The Afterlives of Animals: A Museum Menagerie*, ed. Samuel J. M. M. Alberti, 202–17. Charlottesville: University of Virginia Press, 2011.

McCann, I. Lisa, and Laurie Anne Pearlman. "Vicarious Traumatization: A Framework for Understanding the Psychological Effects of Working with Victims." *Journal of Traumatic Stress* 3 (1990): 131–49.

McGilchrist, Iain. *The Master and His Emissary: The Divided Brain and the Making of the Western World*. New Haven: Yale University Press, 2009.

McHugh, Susan. "Bitches from Brazil: Cloning and Owning Dogs through the Missyplicity Project." In *Representing Animals*, ed. Nigel Rothfels, 180–98. Bloomington: Indiana University Press, 2002.

McKee, Tamar V. S. "Ghost Herds: Rescuing Horses and Horse People in Bluegrass Kentucky." PhD dissertation, University of British Columbia, 2014.

Méniel, Patrice. *Les Sacrifices d'animaux chez les Gaulois*. Paris: Editions Errance, 1992.

Merleau-Ponty, Maurice. *Phenomenology of Perception*. London: Routledge, 1962.

Midgley, Mary. *Utopias, Dolphins and Computers: Problems in Philosophical Plumbing*. London: Routledge, 1996.

Miller, Lila, and Stephen Zawistowski. *Shelter Medicine for Veterinarians and Staff*. 2nd ed. Hoboken: Wiley-Blackwell, 2013.

Mills, Wesley. *The Dog in Health and in Disease*. New York: D. Appleton, 1892.

Milner, Nicky, and Dorian Q. Fuller. "Contending with Animal Bones." *Archaeological Review from Cambridge* 16 (1999): 1–12.

Mithen, Steven J. *After the Ice: A Global Human History, 20,000–5000 BC*. Cambridge, MA: Harvard University Press, 2004.

Morgan, David. *Acquaintances: The Space between Strangers and Intimates*. Maidenhead: Open University Press, 2009.

Morley, Christine, and Jan Fook. "The Importance of Pet Loss and Some Implications for Services." *Mortality* 10, no. 2 (2005): 127–43.

Morris, Desmond. *Horsewatching*. New York: Crown, 1988.

Morris, James. "Animal 'Ritual' Killing: From Remains to Meanings." In *The Ritual Killing and Burial of Animals: European Perspectives*, ed. Aleksander Pluskowski, 8–21. Oxford: Oxbow, 2012.

———. "Associated Bone Groups: One Archaeologist's Rubbish Is Another's Ritual Deposition." In *Changing Perspectives on the First Millennium BC: Proceedings of the Iron Age Research Student Seminar 2006*, ed. Oliver Davis, Niall Sharples, and Kate Waddington, 83–98. Oxford: Oxbow, 2008.

———. *Investigating Animal Burials: Ritual, Mundane and Beyond*. Oxford: Archaeopress, 2011.

Morris, James, and Ben Jervis. "What's So Special? A Reinterpretaion of Anglo-Saxon 'Special Deposits.'" *Medieval Archaeology* 55 (2011): 66–81.

Morris, Patricia. *Blue Juice: Euthanasia in Veterinary Medicine*. Philadelphia: Temple University Press, 2012.

Murti, Vasu. *They Shall Not Hurt or Destroy: Animal Rights and Vegetarianism in the Western Religious Traditions*. Cleveland: Vegetarian Advocates, 2003.

National Canine Defence League. "September Holocaust." *The Dogs' Bulletin* 114 (December 1939).

Natsume Sōseki. *Ten Nights' Dreams and Our Cat's Grave*. Trans. Sankichi Hata and Dofu Shirai. Tokyo: Tokyo News Service, 1934.

Nelson, Katherine. "Event Representations, Narrative Development, and Internal Working Models." *Attachment & Human Development* 1, no. 3 (1999): 239–52.

Nicholls, Henry. "Ham the Astrochimp: Hero or Victim?" *The Guardian*, December 16, 2013.

O'Connor, Terry. *Bones from Anglo-Scandinavian Levels at 16–22 Coppergate*. Fasc. 3 of *The Archaeology of York*, vol. 15, *The Animal Bones*. York: Council for British Archaeology, 1989.

Ogle, Maureen. *In Meat We Trust: An Unexpected History of Carnivore America*. Boston: Houghton Mifflin, 2013.

Oliver, Kelly. "Pet Lovers, Pathologized." *New York Times*, October 30, 2011.

O'Malley Halley, Jean. *The Parallel Lives of Women and Cows: Meat Markets*. New York: Palgrave Macmillan, 2012.

Pachirat, Timothy. *Every Twelve Seconds: Industrialized Slaughter and the Politics of Sight*. New Haven: Yale University Press, 2013.

Pallotta, Nicole R. "Becoming an Animal Rights Activist: An Exploration of Culture, Socialization, and Identity Transformation." PhD dissertation, University of Georgia, 2005.

Panksepp, Jaak, and Lucy Biven, eds. *The Archaeology of Mind: Neuroevolutionary Origins of Human Emotions*. New York: W. W. Norton, 2012.

"Paragraphs of Natural and Unnatural History." *Current Literature* 1, no. 4 (1888): 350.

Park, Crystal L. "Making Sense of the Meaning Literature: An Integrative Review of Meaning Making and Its Effects on Adjustment to Stressful Life Events." *Psychological Bulletin* 136, no. 2 (2010): 257–301.

Parker, Gail. "The Dickin Medal and the PDSA Animal Cemetery." *After the Battle* 140 (2008): 46–55.

Partridge, Frances. *A Pacifist's War: Diaries, 1939–1945*. Vol. 1. London: Phoenix, 1999.

PDSA, *Annual Report 1945*. (London: PDSA 1946).Patton, Paul. "Language, Power, and the Training of Horses." In *Zoontologies: The Question of the Animal*, ed. Cary Wolfe, 83–99. Minneapolis: University of Minnesota Press, 2003.

People's Dispensary for Sick Animals. *A Commemorative Brochure Documenting 80 Years of the People's Dispensary for Sick Animals*. Telford: PDSA, 1997.

———. *PDSA Dickin Medal*. Telford: PDSA, 2014.

Peterson, Buck. *Original Road Kill Cookbook*. Berkeley: Ten Speed Press, 1985.

Peterson, Rick. "Social Memory and Ritual Performance." *Journal of Social Archaeology* 13 (2013): 266–83.

Phillips, Mary T. "Proper Names and the Social Construction of Biography: The Negative Case of Laboratory Animals." *Qualitative Sociology* 17, no. 2 (1994): 119–42.

Philo, Chris. "'To Go Back up the Side Hill': Memories, Imaginations, and Reveries of Childhood." *Children's Geographies* 1, no. 1 (2003): 7–23.

Philo, Chris, and Chris Wilbert, eds. *Animal Spaces, Beastly Places: New Geographies of Human–Animal Relations*. London: Routledge, 2000.

Pierce, Jessica. *The Last Walk: Reflections on Our Pets at the End of Their Lives*. Chicago: University of Chicago Press, 2012.

Pluskowski, Alek. "The Dragon's Skull: How Can Zooarchaeologists Contribute to Our Understanding of Otherness in the Middle Ages?" In *Animals and Otherness in the Middle Ages: Perspectives across Disciplines*, ed. Francisco de Asis García García, Mónica Ann Walker-Vadillo, and María Victoria Chico Picaza, 109–24. Oxford: Archaeopress, 2013.

Podberscek, Anthony L. "Good to Pet and Eat: The Keeping and Consuming of Dogs and Cats in South Korea." *Journal of Social Issues* 65, no. 3 (2009): 615–32.

Podberscek, Anthony L., Elizabeth S. Paul, and James A. Serpell. *Companion Animals and Us*. Cambridge: Cambridge University Press, 2000.

Poliquin, Rachel. *The Breathless Zoo: Taxidermy and the Cultures of Longing*. University Park: Pennsylvania State University Press, 2012.

Potter, Will. *Green Is the New Red: An Insider's Account of a Social Movement under Siege*. San Francisco: City Lights Publishers, 2011.

Powell, Eric A. "Messengers to the Gods." *Archaeology*, March/April 2014, 48–52.

Preece, Rod. *Awe for the Tiger, Love for the Lamb: A Chronicle of Sensibility to Animals*. London: Routledge, 2002.

"Preliminary Autopsy Results: Knut May Have Died of Brain Disease." *Spiegel Online*. March 22, 2011.

Price, Frances. "Now You See It, Now You Don't: Mediating Science and Managing Uncertainty in Reproductive Medicine." In *Misunderstanding Science? The Public Reconstruction of Science and Technology*, ed. Alan Irwin and Brian Wynne, 84–106. Cambridge: Cambridge University Press, 1996.

Primatt, Humphrey. *A Dissertation on the Duty of Mercy and Sin of Cruelty to Brute Animals*. London: R. Hett, 1776.

Proops, Leanne, Karen McComb, David Reby, and Jeanne Altmann. "Cross-modal Individual Recognition in Domestic Horses (*Equus caballus*)." *Proceedings of the National Academy of Sciences* 106, no. 3 (2009): 947–51.

Rag, Jack, ed. *Streetology of London*. London: James S. Jodson, 1837.

Ramstad, Evan, and Jaeyeon Woo. "Foot-and-Mouth Disease Roils Farms." *Wall Street Journal*, January 11, 2011.

Rando, Therese A. *How to Go on Living When Someone You Love Dies*. New York: Bantam Books, 1991.

———. "Vicarious Bereavement." In *Death and the Quest for Meaning*, ed. Stephen Strack, 257–74. Northvale: Jason Aronson, 1997.

Rapport, Nigel. "The 'Contrarieties' of Israel: An Essay on the Cognitive Importance and the Creative Promise of Both/And." *Journal of the Royal Anthropological Institute* 3, no. 4 (1997): 653–72.

Redmalm, David. "An Animal Without an Animal Within: The Powers of Pet Keeping." Doctoral thesis, Örebro University, 2013.

———. "Pet Grief: When Is Non-Human Life Grievable?" *Sociological Review* 63, no. 1 (2015): 19–35.

Reeve, Charlie L., Steven G. Rogelberg, Christiane Spitzmüller, and Natalie DiGiacomo. "The Caring-Killing Paradox: Euthanasia-Related Strain among Animal-Shelter Workers." *Journal of Applied Social Psychology* 35, no. 1 (2005): 119–43.

Reitz, Elizabeth J., and Myra Shackley. *Environmental Archaeology*. New York: Springer, 2012.

Reitz, Elizabeth J., and Elizabeth S. Wing. *Zooarchaeology*. Cambridge: Cambridge University Press, 1999.

Ricoeur, Paul. "Memory and Forgetting." In *Questioning Ethics: Contemporary Debates in Philosophy*, ed. Richard Kearney and Mark Dooley, 5–11. New York: Rouledge, 2002.

Ritvo, Harriet. *The Animal Estate. The English and Other Creatures in the Victorian Age*. Cambridge, MA: Harvard University Press, 1987.

Rogelberg, Steven G., Natalie DiGiacomo, Charlie L. Reeve, Christiane Spitzmüller, Olga L. Clark, Lisa Teeter, Alan G. Walker, Nathan T. Walker, and Paula G. Starling. "What Shelters Can Do About Euthanasia-Related Stress: An Examination of Recommendations from Those on the Front Line." *Journal of Applied Animal Welfare Science* 10, no. 4 (2007): 331–47.

Rollin, Bernard. "Euthanasia and Moral Stress." In *Suffering: Psychological and Social Aspects in Loss, Grief, and Care*, ed. Robert DeBellis, Eric Marcus, Austin H. Kutscher, Carole Smith Torres, Virginia Barrett, and Mary-Ellen Siegel, 115–26. London: Routledge, 2014.

Romain, Tiffany. "'Fertility. Freedom. Finally.': Cultivating Hope in the Face of Uncertain Futures among Egg-Freezing Women." In *The Anthropology of Ignorance: An Ethnographic Approach*, ed. Casey High, Ann H. Kelly, and Jonathan Mair, 189–216. New York: Palgrave Macmillan, 2012.

RSPCA 117th *Annual Report*, 1940, (London: RSPCA, 1940)

Russel, W. M. S., and R. L. Burch. *The Principles of Humane Experimental Technique*. London: Methuen, 1959.

Russell, Nerissa. *Social Zooarchaeology: Humans and Animals in Prehistory*. Cambridge: Cambridge University Press, 2012.

Ryder, Richard D. *Animal Revolution: Changing Attitudes towards Speciesism*. Oxford: Berg, 2000.

Rydge, John. *The Veterinary Surgeon's Vade Mecum: A Complete Guide to the Cure of All Diseases Incident to Horses, Cattle, Sheep, and Dogs*. London: Clerc Smith, 1827.

Rydgrens, Jens. "Shared Beliefs about the Past: A Cognitive Sociology of Intersubjective Memory." In *Frontiers of Sociology*, ed. Peter Hedstrom and Bjorn Wittrock. Leiden: Brill, 2009.

Samashev, Z., G. Bazarbaeva, G. Zhumabekova, and S. Sungatai. Beryl. Almaty, Kazakhstan: O.F. Beryl, 2000.

Sanders, Clinton R. "Killing with Kindness: Veterinary Euthanasia and the Social Construction of Personhood." *Sociological Forum* 10, no. 2 (1995): 195–214.

Sankey, Carol, Marie-Annick Richard-Yris, Hélène Leroy, Séverine Henry, and Martine Hausberger. "Positive Interactions Lead to Lasting Positive Memories in Horses, *Equus caballus*." *Animal Behaviour* 79, no. 4 (2010): 869–75.

Sartre, Jean-Paul. *Being and Nothingness: An Essay on Phenomenological Ontology*, trans. Hazel E. Barnes. New York: Routledge, 1984.

"SD Lawmakers Approve Making Animal Cruelty a Felony." *Rapid City Journal*, March 11, 2014.

Seiler, Andreas, and J.-O. Helldin. "Mortality in Wildlife Due to Transportation." In *The Ecology of Transportation: Managing Mobility for the Environment*, ed. John Davenport and Julia Davenport, 166–68. New York: Springer, 2006.

Shakespeare, William. *Macbeth* (New York: Simon & Schuster, 2014).

Shapiro, Kenneth. "The Caring Sleuth: Portrait of an Animal Rights Activist." *Society & Animals* 2, no. 2 (1994): 145–65.

Shell, Marc. "The Family Pet." *Representations*, no. 15 (1986): 121–53.

Simmonds, P. L. *Waste Products and Undeveloped Substances: A Synopsis of Progress Made in Their Economic Utilisation during the Last Quarter of a Century at Home and Abroad*. London: Robert Hardwicke, 1873.

Simmons, James R. *Feathers and Fur on the Turnpike*. Boston: Christopher Publishing House, 1938.

Sinclair, Rebekah. "Who's on Butler's Plate: Mourning, Vulnerability, and the Consumption of Others." Paper presented on the panel "Women, Animals and Religion: From Fleshy Objects to Embodied Subjects" at the American Academy of Religion National Conference, Atlanta, Georgia, October 30–November 1, 2010.

Smith, Horace. "The Old White Hat—and the Old Grey Mare." In *Gaieties and Gravities: A Series of Essays, Comic Tales, and Fugitive Vagaries*, 61–62. London: Henry Colburn, 1825.

Snowden, R. W. "The Life after Death." *Street Railway Review* 1 (1891): 560–61.

Soron, Dennis. "Road Kill: Commodity Fetishism and Structural Violence." In *Critical Theory and Animal Liberation,* ed. John Sanbonmatsu, 55–70. New York: Rowman & Littlefield, 2011.

Stanescu, James. "Species Trouble: Judith Butler, Mourning, and the Precarious Lives of Animals." *Hypatia* 27, no. 3 (2012): 567–82.

Stephens, Debra Lynn, and Ronald Paul Hill. "The Loss of Animal Companions: A Humanistic and Consumption Perspective." *Society & Animals* 4, no. 2 (1996): 189–210.

Stone, Sherril. "Human Facial Discrimination in Horses: Can They Tell Us Apart?" *Animal Cognition* 13, no. 1 (2010): 51–61.

Styles, John. "The Knacker's Yard." In *The Animal Creation: Its Claims on Our Humanity*, 328. London: Thomas Ward, 1839.

Sullender, R. Scott. "Vicarious Grieving and the Media." *Pastoral Psychology* 59 (2010): 191–200.

Swart, Sandra. "Horses in the South African War, c. 1899–1902." *Society & Animals* 18, no. 4 (2010): 348–66.

Sykes, Naomi. *Beastly Questions: Animal Answers to Archaeological Issues*. London: Bloomsbury, 2014.

Tarlow, Sarah. "The Archaeology of Emotion and Affect." *Annual Review of Anthropology* 41 (2012): 169–85.

Taylor, Chloë. "The Precarious Lives of Animals: Butler, Coetzee, and Animal Ethics." *Philosophy Today* 52 (2008): 60–72.

———. "Respect for the (Animal) Death." In *Animal Death*, ed. Jay Johnston and Fiona Probyn-Rapsey. Sydney: Sydney University Press, 2013, 85–102.

Taylor, George B. *Man's Friend, the Dog*. New York: Frederick A. Stokes, 1891.

Taylor, Nik. "Animal Shelter Emotion Management: A Case of in situ Hegemonic Resistance?" *Sociology* 44, no. 1 (2010): 85–101.

Thomas, Keith. *Man and the Natural World: Changing Attitudes in England, 1500–1800*. London: Penguin Books, 1984.

Thomas, Richard. "Perceptions versus Reality: Changing Attitudes towards Pets in Medieval and

Post-Medieval England." In *Just Skin and Bones? New Perspectives on Human–Animal Relations in the Historical Past*, ed. Aleksander Pluskowski, 95–105. Oxford: Archaeopress, 2005.

Tipper, Becky. "'A Dog Who I Know Quite Well': Everyday Relationships between Children and Animals." *Children's Geographies* 9, no. 2 (2011): 145–65.

———. "Creaturely Encounters: An Ethnographic Study of Human–Animal Relations in a British Suburban Neighbourhood." PhD dissertation, University of Manchester, 2012.

Tipping, Richard. "'Ritual' Floral Tributes in the Scottish Bronze Age—Palynological Evidence." *Journal of Archaeological Science* 21 (1994): 133–39.

Toray, Tamina. "The Human–Animal Bond and Loss: Providing Support for Grieving Clients," *Journal of Mental Health Counseling* 26 (2004): 244–59.

Toynbee, Jocelyn. *Animals in Roman Life and Art*. Ithaca, NY: Cornell University Press, 1973.

Turner, James. *Reckoning with the Beast: Animals, Pain, and Humanity in the Victorian Mind*. Baltimore: Johns Hopkins University Press, 1980.

"Unwanted Horses: How the Industry Is Dealing with Life after Racing." *The Blood-Horse*, no. 40 (October 2, 2010).

van Dierendonck, Matcheld C., and Debbie Goodwin. "Social Contact in Horses: Implications for Human-Horse Interactions." In *The Importance of Social Relationships in Horses*, ed. M. C. van Dierendonck, 28–44. Utrecht: Proefschrift Universitat Utrecht, 2006.

van Dooren, Thom. "Pain of Extinction: The Death of a Vulture," *Cultural Studies Review* 16, no. 2 (2010): 271–89.

Van Manen, Max. *Researching Lived Experience: Human Science for an Action Sensitive Pedagogy*. London, ON: Althouse Press, 1990.

Veldkamp, Elmer. "Aiganken to shokuyōken no aida: Kankoku no inuronsō ni kansuru ikkōsatsu" [Between Pet Dogs and Food Dogs: On the Dog Debate in Modern Korean Society]. In *Higashi Ajia kara no jinruigaku: kokka, kaihatsu, shimin*, ed. the Editorial Board for the Festschrift of Professor Ito Abito, 181–93. Tokyo: Fūkyōsha, 2006.

———. "Commemoration of Dead Animals in Contemporary Korea: Emergence and Development of *Dongmul Wiryeongje* as Modern Folklore." *Review of Korean Studies* 11, no. 3 (2008): 149–69.

———. "Densetsu no inu ga yomigaetta toki: kōhi no gugenka wo tōshite miru Kankokujin no shizenkan" [When a Legendary Dog Comes Back to Life: Korean Views of Nature Seen Through the Concretization of Oral Literature]. In *Sekaiisanjidai no minzokugaku*, ed. Iwamoto Michiya, 349–77. Tokyo: Fūkyōsha, 2013.

———. "The Emergence of 'Pets as Family' and the Socio-Historical Development of Pet Funerals in Japan." *Anthrozoös* 22, no. 4 (2009): 333–46.

Vialles, Noëlie. *Animal to Edible*. Cambridge: Cambridge University Press, 1994.

Villagra, Analía. "Cannibalism, Consumption, and Kinship in Animal Studies." In *Making Animal Meaning*, ed. Linda Kalof and Georgina M. Montgomery. East Lansing: Michigan State University Press, 2011.

Wagman, Bruce A., Sonia S. Waisman, and Pamela D. Frasch. *Animal Law: Cases and Materials*. 4th ed. Durham, NC: Carolina Academic Press, 2010.

Wagner, Allen. "S. Korea Foot-and-Mouth: Over a Million Animals Culled." *Time*, January 18, 2011.

Walraven, Boudewijn. "Bardot Soup and Confucians' Meat: Food and Korean Identity in Global Context." In *Asian Food: The Global and the Local*, ed. Katarzyna Cwiertka and Boudewijn Walraven, 95–115. Richmond: Curzon, 2002.

Ward-Jackson, Philip. *Public Sculpture of the City of London*. Liverpool: Liverpool University Press, 2003.

———. *Public Sculpture of Historic Westminster.* Vol. 1. Liverpool: Liverpool University Press, 2011.

Werner-Lin, Allison, and Teresa Moro. "Unacknowledged and Stigmatized Losses." In *Living beyond Loss: Death in the Family*, ed. Froma Walsh and Monica McGoldrick, 2nd ed., 258–61. New York: W. W. Norton, 2004.

White, Debra J., and Ruth Shawhan. "Emotional Responses of Animal Shelter Workers to Euthanasia." *Journal of the American Veterinary Medical Association* 208, no. 6 (1996): 846–49.

Willich, A. F. M. "Bones." In *The Domestic Encyclopedia*, 263. Philadelphia: Abraham Small, 1821.

Wisch, Rebecca F. "FAQs on Emotional Support Animals," Animal Legal & Historical Center, 2015. Https://www.animallaw.info.

Wiser, Mike. "PETA Wants Memorial to Turkeys Killed in Sioux City Crash." *Sioux City Journal*, April 23, 2014.

Witt, David D. "Pet Burial in the United States." In *Handbook of Death and Dying*, ed. Clifton D. Bryant and Dennis L. Peck, 757–67. Thousand Oaks, CA: Sage Publications, 2003.

Wolfson, David J., and Mariann Sullivan. "Foxes in the Hen House: Animals, Agribusiness, and the Law; a Modern American Fable." In *Animal Rights: Current Debates and New Directions*, ed. Cass R. Sunstein and Martha C. Nussbaum, 205–33. Oxford: Oxford University Press, 2005.

Woods, Tania. "Mourning the Loss of a Companion Animal: An Evaluation of the First Six Years of a Pet Loss Support Service." *Bereavement Care* 19, no. 1 (2000): 8–10.

Woodward, Ann. *British Barrows: A Matter of Life and Death.* Stroud: Tempus, 2000.

Wrobel, Thomas A., and Amanda L. Dye. "Grieving Pet Death: Normative, Gender, and Attachment Issues." *Omega* 47 (2003): 385–93.

Yi Shin-sŏng. *Han'guk kojŏnmunhak kyojaeyŏn'gu.* Seoul: Bogosa Books, 2004.

Yorke, Jan, Cindy Adams, and Nick Coady. "Therapeutic Value of Equine–Human Bonding in Recovery from Trauma." *Anthrozoös* 21, no. 1 (2008): 17–30.

Zapoleon, L. B. *Inedible Animal Fats in the United States.* Stanford: Stanford University Press, 1929.

Ziegler, Philip. *London at War, 1939–1945.* London: Sinclair-Stevenson, 1995.

Contributors

Gala Argent is an interdisciplinary scholar and lifelong equestrienne whose work concerns the relational ways humans and other animals come together to create mutually interdependent lives and selves. She holds a PhD in archaeology and MA and BA degrees in human communication studies and teaches or has taught in departments of art, communication studies, anthropology, and animal studies.

Jessica Austin serves as a consultant at the Centers for Disease Control and Prevention. Her career in public health and health policy has inspired interest in the linkages between nonhuman animals and various aspects of human well-being, including animal abuse's relationship to domestic violence and the benefits of interspecies interaction. She has published and presented on the state of emergency preparedness for companion animals in the United States. Her other research interests include veterinary ethics, relationships between humans and domestic felines, and evolving attitudes toward animals in legal and public policy domains. Austin received her Bachelor of Arts in psychology from Michigan State University, her Master of Public Administration from Western Michigan University, and her Master of Science in Anthrozoology from Canisius College.

Linda Brant is a visual artist and a psychologist from Orlando, Florida. Her academic interests extend across the disciplines of psychology, human–animal studies and visual art. She uses interviews, fieldwork, concept mapping, sculpture, and photography to explore the complexities of interspecies relationships in her art. She is especially interested in the process and function of honoring nonhumans. Brant teaches a course in psychology for artists at Ringling College of Art and Design in Sarasota, Florida. She has exhibited her work in shows and galleries across the country including the Women's Research Center Gallery at the University of Central Florida, the J. K. and Sarah Galloway Foundation Gallery in Winter Park, Florida, and the Selby Gallery at Ringling College of Art and Design. She has won numerous awards for her work and has presented papers on her various projects at state and national conferences.

Keridiana Chez is an assistant professor in the English department at the Borough of Manhattan Community College. Her publications appear in the *Victorian Review* and the *Journal of American Culture*.

Ivy D. Collier is an animal advocate guided by the belief that no animal should be abused or neglected. She works for the Delaware SPCA as the director of development, marketing, and communications and has a history of volunteering for animal shelters and animal advocacy organizations. She earned her

221

Bachelor of Science in social psychology and her Master of Public Affairs focusing on fundraising and nonprofit management. As an independent researcher, her interests focus on human–animal studies with a specific lens on companion animals and popular culture, canine selfhood, companion animals and public policy, puppy mills, the no-kill movement, shelter management, and the Five Freedoms. She is a council member of the American Sociological Association's Animals & Society section and contributes to the Faunalytics blog and the *Human–Animal Studies* Images and Cinema blogs for the Animals and Society Institute. She is also an independent research volunteer for the Animal and Society Institute.

Christina M. Colvin is a visiting assistant professor of English at Emory University. Her work on animals in American literature and culture has appeared in the *Journal of Modern Literature* and *Evental Aesthetics*. Christina also writes in collaboration with the Kimmela Center for Animal Advocacy to reintroduce people to farmed animals as part of Farm Sanctuary's Someone, Not Something project.

Margo DeMello received her PhD in cultural anthropology from the University of California, Davis in 1995, and is an adjunct professor at Canisius College and Central New Mexico Community College. She is also the Human–Animal Studies Program director for the Animals and Society Institute, and president of House Rabbit Society, an international rabbit advocacy organization. Her books include *Stories Rabbits Tell: A Natural and Cultural History of a Misunderstood Creature* (with Susan E. Davis, 2003), *Why Animals Matter: The Case for Animal Protection* (with Erin E. Williams, 2007), *Teaching the Animal: Human–Animal Studies across the Disciplines* (2010), *Speaking for Animals: Animal Autobiographical Writing* (2012), and *Animals and Society: An Introduction to Human–Animal Studies* (2012).

Anne Fawcett is a companion animal veterinarian and lecturer at the University of Sydney. After completing a Bachelor of Arts degree in philosophy, with an honors thesis on Spinoza, she completed a Bachelor of Veterinary Science and Bachelor of Science (veterinary) at the University of Sydney. Since then she has worked in both veterinary practice and academia, completing her masters in veterinary studies (small animal medicine and surgery) through Murdoch University in 2012. Anne is passionate about all aspects of veterinary medicine and surgery, and as an academic has interests in the study of human–animal interaction and veterinary ethics. She is the author of numerous academic publications, including peer-reviewed journal articles and book chapters, and writes a blog www.smallanimaltalk.com about animal issues, from the perspective of a small animal veterinarian, for pet guardians and animal lovers.

Lori Gruen is professor of philosophy, environmental studies, and feminist, gender, and sexuality studies at Wesleyan University, where she coordinates Wesleyan Animal Studies. She also chairs the faculty committee for the Center for Prison Education. She is the author of *Ethics and Animals: An Introduction* (2011) and *Entangled Empathy: An Alternative Ethic for our Relationships with Animals* (2015). She is the editor of *The Ethics of Captivity* (2014), and coeditor with Carol J. Adams of *Ecofeminism: Feminist Intersections with Other Animals and the Earth* (2014). She developed two websites, one memorializing the first one hundred chimpanzees in research (www.first100chimps.wesleyan.edu), and one following the last one thousand chimpanzees' journey to sanctuary (www.last1000chimps.com).

Mary Shannon Johnstone received her BFA from the School of the Art Institute of Chicago and MFA in photography from Rochester Institute of Technology. She is the recipient of numerous awards including "Pause, To Begin" artist, Critical Mass Top 50 (2009, 2010), and Honorable Mention in Lens

Culture's 2010 International Exposure Awards, and 2014 Review Santa Fe 100. Her most recent project "Landfill Dogs" was a 2013 and 2015 Critical Mass Finalist, and "Best in Show" winner at "Puppy Love 2014." "Landfill Dogs" has been featured in national and international exhibitions and magazines and was most notably on *ABC World News* with Diane Sawyer (December 2013), and CNN.com (November 2014). Johnstone is a tenured associate professor at Meredith College in Raleigh, North Carolina.

pattrice jones is a cofounder of VINE Sanctuary, an LGBTQ-run refuge for farmed animals run from within an ecofeminist understanding of the intersection of oppressions. She is the author of *Aftershock: Confronting Trauma in a Violent World* (2007) and *The Oxen at the Intersection: A Collision (2014)*.

Hilda Kean is visiting professor at the University of Greenwich and adjunct professor at the Australian Centre for Public History, University of Technology, Sydney and former dean of Ruskin College, Oxford. Having published widely on cultural/public history and on nonhuman animals her many articles on animals (and their representation) include those published in *Anthrozoös, Australian Cultural History Journal, European Review of History, History Workshop Journal, International Journal of Heritage Studies, London Journal*, and *Society & Animals*, where she has been history associate editor. Recent articles on animals and war memorials and pet cemeteries were included in *Animals and War*, ed. Ryan Hediger (2012); *Lest We Forget*, ed. Maggie Andrews (2011); and *Animal Death*, ed Jay Johnston and Fiona Probyn-Rapsey (2013). Her many books include *Animal Rights: Political and Social Change in Britain since 1800* (2000). She has served on the advisory board for Minding Animals International and the Oxford Centre of Animal Ethics.

Emma Kisiel is a photography artist with a BFA from the University of Colorado Denver. In her work, she documents and ponders her emotional and physical closeness to animals, both living and dead; the significance and future of taxidermy in museums of natural history; and the twenty-first-century culture of places where visitors can experience captive and preserved animals. Kisiel is also the author of the blog and online artist index Muybridge's Horse. She is based in Portland, Oregon.

Liza Wallis Margulies is a photographer whose passion is photographing animals. She began photographing her own pets, and from there she began to document the lives of other animals—and humans—as well. Even though she's never lived far from the Hartsdale Pet Cemetery, it wasn't until she lost her dog, Ben, that she went inside the gates for the first time and found herself surrounded by the love that people have had for their departed animals. She returns to the cemetery from time to time to photograph the headstones, which bring peace to family members whose pets are buried there.

Alma Massaro received a PhD in philosophy from the University of Genoa, Italy. In her doctoral research she investigated the Christian roots of contemporary animal concerns. She coedited *Emotività animali: Ricerche e discipline a confronto* (2014) and *L'anima del cibo: Percorsi fra emozioni e coscienza* (2014). She is also the author of *Gli animali in Lucrezio* (2014) and of several articles about the history of Christian animal ethics. She is an associate editor of the journal *Relations: Beyond Anthropocentrism*.

Jo-Anne McArthur, an award-winning photojournalist, has been documenting the plight of animals on all seven continents for over a decade. Her documentary project, *We Animals*, is internationally celebrated, and over one hundred organizations have benefited from her photography and continue to work closely with her on campaigns and investigations. Her work has been featured in publications such as *Elle Magazine, More, Parabola, National Geographic Traveler, Photolife,* DAYS Japan and

Helsingin Sanomat. Awards and accolades for Jo-Anne's work include the 2014 Institute for Critical Animal Studies Media award; one of CBC's Top 50 Champions of Change; HuffPost Women's "Top 10 Women trying to change the world"; and one of twenty activists featured in the book *The Next Eco Warrior*. Jo-Anne is the featured human subject in *The Ghosts in Our Machine*, an award-winning documentary by Canadian filmmaker Liz Marshall. She hails from Toronto, Canada.

Tamar V. S. McKee is an anthropologist, writer, curator, and filmmaker fundamentally interested in what it means (and costs) to be human and humane in the Anthropocene. Her research interests have included the persistence, persecution, and politics of Tibetan cultural identity as evidenced through contemporary art and horse festivals and how the famed horse culture of Bluegrass Kentucky is morally, ethically, and economically challenged by the emerging practice of rescuing Thoroughbred ex-racehorses, particularly as it involves human incarceration and globally faltering economic times. McKee holds a PhD (anthropology, 2014) from the University of British Columbia, an MA (anthropology) and MS (museum and field studies) from the University of Colorado, and is a professor of anthropology in the social sciences division at Quest University Canada.

Linda Monahan is a vegan scholar-activist holding a BA and MA in American studies, completed respectively at American University and the College of William and Mary. As the archivist for the oldest animal shelter in Washington, D.C., she authored a commemorative book, *"Such Courage, Such Heart": A Centennial History of the Washington Animal Rescue League* (2014). Her work explores interspecies relations and advocates for a vegan world.

James Morris is a lecturer in archaeology at the University of Central Lancashire. He specializes in archaeozoology, with a particular emphasis on the use of archaeological animal remains to explore past social concepts. He has published widely on animal burials from archaeological contexts including his book *Investigating Animal Burials: Ritual, Mundane and Beyond* (2011). His work has also been published in the journals *Anthropozoologica*, *Antiquity*, *Archaeological and Anthropological Science*, *Journal of Archaeological Science*, *Medieval Archaeology*, and *Oxford Journal of Archaeology*. He is an elected committee member of the Association for Environmental Archaeology and is a member of the International Council of Archaeozoologists.

Carolyn Merino Mullin is the founder and executive director of the National Museum of Animals & Society, the first museum of its kind dedicated to enriching the lives of animals and people by exploring our shared experience, particularly through the living history of the animal protection movement, animal studies, and humane education. She holds a Bachelor's in religion studies, with a focus in religion and nature, from the University of Florida and a Master's in nonprofit management from Regis University in Denver, Colorado. Her writings have been featured in *VegNews* and *Defiant Daughters: 21 Women on Art, Activism, Animals, and the Sexual Politics of Meat*, among other publications.

Nicole R. Pallotta is the student programs coordinator for the Animal Legal Defense Fund (ALDF) and an integral member of ALDF's Animal Law Program, which is dedicated to the development of animal law in academia and legal practice. Prior to joining ALDF, Nicole completed her PhD in sociology at the University of Georgia, where she developed and taught the school's first Animals and Society course. Her writing has appeared in *Sociological Perspectives*, *Society & Animals*, *Journal for Critical Animal Studies*, the *Portland Tribune*, and *Animal Wellness Magazine*.

Michał Piotr Pręgowski is a sociologist (PhD, 2008) and an assistant professor at the Warsaw University of Technology. His specialties include sociology of norms and values, as well as animal studies/anthrozoology. His research projects include analyzing the roles and status of dogs in the West, social practices of dealing with the death of companion animals, as well as the history and ethics of dog training. Michał is a Fulbright alumnus who served as visiting professor at Eastern Kentucky University and its animal studies program from 2014 to 2015. He is the coeditor of *Free Market Dogs: The Human-Canine Bond in Post-Communist Poland*.

Teya Brooks Pribac has a background in literature and linguistics. She works as a freelance translator and in animal advocacy between Australia and Europe, engages in different visual and verbal art forms as a hobbyist, and is currently a doctoral candidate at the University of Sydney researching animal grief, though her research interests extend to other aspects of emotions as well as to spirituality in human and nonhuman animals. She lives in the Blue Mountains of New South Wales with various rescued animals.

David Redmalm is a researcher in the Department of Sociology and Department of Industrial Engineering and Management at Uppsala University. His doctoral thesis, which he defended in November 2013, concerned nonhuman animals' place in sociology. He has published an article about dogs in popular culture in *International Journal of Cultural Studies*, and other previous publications have focused on the theory of social psychology.

Joshua Russell is an assistant professor at Canisius College, teaching in both their undergraduate program in animal behavior, ecology, and conservation as well as their graduate program in anthrozoology. His interdisciplinary research focuses on children's relationships with animals, with a particular emphasis on the ethical and pedagogical implications of children's experiences of life and death within a variety of multispecies communities. His chapter in this volume was supported in part by the Animals and Society Institute's Human–Animal Studies Fellowship.

Julia Schlosser is a Los Angeles based artist, art historian, and educator. Her artwork elucidates the multilayered relationships formed between people and their pets. Her writing and research interests focus on contemporary photographic artwork that depicts animals' lives and deaths. Her photographs appeared in "The Lives of Others: The Work of Julia Schlosser," Ciara Ennis (curated image portfolio and essay) in *exposure: The Journal of the Society for Photographic Education*, fall 2012. Her book chapter entitled "Tangible Affiliations: Photographic Representations of Touch between Human and Animal Companions" was published in *Experiencing Animal Minds* (ed. Julie A. Smith and Robert Mitchell, 2012). She is a lecturer at California State University, Northridge, where she teaches the practice and history of photography. She completed her MA in art history at California State University, Northridge, with a thesis entitled "The Postmodern Pet: Images of Companion Animals in Contemporary Photography and Video," and has also received an MFA in photography from California State University, Fullerton.

Becky Tipper received her PhD in sociology from the University of Manchester. Her doctoral thesis was an ethnographic study of a range of everyday human–animal relationships in suburban Britain. She is an Honorary Research Fellow at the Morgan Centre for Research into Everyday Lives at the University of Manchester.

Elmer Veldkamp is an assistant professor in cultural anthropology at University College Roosevelt in Middelburg, the Netherlands. He received MA degrees in Japan studies (Leiden University, 1998) and cultural anthropology (University of Tokyo, 2004), and then obtained a PhD in cultural anthropology from the University of Tokyo in 2010, with a dissertation titled "What Feels Natural: The Changing Realities of Human–Animal Relations in Korea and Japan," focusing on the processes of cultural construction that have resulted in present-day animal-related practice such as memorial services for animals, pet culture, and pet funerals. His research interests include human–animal relations in East Asia (Korea and Japan in particular), the utilization of animal-related folklore in present-day tourism, intangible cultural heritage, and museum anthropology.

Chrissie Wanner is a PhD candidate in social anthropology at the University of Edinburgh. She has been studying pedigree dog breeders in the UK since 2008, initially focusing on working sled dogs. She has received funding from the Economic and Social Research Council to conduct research into health, heredity, and the ethics of breeding in the dog-showing community. She is coeditor of the *Interspecies Encounters* book series and founder and coeditor of the website Multispecies.net.

Index

A

Act on Processing Livestock (South Korea), 55
American Stuffers, 68–69
Anglicanism, 31–35
Animal Protection Law (S. Korea), 56
animal rights, 95
Animal Welfare Act (AWA), 181
animal-assisted therapy, 180
Animals in War memorial, 120
anthropocentricism, 101, 105–6; violence and, 194, 195
articulated or associated animal bone groups, 3, 8
artificial insemination, 74–76. *See also* reproduction technologies
At Rest, 156

B

Brave Beasts, 123–24
Buddhism, xix, xxi, xxii, 5, 56–57, 59–62. *See also* religion
burial practices, xx, 3–4, 47, 49, 50; Anglo-Saxon, 13–16; death care industry, xvii; foundation offering/deposits and, 3, 11; for foxes, 4; grave goods and, 21; in the Iron Age, 13–16; Natufian and pre-Natufian, 4; Pazyryk horse burials, 21–22, 23–26; pet caskets and, 56; pet cemeteries, 47–53; pet funerals and, xix, xxi, 6, 7; problems interpreting, 11–12; Roman, 13, 16; and the unburiable, 144, 145

C

cannibalism, 143, 146, 147
Cartesian theory, 31, 32–33
cats: condolence cards and, 102–5; Egyptian relationships with, xx, 4–5; taxidermic, 68–70; in war, 115, 116;
cemeteries. *See* burial practices; pet cemeteries; whole family cemeteries
Cher Ami (pigeon), 123
chickens, 188–89
children: Erica Fudge on pets and, 83; pedagogy and, 82–83
chimpanzees, 188, 191
Christianity, xix, xxi, 13, 31–35, 57, 103. *See also* religion
cloning, 74. *See also* reproduction technologies
Coexistence of Animal Rights on Earth, 60–61
Communism, 47
companion animals: burials of, xvii–xix, 3–7, 12, 16, 47–53; condolence cards for, 101–6; euthanasia of, 165–68, 172–74; killed at war, 115, 119–20; memorial services for, 55–57; mourning of, 168–70, 175–77, 180–82; and the Rainbow Bridge, xxi–xxiii; the rise of dogs as, 144–47; taxidermy of, 66–70. *See also* children
compassion fatigue, animal shelter workers, 165–68
condolence cards, 93–94, 177; and grief, 101–2, 104, 105; replaceability theme in, 102–3
Confucian beliefs, 55
cremation, xx, 56–57
cryopreservation, 73–78. *See also* reproduction technologies

D

Dean, Richard, 33, 34, 35
Descartes, 31, 32–33
Dickin Medal, 118
dogs: Alec, 182–83; in Anglo-Saxon burials, 13–16; breeding, 73–78; burials of, xx; in condolence cards, 103; death of family pet, 81–82, 83, 86; during the Dunkirk evaluation, 119–20; Egyptian beliefs about, 4; euthanasia of, 168, 173, 174; Hachikō, 125–26; and Hurricane Katrina, xxiii; as meat, 55–56; pedigreed, 73–78; in Polish cemeteries, 51–52, 53; and the Rainbow Bridge, xviii, xxi; rise of, as pets, 143–47; search and rescue, 124; taxidermy of, 68–69; at war, 115, 116, 117, 118

228 | Index

Drummond, William H., 34–35
Dunkirk evacuation, 119–20

E

Egypt, 4–5
emotional support animals, 180
ethnoethology, 21
ethnozooarchaeology, 21
euthanasia, xvii, 27, 104, 105, 109, 106; by animal shelter workers, 165, 167, 168–69; guilt and, 173; by veterinarians, 171, 173–76

F

Faith (cat), 116
farmed animals, 151, 181–83, 184, 187, 188–89
foot-and-mouth disease, xxiii, 61

G

gravestones, xix–xx; in Poland, 50–53
green burial, xvii. *See also* burial practices
grief: by animal advocates, 193–98; by animal shelter workers, 165; disenfranchised, xii, 172, 193; and edibility, 142–44, 147; of farmed animals,187–92; and grievability, xviii, xxiii, 106, 179, 181, 184; of horses, 27, 141, 144–42; interpretations of, 16, 18; Judith Butler on, 96, 101–2, 105; overload, 189; of pets, 12–13, 48, 50, 51, 65, 68, 69, 70; and roadkill, 153, 156; by veterinarians, 175–77; vicarious, 194–96

H

Hachikō (dog), 125–26
Ham (chimpanzee), 128–29
Hammam, Uyun al-, 4, 47
Hartsdale Pet Cemetery, 6, 7, 39, 50
heaven, xix, xxi–xxii
Hildrop, John, 32, 33, 35
Hinduism, xix, xx
horses, 14, 55, 102, 107, 117; Pazyryk burial practices, 23–25; racehorses, memorial services for, 137–39; riders and, 21–23, 27; slaughter of, 141; used for meat, 144–45, 147
Humane Methods of Slaughter Act (U.S.), xxivn6
Humane Society of the United States, 152
human-nonhuman boundary, 27
hunting trophies, xxi, 65, 70

I

Immortalized, 66–67
Invisible Ink (racehorse), 137–42
Islam, xix. *See also* religion

J

Japan, xvii, xx–xxi, 5, 59, 62
Judaism, xix. *See also* religion

K

Kentucky Horse Park, 137–39
Knut (bear), 124–25
Korean Association for Animal Protection, 60–61

L

laboratory animals, vii, 60, 61, 181, 201

M

Martha (passenger pigeon), 127
meat, 153, 201; dog, 55–56; horse, 143–47
memorial services, 55, 57–61, 137–39
memory, 83–84, 85–86, 87–88
military animals. *See* World War II
mourning: by animal rights advocates, 179, 193–97; by animal sanctuary workers,183, 189, 190, 191–92; by animal shelter workers; 165–70; and cryopreservation, 74–75, 77, 78; interpretations of, 12, 14; in Korea, 61–62; mournability, 141, 144, 146; Pazyryk, 27–28; of racehorses,139; of roadkill, 151–56; and taxidermy, 70; the unmournable, 180–82; by veterinarians, 171–77
mummification, xx, 5
museum exhibits, 65–67, 70; Hachiko, 125–26; Ham, 128–29; Martha, 127–28; war memorials, 123–24; zoo animals, 124–25

N

National September 11 Memorial & Museum, 124

O

Original Road Kill Cookbook, 153
original sin, 32
Orville, 69–70

P

Passenger Pigeon Memorial, 127–28
Pazyryk horses. *See* burial practices; horses
People for the Ethical Treatment of Animals (PETA), 154–55, 156
People's Dispensary for Sick Animals (PDSA), 117–18
pet cemeteries, xvii, xviii, xx, 47–53, 56. *See also* burial practices
pet funerals, viii, xix, xxi, 6, 7; treatment of the body, 56. *See also* burial practices
Pet Memorial Day, 49

pet taxidermy, 66–70
pets. *See* companion animals
pigeons. *See* Cher Ami; Martha
pigs, 14–15, 60–61
Poland, 47–53
Price of Freedom: Americans at War, The, 123
Primatt, Humphrey, 33–34, 35
Psi Los, 48; gravestone inscriptions, 50–53; symbolism in, 49
public memorials, 116–17, 123–24
public vigils, 198

R

racehorses. *See* horses
Rainbow Bridge, xviii, xix, xxi–xxiii, 50, 103
religion: animal afterlife, xvii, xviii–xxii, 31–35; animal cults, 11; animal souls, xvii–xx, 31–35, 59–60; sacrifice and, xx, 3, 11, 14, 18, 21–28; salvation, 33
reproduction technologies, 74–76, 77–78. *See also* artificial insemination; cryopreservation
roadkill, 60, 131, 151–56
Royal Society for the Prevention of Cruelty to Animals, 117, 119

S

sacrifices, xx, 3, 11, 14, 18, 21–28
sanctuaries, 187–92, 201
secondary losses, 179–83
Sergeant Stubby (dog), 123
shelter workers, 165–70
Sirius (dog), 124
slaughter, x, xii, xviii, 55, 59, 139–41, 144, 146

South Korea: memorial services, 57–61; pet cremation, 56–57; relationships with animals, 55–56
speciesism, 194
stewardship, 32

T

taxidermy, 65–67, 131. *See also under* companion animals
tombstones. *See* gravestones

U

United Poultry Concerns, 189

V

veterinarians, viii, xvii, xi–xii, 169, 171–77
vicarious traumatization, 194
Vincent (cat): community mourning of, 92–94; death of, 91–92; larger response to, 95–97

W

war memorials. *See* public memorials
werewolves, 106
whole family cemeteries, xvii
World War II: animal deaths in, 115–17; Dunkirk evacuation and, 119–20; PDSA Cemetery and, 117–18

Z

zoo animals, 124–25
zooarchaeology, 11